Tabloid Journalism in South Africa

T0317210

HERMAN WASSERMAN

Tabloid Journalism in South Africa

True Story!

INDIANA UNIVERSITY PRESS
Bloomington and Indianapolis

This book is a publication of

Indiana University Press
601 North Morton Street
Bloomington, Indiana 47404-3797 USA

www.iupress.indiana.edu

Telephone orders	800-842-6796
Fax orders	812-855-7931
Orders by e-mail	iuporder@indiana.edu

Manufactured in the United States of America

Library of Congress Cataloging-in-Publication Data

Wasserman, Herman, [date]
    Tabloid journalism in South Africa : true story! / Herman Wasserman.
        p. cm.—(African expressive cultures)
    Includes bibliographical references and index.
    ISBN 978-0-253-35492-1 (cloth : alk. paper)—ISBN 978-0-253-22211-4 (pbk. : alk. paper)   1. Tabloid newspapers—South Africa.   2. Sensationalism in journalism—South Africa.   3. Journalism—Social aspects—South Africa.   I. Title.
    PN5477.T33W37 2010
    079'.68—dc22

                                                                                    2009045608

1   2   3   4   5   15   14   13   12   11   10

For Helena, the original journalist. And for my children, Lukas, Daniel, and Sophie, who daily bring sun and sensation into my life.

We see many things planned for us, promised to us, and written about us in the newspapers but there is never our voice—always it is the words and the empty promises and the visions of the politicians, the so-called leaders, and the Municipality.

—Press statement from the "shack-dwellers" social movement
Abahlali baseMjondolo bakuAsh Road,
June 24, 2008

I think we blew everything up. Boom. When this thing started working as I knew it would, everything was no longer true.

—Deon du Plessis, personal communication,
February 1, 2007

"Mum tries to cook baby!" You see? That's a true story!

—Anonymous *Daily Sun* reader in the BBC documentary
Black, White and Read All Over

In this country we all have stories.

—Former sub-editor at the *Daily Sun*

Contents

Preface

At the entrance to the *Daily Sun*'s offices in Johannesburg, a mannequin is displayed reading a copy of the newspaper. This is the "man in the blue overalls" that the paper's publisher says forms the core of the paper's readership, and that the paper remains fiercely loyal to, even as it is accused of journalistic sins like sensationalism, "dumbing down," sexism, and xenophobia.

In the clamor of controversy around the emergence of the highly popular *Daily Sun* and its tabloid counterparts in South Africa, the voices of these men and women in their blue overalls have not often been heard. This is not to say that the professors, commentators, and members of the professional journalistic fraternity did not have a right to present their own views—which in the majority of cases were damning—about these papers. Certainly there is much in these papers that invites criticism. But in the shorthand of public debate, the words "tabloid" or "tabloidization" have too easily become catch-all pejoratives for all that is wrong with South African journalism. The perspective from which these papers have been debated and criticized often is that of a professional elite that has not bothered to find out why these papers are popular, what they mean to their readers or how they articulate an experience of daily life in post-apartheid South Africa that differs vastly from theirs. Often the criticism directed at the tabloids centers around incredulity or ridicule at stories that defy belief. How could stories about supernatural events, strange sightings, or sidewalk rumors qualify as news? This book grapples with the question of why tabloids are considered by millions of readers in the country as telling a "true story" even as they are dismissed as trash by others.

What exactly it means to tell a "true story" is more complicated than just doing fact checking. It means telling stories so that they resonate with the narrative of people's daily lives, which, for millions of people in post-apartheid South Africa, remain precarious, dangerous, difficult, and uncertain. What would a "true story" about politics, transformation of society, crime, and poverty look like for readers who have lost faith in the "facts" of sound statistics, verifiable political soundbites, or expert scientific evidence? Yet the "true story" of life in South Africa is also about more than hardship. People use media to socialize, to facilitate their interactions, to be entertained. This is as true of tabloids as it is of the "quality" papers, which also have their share of rumor, gossip, and showbiz news. For a newspaper to tell a "true story" in this sense might mean that it uses the idiom, frame of reference, and spectrum of interests of one set of readers, which to another set of readers might seem banal or far removed from reality. Yet readers should be given credit for decoding, reading between the lines, and appropriating media content in a way that is sometimes more of a ritual than a deliberation. From this point of view, what would the "true story" of the pleasures and diversions of an ordinary life—if there is such a thing—look like for readers who prefer tabloids to other newspapers?

The debate about South African tabloids also poses questions for scholars studying journalism and the media. Too often, generalizations are made about the state of journalism, its future, and its social functions that are premised on the conditions in the media-saturated, developed countries of the Global North. Taking South African tabloids seriously—to borrow the title of Barbie Zelizer's well-known book about journalism studies—would also entail revisiting some of the dominant assumptions that govern scholarly debates about journalism today. For one, South African tabloids show that the future of print media does not look the same all around the world, nor does it look the same for different types of print media within the same country. A study of South African tabloids reiterates the importance of viewing media and journalism within its social context, against the background of specific histories, and from the perspectives of all the various participants in the communication process.

The book is not an apology for the South African tabloids. The fact that it does not dwell on tabloid transgressions does not mean that no transgressions could be found, but that the book is not primarily intended as an evaluation or assessment of the "quality" or ethical standards of tabloid papers. Instead, it wants to understand how criteria for measuring "quality" or journalistic standards come about in the first place, how these norms relate to the construction of journalistic professionalism in a transitional society, and how these norms are viewed from the perspective of the readers. This book aims to go beyond moralistic dismissals of tabloids as an inferior form of journalism, or as one which is inappropriate for a young, developing democracy, to try to understand why these papers emerged when they did, why they became so popular so quickly, and what they mean to their readers—without assuming that 'tabloid readers' represents a homogenous or stable mass audience (Barber 1997, 4). In summary, tabloids are viewed in this book not so much as journalistic products to be measured against a scale of good to bad performance, but as social phenomena that tell us something about the society in which they exist and the role of media in that society.

By taking tabloids seriously, the book invests popular culture with legitimacy, even as the notion of "the popular" in African society is a complex and conflicted one, as Karin Barber has pointed out (1997, 3). The emphasis in this book is on the importance of the audience in that process of understanding. This perspective raises a dilemma for a researcher who is himself not part of the target readership demographic and who therefore has to account for his own position when representing the views of readers. While methodological steps have been taken to address this problem, there are limits to how well an academic study such as this one can represent the voices and perspectives of readers. Nevertheless, this book is not intended as a comprehensive account of tabloid reading in South Africa, but as an attempt to shift the focus of the debate and reframe the tabloid controversy to include a wider range of perspectives that has been the case up until now. It is hoped that this book will contribute to a critical reassessment not only of these tabloids themselves, but of the role of journalism in a transitional, unequal, and young democracy such as South Africa's.

Acknowledgments

I owe the initial spark of an idea for this book to a teatime conversation I had with Professor Larry Strelitz during a colloquium at Rhodes University, Grahamstown, South Africa, in 2005. Larry's views on the cultural significance of tabloid media in the post-apartheid public sphere went against the grain of the dominant discourse at the time, namely a hysterical condemnation of tabloids for their perceived lack of ethics, "dumbing down" of journalism and overall detrimental effect on the country's media. Larry's input in a subsequent meeting of a pilot research group as well as his subsequent article (with Lynette Steenveld) in *Ecquid Novi* 26(2) made it clear to me that the South African tabloids deserved to be taken seriously.

Along the way I benefited greatly from the comments, suggestions, and constructive criticism of colleagues, especially Arnold de Beer, Sean Jacobs, Winston Mano, and Wendy Willems, as well as numerous respondents who raised questions and comments when I presented parts of the book as conference or seminar papers.

The book would also not have been possible without the editors, journalists, and tabloid readers who gave generously of their time and allowed me to interview them, conduct focus groups, and spend time as a nosy observer in their newsrooms and who gave permission to reproduce visual material. Family members, colleagues, and friends who helped me obtain copies of tabloids and set up interviews include Todani Nodoba, Fadia Salie, Danie and Alphia Schutte, Gladys van Rooyen, Herman and Marietjie Wasserman, Tobie Wiese, Wendy Willems, and Lijuan Williams. Wadim Schreiner and Richard Kunzmann of Media Tenor South Africa also kindly provided data on tabloid content, Fienie Grobler of *The Media* magazine gave me access to useful circulation information, and Betsi Grabe from Indiana University and Ilana van Wyk from the London School of Economics pointed me toward relevant literature. David Baines at Newcastle University helped me with newspaper terminology, while Ané Honiball and Ylva Rodny-Gumede provided kind assistance with visual material.

I wish to thank the universities of Stellenbosch, Newcastle, and Sheffield for support to attend conferences where some of these chapters were first presented as papers. These conferences and seminars include the London School of Economics and Political Science's African Anthropology Seminar Series and Media, Communication, and Humanity conference; Westminster University Communication and Media Research Institute's Africa Media Series; the African Studies Association of the United Kingdom's annual conference in Preston, Lancashire; the AEGIS European Conference on African Studies in Leiden, Netherlands; the Future of Newspapers conference at Cardiff University; the Cultural Studies

Now conference at the University of East London; the 12th General Assembly of the Council for the Development of Social Science Research in Africa (Codesria) in Yaoundé, Cameroon; the South African Communication Association's annual conference in Tshwane, South Africa; and the research seminar at the Law Faculty, University of the Western Cape, Bellville, South Africa. I also thank colleagues for sharing their thoughts and suggestions on these occasions, which made me rethink and revisit my ideas.

An earlier version of chapter 2 appeared in *Journalism Studies* 9(5), a version of chapter 4 in *Communicare* 25(1), and a version of chapter 7 in *Australian Journalism Review* 31(2). These articles are drawn upon for this book with the kind permission of the respective journals.

My publisher, Indiana University Press, and specifically senior sponsoring editor Dee Mortensen, who believed in the project from the start and patiently guided the manuscript toward publication, deserve a special word of thanks.

Like my other academic pursuits and obsessions, this book took a substantial amount of time which I could have spent with my family instead. For allowing me the space and time to work on this and other projects, I remain very grateful to Helena, Lukas, Daniel, and Sophie.

I recognize that as a member of the historically privileged class in South Africa, spending periods living abroad, my lived experience differs vastly from the majority of South Africans whose stories are recounted in the tabloids. In a sense I therefore study the tabloid media as an outsider, even though my work experience as a journalist and journalism educator in South Africa has given me wide exposure to the country's media industry. I remain fascinated by my country, its vibrant media, and the resilience of its people. One cannot ask for a richer, more challenging area of study.

The main players in the story of South Africa's "tabloid revolution" are its readers, who struggle, hope, and dream often in proud defiance of their circumstances. I hope that this book will contribute to the wider recognition of the stories of their lives.

Tabloid Journalism in South Africa

1. Shock! Horror! Scandal! The Tabloid Controversy and Journalism Studies in Post-Apartheid South Africa

In many regions of the world, the death of newspapers is expected soon. One critic (Meyer 2004) famously predicted that the last newspaper will be read and recycled in April 2040. Amid this panic about the future of printed news, a newspaper revolution has taken place in South Africa.

The newspaper market in that country has been conquered convincingly by the entry of the new tabloid newspapers that have turned the local media landscape upside down and created heated controversy in South African journalism circles (Wasserman 2006b) to such an extent that the tabloid "revolution" has attracted international attention.[1]

The *Daily Sun* is the country's biggest daily newspaper, with a circulation of around 500,000 copies per day, which translates into around 4.7 million regular readers.[2] Its closest daily rival in terms of circulation (although aimed at a different market) is "quality" newspaper *The Star,* published in Gauteng province, with around 178,000 copies. The *Daily Sun* also competes with the weekly *Sunday Times* in terms of copies sold (the ABC figures for the corresponding period show 504,000 copies per week for the *Sunday Times*). Importantly, the *Daily Sun* has almost a million more readers than the *Sunday Times* (which has 3.8 million according to the AMPS for the corresponding period). This is because the newspaper is shared among more people, creating a community of readers. The publisher, Deon du Plessis, claims that there is even a second-hand market for copies—such is the demand for the paper among those that can barely afford it.[3]

Although the *Daily Sun* is the most successful tabloid in the country, it is not the only one that has recently entered the South African media landscape. It forms part of a wave of tabloid newspapers that have swept the country since the mid-2000s, challenging the dominant journalistic norms and sparking heated debate in industry and academic circles. But most importantly, these tabloids have created a mass readership out of the poor and working-class Black majority of the country that had hitherto been largely ignored by the post-apartheid mainstream press,[4] which had been concentrating on middle-class and elite readerships.

Why Think about Tabloids?

Why a book on the South African tabloids? In the first, and most general, instance, it is noteworthy that in an era where the existence of newspapers is under threat in many parts of the world, a new print-media genre introduced in a developing country has met with unprecedented commercial success. For scholars of journalism and media, this development underscores the need for scholarship to take a global view, the importance of more comparative research instead of unproblematically extrapolating the circumstances and experiences of media contexts in the developed world. The emergence of the South African tabloids is significant not only as a case study that might contribute to a richer understanding of global journalism, but also for what they say about the mediated public sphere in emerging democracies. The genesis and growth of these tabloids are linked to the changing socio-political context and the shifting media landscape in the country since the demise of formal apartheid in the 1990s. Studying the social, cultural, and political meanings of tabloids within the transitional South African democracy can therefore also indicate to us some of the conditions under which this transition is mediated, and the potential and limitations of the popular press within such a context. The South African tabloids can provide an example of how societal shifts in transitional settings are influenced by (and prey to) local and global market forces; they offer a picture of how popular culture, mediated politics, and discourses of citizenship can converge in a young democracy; and they illustrate how local and global cultural forces interact in shaping media formats and content. Of importance in such a study is not only tabloid content, but also the views and experiences of tabloid producers and tabloid readers.

Tabloids and the Post-Apartheid Media Sphere: Economic Shifts

In particular, this book hopes to contribute to the debates about the multi-leveled shifts occurring in South African society after the demise of apartheid, especially as these concern journalism and the media. With the arrival of formal democracy in the country in 1994, the public sphere was broadened in major ways—freedom of speech was guaranteed in the Constitution, race was no longer a formal preclusion to participation in public debate and political processes, the media were revitalized as apartheid-era restrictions were lifted and replaced by self-regulation, and the media achieved wider legitimacy as the demography of newsrooms changed to better represent the country's ethnic and racial profile.

But the public sphere also contracted. Under apartheid, there had been a vibrant alternative press which found its raison d'être in the struggle against apartheid. Consequently, alternative opinions to those in the mainstream media were in wide circulation, even while they were suppressed by the apartheid regime's intricate set of impediments on press freedom. In the post-apartheid era, virtually all these alternative voices disappeared, leaving the media landscape to be dominated by commercial media—even as attempts were made to develop the community media sector through the establishment of the Media Diversity and Development Agency (MDDA) and the awarding of community radio broadcasting licenses (we will return to the point about alternative media in the next chapter). Progressive social movements like the Treatment Action Campaign, Abahlali baseMjondolo, and the Anti-Privatisation Forum have, to varying extents and with varying levels of success, used new media technologies to amplify other methods of communication with target audiences (Wasserman 2007). But as far as the printed press is concerned, the post-apartheid era has seen the dominance of a corporatized, professionalized commercial news industry. On one level, the tabloids can be seen as an extension of this move toward market-driven (as opposed to explicitly ideologically motivated) media. They belong to big conglomerates set on extracting as much profit as possible from the communities they cater to—if they manage to contribute to the good of society in the process, this might be seen as a positive spin-off rather than the main aim.

But on another level, the tabloids could be seen as stepping into the gap left by the demise of alternative media (although referring to the South African tabloids as alternative media in and of themselves would certainly be stretching this definition too far). The dominance of commercial media in the post-apartheid era meant that the logic of selling lucrative audiences to advertisers held sway over newspapers, and the working-class and unemployed majority in the country did not count among these readerships.[5] The major newspapers catering to a Black readership, like the *Sowetan* and *City Press,* had their sights trained on the middle class and elites. A number of free "knock-and-drop" newspapers had been circulating in Black townships, but these were small operations, mostly vehicles for local advertising. These small publications did not influence the mainstream news agenda, nor did they have a significant impact on debates about the media industry or journalism in the country in the way that the tabloids started doing. This climate made it possible for the tabloids to become ersatz community or alternative papers.

The tabloids seem to have turned the received orthodoxy about newspaper business models around, creating a mass readership among the poor and the working class (the latter also consisted of a young, upwardly mobile group that had the potential to become big spenders). For the first time since the end of apartheid, the poor majority of South Africans had a big print-media outlet that viewed news items from a perspective they recognized as familiar, that addressed them on their terms rather than from above, that articulated their opinions and views, and that dared to challenge dominant journalistic conventions in the process.

The tabloids' brash, defiant attitude did not win them many friends in the journalistic establishment. The journalistic fraternity responded harshly to these new kids on the block and even considered barring tabloid journalists from the professional body for editors, the South African National Editors Forum (SANEF) (this and other responses will be discussed in chapter 4). The tabloids' entry into the post-apartheid mediated public sphere also came under pressure from the journalistic community itself.

Tabloids and the Post-Apartheid Media Sphere: Political Pressures

If the mediated public sphere contracted as a result of economic forces, it has also been subject to political pressures. As with many other aspects of the media in contemporary South Africa, the political dimension of tabloid newspapers is best understood against a historical background.

Under apartheid, the White press was a "pivotal institution in the racially and ethnically based struggles for economic and political power" (Horwitz 2001, 36). The mainstream commercial print media were broadly divided along ideological lines that corresponded with ethnic and linguistic differences in the White community. They made only limited attempts to cater to Black or "Coloured" (mixed-race) audiences (e.g., in separate, "extra" editions). While English-language newspapers were linked to the interests of mining capital (and provided a limited, liberal critique of apartheid), Afrikaans-language newspapers supported Afrikaner nationalism and the apartheid state. They served as key institutions for the articulation of nationalist ideology, even while some of them questioned the establishment from time to time (Tomaselli and Dunn 2001; Horwitz 2001). In the post-apartheid era, the Afrikaans and English press became de-linked from these ideologies, repositioned themselves according to the new political landscape, and adopted a more commercialized approach.

The apartheid regime put an extensive set of legal measures in place to control the media and limit criticism of itself. For instance, it was forbidden to quote or publish photographs of certain leaders in the freedom struggle (like Nelson Mandela) or to publish information that could be perceived as threatening the security of the state. Critical journalists and editors from the anti-apartheid press were censored, banished, harassed, and imprisoned (see Wasserman and De Beer 2005). This history of both complicity with the apartheid regime (on the part of the Afrikaans press and the SABC) and government interference and repression (especially with regard to journalists with a "struggle" background) resulted in the post-apartheid media being extremely vigilant of any attempt by the government to meddle in its affairs and suspicious of any media that could be seen to toe the government line. Although freedom of expression was guaranteed in the post-apartheid constitution agreed upon in 1996, this right has often been understood in different ways. As a result, the media and the government were in disagreement on several occasions (De Beer 2002; Fourie 2002; Shepperson and Tomaselli 2002).

The initial years of democracy were marked by a mutual mistrust between media and government. The government had misgivings about the media's demographic representation, seeing ownership and editorial staff as being too White (see Mandela 1994a). For their part, many members of the media industry anticipated that the new ruling party, the African National Congress (ANC), would pose a threat to media freedom. This pessimistic expectation could perhaps be understood against the trends of governmental interference in the media elsewhere in Africa (Duncan 2003, 5), but has also been linked to "racist and misplaced associations" of the new government with authoritarianism (Jacobs 2003, 132).

The tense relationship between the new government and the media became especially evident during two investigations into the media conducted soon after the formal democratic transition took place. The first investigation, into the media's role during the apartheid era, formed part of the Truth and Reconciliation Commission's (TRC) hearings (1996). The second investigation was conducted by the Human Rights Commission (HRC) (1999/2000), following a complaint by the Black Lawyers Association and the Association of Black Accountants of South Africa about alleged racism in the media.

These investigations provided some of the earliest instances of friction between the media sector and the newly elected government and its related institutions that would only increase over the coming years despite formal efforts to manage the relationship through initiatives like the Government Communication and Information System (GCIS), which was tasked with facilitating government's communication with the media. In the case of the TRC, the Afrikaans media giant Naspers, whose publications (albeit in varying degrees) had supported the apartheid regime, refused to testify in front of the commission—which resulted in a small rebel group of journalists submitting their own declaration. In the case of the HRC investigation, the media in general met the commission with "scorn and incredulity" and responded with discursive strategies of denial of racism (Durrheim et al. 2005). Critical questions were asked of the media's role in society after apartheid, but both commissions approached racism largely in terms of prejudice and representation and failed to ask broader, structural questions regarding the intersection of the South African media, the market, and race (see Krabill 2001, 591–596; *Rhodes Journalism Review* 1997; Johnson and Jacobs 2004).

Whereas the media were objects of scrutiny under the Mandela presidency, it often clashed outright with Mandela's successor, Thabo Mbeki. Mbeki's relations with the media have been generally poor (Chotia and Jacobs 2002, 157). The bulk of the debate in professional and academic journalistic circles during the Mbeki presidency was framed in terms of "media freedom" and "independence." The government was seen as encroaching upon the media's constitutionally guaranteed freedom, among other things through attempts by senior ANC members to acquire ownership of Johncom,[6] a company which owns several influential newspapers; a proposed Film and Publications Amendment Bill which would make pre-publication censorship of the news media possible; and ANC plans to establish a media tribunal as an alternative to self-regulation by the Press Ombudsman (who adjudicates complaints by the public against the press) (SANEF 2007). The perceived influence by the government on the public broadcaster, the South African Broadcasting Corporation (SABC), has become a recurring theme in media reports, and an antagonistic relationship between the print media and the

SABC has developed. In 2007, this antagonism came to a head when the SABC withdrew from the South African National Editors' Forum after the *Sunday Times* published allegations of alcohol abuse on the part of the health minister, Dr. Manto Tshabalala-Msimang, while illegally in possession of her hospital records. This conflict took place in a tense run-up to the election of the new ANC president at the party's general conference in Polokwane in December 2007. When Jacob Zuma emerged victorious from this conference, he was immediately scrutinized for his view of the media. In one of his first weekly emailed "Letters from the President," Zuma slammed the media,[7] writing that it was "politically and ideologically out of synch with the society in which it exists . . . a product of the various political, social, economic and cultural forces that exist within a society," and a "major arena in the battle of ideas" between those with economic power that seek to "reinforce their privileged position" and those who "campaign for a media that serves the cause of a more equitable society" (ANC 2008). For this criticism, Zuma was branded by the South African National Editors Forum as harboring a "hostile state of mind towards the media" (SANEF 2008).

Tabloids and the Post-Apartheid Media Sphere: Race, Ethnicity, and Class

The roles of race, ethnicity, and class in shaping the post-apartheid media sphere are a further consideration in studying the significance of tabloids. The relationship among race, ethnicity, class, and media markets has not yet been adequately studied in the South African context. The TRC, by focusing its attention on press-freedom issues and professional media institutions in a functionalist fashion, neglected the larger issues of the political economy of the media. In turn, the HRC investigation displayed methodological failures (Tomaselli 2000b), opting to highlight individual cases of alleged racism to make the general point that the South African media was "racist." It focused largely on issues of representation, and, similar to the TRC inquiry, passed up on the opportunity to investigate the bigger questions about the more intricate power relations between race and ethnicity, the media market, and the state. Although these links were left underexplored, the continued impact of race and ethnicity on the media landscape of post-apartheid South Africa cannot be ignored. The emergence of tabloids has made it clear that South African media audiences remain marked by race, ethnicity, and class, and that this segmentation continues to shape debates about what the post-apartheid mediated public sphere should look like. But although tabloids have succeeded in creating a new, largely racially defined market that had previously not been catered to by the mainstream print media, they are worth studying for more than merely market reasons. Reader responses to tabloids (discussed in chapter 6) have suggested that these publications have also had a profound influence on the lives of their readers. They seem to have instilled a measure of trust in at least one section of the media and created a sense of ownership over it, provided daily companionship and assisted in confirming a civic identity for a large section of the public who had felt left out or forgotten in the post-apartheid media sphere. The tabloids should therefore also be studied in terms of questions about culture, identity, and citizenship in contemporary South Africa.

Such consideration of the influence of race and ethnicity on the South African media sphere should be seen in conjunction with persisting socio-economic legacies of apartheid such as illiteracy and lack of access to communications infrastructure, which also impact how the broader public can participate in the public sphere. In short, the impact of race, ethnicity, and class on the media landscape of post-apartheid South Africa should be seen not only in textual terms—how the racial Other of apartheid has been represented in the media—but as a structural problem with historic antecedents and contemporary policy implications.

Contested Terrain: Tabloids and Society

Although this book takes only a snapshot of the new South African tabloids, it does so out of an interest in the wider picture of South African media and society. An investigation into the emergence and popularity of the tabloids, their relationship with society in the broader sense but with their readers in particular, the response they received from the professional collective of journalists, and their political significance provide us with a vantage point from which the broader media landscape in the country can be viewed. This landscape is a contested one in which local and global political, economic, and socio-cultural interests are increasingly mediated. This mediation does not, however, take place by means of a disinterested media that serves merely as a conduit for information. In the as-yet-incomplete transition to a democratic society, the media themselves have become important roleplayers and stakeholders, facilitating the re-orientation of these interests in relation to established and shifting centers of power. It might not be too implausible to consider the emergence of the tabloids themselves as directly linked to the country's democratization process, even as they might point toward the limits of liberation (Robins 2005) and complicate notions that are central to the democratic discourse in the country, such as citizenship, human rights, freedom of the press, and the media's social responsibility.

Notes on Approach

Because the new tabloids and the controversies surrounding them are significant for post-apartheid South African media and society on different levels, it follows that a combination of approaches would be needed to study them. This book therefore aims to follow the varied approach to the study of South African tabloid media suggested by Steenveld (2006, 20)—namely, a combination of a textual exploration, a study of audience responses, and a critical political-economic approach that seeks to situate tabloids at the intersection of local and global media discourses. The book addresses tabloid journalism through the "multivariegated lens" suggested by Zelizer (2008, 90), seeing journalism as a form of communication but also as a form of culture and critique:[8]

> Journalism as *communication* privileges the important role in information gathering and disseminating which journalism fulfills. Journalism as *culture* addresses the function of journalism in imparting value preferences and mediating meaning about how the world does and should work. Journalism as *critique* highlights the particular value of criticism and opinion as a modality through which journalism can make explicit its response to events and issues of the public sphere.

Staying with Zelizer's triptych of journalism as communication, culture, and critique, the book's scope can be outlined as follows.

- *Tabloids as communication:* What information is being disseminated? How does this information differ from that which had already been disseminated by other print media in contemporary South Africa? To which audience is this information being disseminated, and how should the construction of this audience or market be understood against the historical background of the press in South Africa? Who owns the means of communication? Does this communication take the form of a one-way process or an interactive one? How do those who participate in this process view their roles?
- *Tabloids as culture:* What cultural values, meanings, and symbolic framework are imparted by the tabloids? Is South African tabloid culture different from or similar to tabloid culture in other parts of the world? How should such differences or similarities be understood? How does the tabloid culture in South Africa fit into the broader journalistic culture, and what tensions and frictions have arisen between the country's different journalistic cultures? What do these tensions and frictions tell us about the dominant value framework within which journalism operates in a post-apartheid, democratic South Africa? How well do the tabloids reflect the lived experience of their readers?
- *Tabloids as critique:* A familiar criticism of popular media like tabloids, informed by neo-Marxist critical studies, is that they feed people entertainment as a diversion from political engagement. Scholars viewing media from a cultural studies perspective have in turn pointed out that it is possible to give a political reading of these media. What is the situation with regard to South African tabloids? Can they have a political influence? How does such influence work—how can popular tabloids, known more for entertainment and diversion than political news, be read politically? What impact might the South African tabloids have on the country's politics? Do these tabloids offer a critical perspective on social, economic, and political reality in the country? Can the very existence and huge popularity of these tabloids be seen as a form of criticism against the mainstream post-apartheid media?

Such a multi-dimensional approach to tabloid journalism brings with it a certain theoretical and methodological eclecticism. These questions will not be asked in sequence, but will underpin the discussion of the various aspects of the South African tabloids. Some answers may emerge, but this book is more about asking questions in order to shift or reframe the dominant debates in the South African media and in scholarly circles than providing conclusive answers. The different dimensions of tabloid journalism—communication, culture, and critique—cannot be separated neatly, but are interlinked as constitutive elements of journalism as a practice, an occupation, a signifying framework, a discursive structure, and so on. For this reason, these elements will be interwoven through the chapters rather than discussed separately or in isolation of each other. Themes and issues pertaining to the tabloids, located within post-apartheid society and culture, will be discussed and illustrated by examples. Although tabloid content will be referred to in order to elucidate this discussion and to illustrate arguments, there will not be a systematic content analysis or a detailed political-economic dissection of the ownership and management structure of the tabloids nor a long-term ethnographic study of tabloid audiences. In contrast, the preferred multi-level approach to tabloids made an in-depth study of one dimension of tabloids—for instance a longitudinal content analysis of the communicative aspects of tabloids, or a long-term participant observation or ethnography of producers or audiences with the objective of providing a rich, "thick description" (Geertz 1973) of audience preferences or behavior—impossible within the scope of this book.

Instead, this book employs a variety of methods to outline the various lenses through which tabloids could be viewed, to raise critical questions, to put certain key topics on the agenda with a view to shift the dominant frame of discussion of South African tabloids, to unsettle some of the assumptions, and to lay the groundwork for further in-depth study. Some might take this book as a hagiography for tabloids, since it goes against the grain of what has become a very predictable and often elitist discussion of tabloids in the country—one which routinely ends in condemnation or dismissal of these papers. Although this book highlights some of the positive potential of tabloids, it certainly also takes a critical view of other aspects of these publications.

What are the objectives of the book? This book views tabloids as connected to larger socio-cultural and political-economic phenomena, best understood not in isolation, but rather in relation to the South African society's transition to democracy. One of this book's first objectives is therefore to locate the South African tabloids within the recent history and socio-political context of the media in post-apartheid South Africa. This book aims to be more than a case study of an example of African media in the area studies tradition, however. Although discussing the emergence of a particular type of newspaper in a specific time and place, and seeing these media as inextricably linked with the context of their emergence, the book also establishes links between the particular and the more general, or between local media and global trends. It first compares the South African tabloids with their counterparts in other parts of the world, but also uses the specific example of South African tabloids inductively as a point of departure from where more general themes and issues around the future of newspapers, the globalization of media formats and genres, and the role of media in society can be discussed.

By approaching the South African tabloids in this way, this book goes beyond an analysis of media in a particular time and place to contribute to our comparative understanding of global media and journalism theory. Even in the era of accelerated globalization, there is still too little evidence from non-Western contexts entering into debates in the fields of journalism and media studies. Theoretical debates in these fields frequently take place in ignorance or disregard of conditions in the Global South, with the result that theoretical frameworks and future predictions are often arrived at by extrapolating the experiences of a limited range of countries and regions to assume universal relevance. When media in the South are paid attention to, they are often approached as case studies in isolation, as examples of media "elsewhere." This approach has succinctly been summarized by Shiva (1989, 118) as using the "West as theory, East as evidence."[9] It is therefore important that when media from contexts such as the South African one are studied, these media are not treated merely as evidence to support extant theories developed elsewhere, nor to paint a descriptive picture that does not impact theory. Instead, such evidence should be scrutinized for the way it complicates the West's "theoretical skeleton" (Chakrabarty 1996, 227).

While more comparative work is called for, such comparative studies often rely on a conceptual framework derived from a British or North American context, which is taken as universal and then applied in other contexts (cf. Flew 2007, 41). By using existing literature to compare the South African tabloids with their counterparts elsewhere, this book cannot claim to have escaped this problem. However, pointing out both the similarities and differences between South African tabloids and, for instance, British tabloids, may extend the existing body of knowledge on popular journalism while raising questions about some of the assumptions contained therein. The South African case is not only important for enriching the theoretical conversation about popular journalism through a comparison with tabloids in societies in the developed world, but also for the study of journalism in other societies in the developing world that are similarly marked by shifts from an authoritarian-mediated sphere to a highly commercialized, privatized public sphere, where marginalized voices struggle to compete in an arena that has suddenly opened up to global market forces.

The runaway success of the South African tabloids should also remind journalism studies scholars that debates about the future of journalism should remain cognizant of different contexts. Too often these debates are predicated on media-saturated societies with broad access to new media technologies that have extended the range of media choices available to consumers, or on the news habits of audiences whose lived experiences differ vastly from those in other parts of the world.

This is not to argue for a type of cultural relativism that would make any conversation about shared challenges of journalism in diverse contexts impossible.

Nor is it to enter into special pleading for contexts in Africa or elsewhere in the Global South because journalism there has just fallen behind on a trajectory that will, in the end lead, to the same place where journalism in the Global North has already arrived.

Overview of Contents

The discussion of South African tabloids starts by locating these publications contextually. The next chapter, "Attack of the Killer Newspapers! Tabloids Arrive in South Africa," describes the various tabloids that appeared on the scene in the mid-2000s, their target markets, and indicators of their unprecedented popularity. The chapter explains some of the reasons for their emergence at this particular historical juncture by postulating some of the key factors that led to their inception. The success of these tabloids is contrasted with fears in other countries that the newspaper format is on a steep decline, with some preliminary conclusions about why these tabloids are important for scholars of journalism.

The international perspective on South African tabloids continues in chapter 3, "Black and White and Read All Over: Tabloids and the Glocalization of Popular Media." This chapter examines the argument that South African tabloids are just an imitation of British "red-tops" (a name that refers to the red mastheads of papers such as *The Sun, The Daily Mirror, The Daily Star,* and *News of the World*). The contrasting arguments of cultural hybridity and cultural imperialism are considered as alternative frameworks for understanding the influence of global or transnational formats on local media products. Hybridity denotes the mixing and adaptation of existing formats and genres—for instance, tabloid newspapers—to suit local contexts. Cultural imperialism, on the other hand, views the influx of global formats and genres as a threat to local culture and a tool through which Anglo-European culture achieves dominance over the developing world. Chapter 3 also considers the expectation that journalism in the developing world should play a role in the advancement of these societies and asks, what does "journalism for development" mean in the context of South African tabloid media? Can these tabloids help to improve post-apartheid society? Or, as critics have claimed, is the role of tabloids limited to that of sensation and entertainment? Chapter 4, "Not Really Newspapers: Tabloids and the South African Journalistic Paradigm," looks at this and other critical responses to tabloids and at what the antagonism toward tabloids tells us about the professional normative paradigm within which South African journalism is conceived of and practiced. This chapter argues that instead of engaging with the challenge that the new tabloids posed for the existing norms, values, and forms of journalistic practice, the mainstream press rejected the tabloids as a way of defending the existing paradigm within which they operated.

The title of chapter 5, "The Revolution Will Be Printed: Tabloids, Citizenship, and Democratic Politics in Post-Apartheid South Africa," quotes the editor of the *Daily Sun,* Themba Khumalo, who described the entry of tabloids into the South African media market as a "revolution." This might be accurate in terms of sales figures and audience appeal, but how much of a revolution in the political sense did the tabloids bring about? The tabloid genre is usually associated with entertainment and diversion rather than "serious news" which includes political coverage. Tabloids are often criticized for depoliticizing their readers, yet some theorists have argued for a political reading of tabloids even if they do not explicitly engage in the type of political coverage associated with the mainstream press. This chapter investigates the potential that the tabloids have to influence South African politics.

Much of the criticism against tabloids derives from viewpoints held by journalists working for media that serves an elite, or from this elite themselves—including academics. Yet these criticisms often make assumptions on behalf of tabloid readers (even when these readers are patronizingly "defended" against exploitation by tabloids for commercial gain) without bothering to speak to people who choose to buy and read tabloids. Following the work of scholars like S. Elizabeth Bird, who approach tabloid audiences from an anthropological perspective, chapter 6 ("Truth or Trash? Understanding Tabloid Journalism and Lived Experience") attempts a limited, explorative audience study of South African tabloid readers. Through focus-group interviews with tabloid readers representing various demographic sections of the tabloid target market, this chapter explores the role that tabloids play in the everyday lives of their readers. It investigates why these readers prefer tabloids over other newspapers, how the tabloids create a sense of community among readers and assist them in exercising their civic duties and claiming their rights as citizens, and how tabloid readers view value concepts like "truth" and "accuracy" in the tabloid context. These responses are then compared with those of tabloid readers in other countries as documented in the literature. The chapter aims to understand South African tabloid readers as active participants in meaning-making and not as the guileless, gullible victims that they are often made out to be in journalistic and academic debates.

The views of tabloid editors and journalists are also explored. Chapter 7, "Often They Cry with the People: The Professional Identities of Tabloid Journalists," outlines the complex relationships between different participants and stakeholders in the tabloid-production process. It also examines some of the contradictions of tabloid journalism in the post-apartheid era. What are the implications of tabloids aimed at working-class Black South Africans being part of multinational media conglomerates that before had not seen the Black market as worthy of significant newspaper investment? How should one understand the relationships between Black and White journalists, editors, and publishers—are these new relationships forged in a democratic culture, or do they replicate older, hierarchical ones? How do these journalists and editors view themselves, their professional identities and their relationship with the journalistic establishment? Interviews with journalists and editors explore their approach to tabloid content and ask how they see their role as tabloid journalists as compared to that of their counterparts in the "serious" press. The relationship between editorial staff and readers, which is marked by high levels of trust and interaction, is probed, partly to uncover some of the power relations underpinning this relationship. Tabloid journalists and editors also respond to the criticism they have received from their colleagues in other media and from members of the public and explain the value framework guiding their work.

The last chapter summarizes the preceding chapters and provides some provisional conclusory remarks about the role, impact, and significance of the South African tabloids.

2. Attack of the Killer Newspapers! Tabloids Arrive in South Africa

Before taking a closer look at how tabloids arrived in South Africa, a historical perspective on the form, content, and style of the tabloid genre may be helpful to understand why they continue to cause such controversy.

Form, Content, and the Charge of Sensationalism

The term "tabloid" can refer to the format as well as the content of a newspaper. Etymologically, the word "tabloid" refers to a chemical tablet, initially a term registered as a trademark in the 1800s (Franklin et al. 2005, 258). In newspaper terms, "tabloid" is identified with a smaller size of paper compared to broadsheets, but the term is less often used to describe the physical size than the genre of a particular kind of newspaper. Tabloids are known (and often reviled for) a distinctive type of content—"the human-interest, graphically told story, heavy on pictures and short, pithy, highly stereotyped prose" (Bird 1992, 8)—a reflection of colloquial speech patterns, a melodramatic style, sympathy for the "underdog" in society, and siding with the people against the powerful (Conboy 2006, 5–6). The vehicle for this content is a snappy and lively style of language and a typographical layout that enables quick reading, including screaming "scare-heads" in red and black, introduced in the late nineteenth century by the pioneers of the sensational "yellow journalism" in the United States, Joseph Pulitzer and William Randolph Hearst (ibid., 5).

Tabloid journalism can be seen as a practice of popular culture exactly because it is both widely enjoyed by its audience *and* loathed by the elite, whether they be mainstream journalists, the social elite, or official institutions (Glynn 2000, 9). Tabloids also belong to the realm of popular culture because they can be seen to express the social presence of those who are subordinated, mainly on the grounds of race, economic or social capital, and geographic region—even if arguably they in turn perform exclusions in terms of other categories of disempowerment like ethnicity, sexual orientation, and gender (cf. Glynn 2000, 9). In South Africa, the tabloids have contributed to a stronger presence in the mediated public sphere of people who historically were disenfranchised politically and continue to be marginalized socially and economically in post-apartheid society. Indeed, popular journalism—like popular culture more generally—has implications for politics and social change because it contests the framework within which we make sense of the world, find meaning in our daily lives, and define our roles in society, often in opposition to hegemonic cultural norms and standards (ibid., 9–10):

> Through its transgression of bourgeois "standards" and tastes, its contradiction of the truths circulated in official news, and its emphasis on voices usually marginalized or excluded from the discourse of elite journalism, tabloidism provokes, encourages, and amplifies some of the popular forces that interfere with the extension of imperializing power-bloc knowledges.

Tabloid journalism also refers to a style or a trend that has been seen as "infiltrating" other types of newspapers and the media more generally, in a process often referred to as "tabloidization" or "dumbing down":

> Tabloid journalism conjoins the sentimental and the sensational, and the prurient and the populist, often exploiting personal tragedy for public spectacle with scandal and sensationalism, often masquerading as "human interest." (Franklin et al. 2005, 259)

Understanding the term "tabloid" to refer to content rather than form is all the more important since broadsheets have been changing shape to more closely resemble the tabloids' size, although their content—arguably—has remained the same. Newspapers in several parts of the world, but especially in Europe, have reduced their size in the interest of reading convenience. In changing to a smaller format, "quality" newspapers like the French *Le Monde,* the British *Guardian* and *Observer* (which changed from broadsheet to "Berliner" format, which is still slightly broader and much deeper than the tabloid form), and the British *Times* and *Independent* (which have gone even smaller, to the tabloid size) have remained conscious of the association of smaller newspaper size with down-market content. So strong was reader resistance against the *Times'* smaller format that it was initially forced to continue offering the paper in the broadsheet format as well.[1]

The increasing global popularity of content based on the intersection between popular culture and journalism, such as reality TV in the United States (Glynn 2000) or global "infotainment" (Thussu 2008), also requires a descriptor that denotes its popular approach and the widespread dismissal of these formats as inferior to "serious" or "quality" journalism. For this reason, "tabloid" and "tabloidization" have also been used to describe other media platforms like television (Glynn 2000) and websites (like *Tabloid Column* [http://www.tabloidcolumn .com]) that aggregate tabloid stories from other outlets.

Tabloid content can be described as "subject matter . . . produced at the intersection between public and private life; its style is sensational, sometimes skeptical, sometimes moralistically earnest; its tone is populist; its modality fluidly denies any stylistic difference between fiction and documentary, between news and entertainment" (Fiske 1992, 48), to which Glynn (2000, 7) adds characteristics of tabloid television in particular that also seem applicable to print:

> It prefers heightened emotionality and often emphasizes the melodramatic. It sometimes makes heavy use of campy irony, parody and broad humor. It relies on an often volatile mix of realistic and antirealist representational conventions. It resists "objectivity", detachment, and critical distance. It is highly multidiscursive. It incorporates

voices frequently excluded from "serious" news and often centers on those that are typically marginalized in mainstream media discourse. The "bizarre" and the "deviant" are central to its image repertoire. It is generally offensive to high- and middlebrow tastes. Moreover, it is often equally offensive to masculine tastes. . . . It frequently violates dominant institutional standards and procedures for the production and validation of "truth". It thrives on the grotesque, the scandalous and the "abnormal."

As terms to describe content, "tabloid" and the process of "tabloidization" are closely linked to the concept of "sensationalism." "Sensationalism" was first associated with the "penny press" (a low-price newspaper in the nineteenth century that made journalism accessible to more people) and later intensified with "yellow journalism" in the United States, which in turn influenced the form and content of the British press of the time (Conboy 2006, 5). Sensationalism in journalism has been a "popular topic of fiery discussions for centuries" (Grabe, Zhou, and Barnett 2001, 635), because it is seen to violate "notions of social decency"; it "displaces socially significant stories"; and it is perceived as a recent lapse of journalistic standards in favor of excessiveness (ibid., 636). These three concerns have been countered by scholars who have pointed out that sensationalism maintains the dominant standards of decency and morality by their emphatic display of transgressions of these norms; that the definition of "socially significant" news is relative to social class and gender; and that the conception that sensationalism is a contemporary phenomenon assumes a golden era of scrupulous journalism (ibid.).

Sensationalism can be seen as an approach to content ("soft news" like human-interest stories, or dramatic events like disasters, accidents, etc.) as well as format (e.g., headlines, graphic design or editing techniques) that is aimed at stimulating responses, whether emotional, moral, aesthetic, or sensory (ibid., 637–638).[2] Its purpose is seen mostly as making a profit out of increased reader- or viewership figures, but also to expose wrongdoing and contribute to social justice like in the case of the U.S. "Muckrakers," who exposed corruption and wrongdoing through investigative journalism in the 1900s. Defined in terms of titillation, amusement, or entertainment, sensationalism is contrasted with "proper," rational news, which is assumed to enhance social and political understanding (ibid., 637; see also chapter 4). Contrary perhaps to the panic about deteriorating journalistic standards, it has been shown (Grabe, Zhou, and Barnett 2001, 651) that both in terms of content and format, there remains a "sturdy" dividing line between serious and sensationalist journalism. Experiments in the empiricist/"effects" tradition (measuring physiological responses and recognition and recall measures) of media studies (Grabe et al. 2000; Grabe, Lang, and Zhao 2003) have shown that audiences tend to view news with dramatic formal features as less believable than the "serious" version. While tabloid features caused increased arousal, attention, and recall in the studies (but decreased memory of content detail), participants tended to distrust tabloid news. Qualitative research among South African tabloid readers differed from this experimental finding among U.S. audiences, however. South African tabloid readers tended to take the news in tabloids on the whole very seriously, although in some cases they offered "negoti-ated" or "oppositional" readings (Hall 1970) of certain types of content. A similar distinction between the credibility of South African mainstream news vis-à-vis the dramatic or emotional (and therefore less trusted) tabloid news was, however, made by respondents who are non-readers of tabloids (such as professionals).[3] Trust in tabloids therefore seemed to be influenced by social position.

The association of tabloids with sensationalism, where sensationalism is viewed pejoratively (cf. Franklin's [1997] distinction between "newszak" and news journalism), has been a long-standing point of view in scholarly studies as well as in popular debates. Sensationalism has been seen as a threat to the very practice of journalism since the penny press in the 1830s (Grabe, Lang, and Zhao 2003). In other words, the danger that tabloids supposedly pose for serious jour-nalism has been a concern for more than a century and a half. Let us now turn to a brief overview of this tabloid history.

History of the Genre

The concern that tabloidization is a contemporary phenomenon that sig-nifies a downward slide in journalistic standards is put into perspective by look-ing back at the long historical development of what is known today as tabloid media. Bird (1992, 9) traces the roots of tabloid journalism back to broadside bal-lads (cheap, printed sheets of rhyme or news) and newsbooks (popular book-lets) in the seventeenth century in Europe and America, "packed with tales of strange and wonderful happenings—murders, natural disasters, unusual births, and omens." These popularity of the ballads and newsbooks benefited from the arrival of the printing press, and contained material drawn from oral tradition, word-of-mouth reports, and insider gossip (ibid., 10). Much of this material was based only loosely on facts, recycling old stories or rumor, and characterized by a "moralizing tone" (ibid., 10–11). Johansson (2007, 13) points to the link pro-vided by these early forms of news between a pre-print oral folk culture and a more widespread popular culture—an aspect that we will return to since this orality has also been noted in South African tabloids, and is one of the reasons why tabloids are often seen as inferior to "quality" papers. The shift from an oral to a print culture was also a defining moment in the establishment of the modern nation, as it emerged in Europe from a medieval landscape (Conboy 2006, 20). The "imagined community" of the nation, to use Anderson's (1987) well-known term, was made possible through a print culture which gave citizens a space where they could reflect on their belonging to a greater entity with common in-terests and a common language (Conboy 2006, 2). Anderson (1987, 15) points out that these imagined communities became possible because of "print capitalism," which resulted in material being published in the more popular (and therefore more profitable) vernacular languages rather than in Latin.

The growth of the penny press in the United States is often cited as a signifi-cant event in journalism history. Papers like the *Sun,* founded in 1833, and the *Herald,* founded in 1835, were the first ones directed at a mass readership, with a cover price (one cent) far below that of the mainstream newspapers (six cents).

Their popularity, which caused rapid increases in newspaper circulation, can be attributed to their sensationalist style and focus on human-interest stories, which were written for a general readership rather than the business and political elites of the time (Bird 1992, 12). It was the style, however, not the subject matter, that set the penny-press papers apart from the mainstream papers of the day. The *Sun*'s style was simple and direct, using vivid, active language and colloquialisms, with stories broken up into shorter paragraphs (ibid., 13). Although this style was new in comparison to the mainstream newspapers of the day, Bird (ibid.) points out that it has its roots in broadside ballads and chapbooks (pocket-sized booklets) that continued to influence and be influenced by newspapers, and similarly displayed a "gruesomely moralistic tone" and stereotyped formulas of reporting on crime and punishment. One of these formulas was the "human-interest" story, a format that was pioneered by the penny press and continues to be a stock-in-trade of tabloid (and mainstream) journalism to this day (ibid., 14). Class tensions came to the fore in penny-press attacks on the rich and powerful, with moralizing judgments serving as an excuse to dish up explicit depictions of violence (ibid., 15).

The shift toward the highly visualized content associated with contemporary tabloids started with the founding of the U.S. *Daily Graphic* in 1872, the first illustrated daily newspaper (ibid., 16). During the 1880s in the United States, conditions supported developing newspaper publishing into a more profitable enterprise. Advances in technology made the mass production of newspapers containing illustrations and advertisements easier and more affordable, while increased immigration and higher literacy rates provided the market for these papers, which could be seen as the direct forerunners of contemporary tabloids (ibid.).

The movement known as yellow journalism was started by the famous publisher Joseph Pulitzer when he bought the *New York World* in 1883, cut the cover price by half to a penny, and started a campaign against corruption and scandals, while advocating an American consumer culture through abundant advertising and features like women's pages, advice columns, and etiquette tips. There was less moralizing than with the penny press, however, as a result of the rise of "objectivity" as a journalistic concept (ibid., 16–18). This convergence of a low cover price, a populist approach, and a combination of crusading journalism with the type of consumerism-boosting content that might today be called "lifestyle journalism" is almost a precise description of the formula followed by the South African tabloids, although the details of this approach are of course contextualized differently.

Pulitzer's style was copied and taken further down the road of titillation by William Randolph Hearst, whose San Francisco *Examiner* and New York *Journal* pitted him in a circulation war with Pulitzer. The stage was set for the creation of the first tabloid, the *Daily Continent,* founded in 1891 by Frank A. Munsey, but it could not withstand the competition from Pulitzer and Hearst's big ventures (ibid., 18). The first viable tabloid was established in Britain by Alfred Harmsworth, later Lord Northcliffe. Northcliffe's first attempt at creating a tabloid came when he was invited by Pulitzer to produce a special tabloid edition of the *World*. Although the issue was very popular, he did not manage to convince Pulitzer of the viability of tabloid papers (ibid.). Northcliffe had to demonstrate this in Britain, perhaps the country today most associated with the "riot of competing tabloids" (Conboy 2006, 1), with the launch of the *Daily Mail* in 1896. This is also where the word "tabloid," appropriated from the term for a pill (tablet + alkaloid) to indicate the newspaper's compact size, was first introduced (Johansson 2007, 16). Only after its success in Britain did the tabloid format take off in the United States, with the establishment of the *New York Daily News* in 1919 and later the *Daily Mirror* and the *New York Evening Graphic* (1924), reaching their bloom in the "jazz age" of 1919–1929 (Bird 1992, 20).

Although the development of tabloid media in Britain can be attributed to American influence, this process was more complicated than merely importing a foreign product (Conboy 2006, 4). The establishment of the first tabloid in Britain by Northcliffe was more the culmination of a long process starting in the mid-1800s. Print media in Britain became accessible to a broader public beyond the elite classes from the 1830s onward and developed a tone of language suitable for a broader readership (ibid., 2–3). The founding in 1833 of the *Sun*, the first paper to address readers in the language of the "common man," can be seen as the point in time when a journalism of entertainment developed alongside a journalism of analysis (Michael Schudson cited in Conboy 2006, 5). Although the British market continued to be further liberalized and commercialized from the 1850s, such as with the publication of the *Daily Mail* as a "profoundly respectable and unsensational" yet big-selling paper aimed at the lower middle class, the shift toward a truly tabloid press in Britain only occurred in the 1930s (Conboy 2006, 4)—around the same time that the tabloid form became firmly established in the United States (Bird 1992, 22–23). Although the *Daily Mirror* experimented with a smaller format and more illustrations from 1903, it was the circulation wars of 1930 that led to its relaunch as a truly tabloid paper aimed at the working classes, and it held the upper hand until the *Sun* changed the "face of journalism and the face of Britain" in the 1970s (Conboy 2006, 7–8). The *Sun* today remains an iconic feature of the vibrant, brash, and controversial British tabloid landscape, which also includes its rival, the *Daily Star,* which is seen at times as stooping to the very lowest limits of tabloid journalism (ibid., 8–9).

Although the ancestry of contemporary tabloids can be traced back hundreds of years, the growing popularity of this genre worldwide, and especially its spread from print to other media formats, has been associated with the postmodern era. Late modernity has brought about conditions in which journalism saw rapid and far-reaching changes, many of which have been seen as conducive for the emergence of a global "tabloid culture" (Glynn 2000, 17).[4] These conditions include increasing media and image saturation; prioritization of images over "the real"; instability of distinctions between "public" and "private" and between "reality" and "representation"; a fragmentation of discourses; the commodification of culture; and an increase in cultural products characterized by eclecticism and a skepticism of grand narratives like universality and objectivity (ibid., 18). These conditions have given rise to well-known global "tabloid media events" like the

O. J. Simpson chase, the death of Princess Diana, and more recently, the disappearance of Madeleine McCann (a three-year-old girl who went missing in 2007
while on vacation with her parents in Portugal), with which media consumers
are so inundated that they have become exhausted, yet already hungry for the
next big event (ibid., 19).

The Future of Newspapers?

In debates about the future of newspapers,[5] the consensus in industry,[6] as
well as in the academy (Singer 1997; Kopper, Kolthoff, et al. 2000; Deuze 2004;
Meyer 2004; Quinn 2005), seems to be that newspapers will have to radically
adapt to new technologies and become part of convergence culture (Jenkins
2006) to avoid becoming redundant. Future developments of news, especially in
printed form, are in these debates seen to be predicated largely on technological
advances that facilitate greater interaction between the producers and consumers of news, blurring the line between these two groups. As media become more
and more personalized and interactive, audiences are increasingly fragmented—
one might have to refer to them as "people formerly known as the audience"
(Rosen 2006). The interactivity made possible by new media technologies means
that professional journalists no longer determine what the public "see, hear and
read about the world around us" (Deuze 2004, 146). Buzzwords like "prosumers"
(a combination of "producers" and "consumers") have been coined to epitomize
the actors in this environment, while the technological, professional, and cultural shifts have been termed "networked journalism" (Bardoel and Deuze 2001).

Is this picture of a converged, new media landscape also true of South Africa?
If so, where do the tabloids fit in? The tabloids that have taken the South African
media market by storm in recent years seem at first glance to be out of synch with
the dominant trends in the developed countries of the Global North. These
newspapers seem to follow a much older tradition. To be sure, the shift from conventional journalism to "networked journalism"—the former being "hierarchical, professionalized, and formulaic: it has deadlines, packages, and messages for
its mainly passive consumers" and the latter displaying a "linear process to networked interactivity, where there is constant communication and exchange of
information between journalists and society" (Beckett and Kyrke-Smith 2007,
56)—can also be noted in some South African media.

The "quality" press in South Africa have been quick to adapt to international
trends in convergence (the combination of old print media and new technologies
such as blogs, video clips on websites, and cell phone news services, as well as
new platforms like Facebook and Twitter) and interactivity (including readers'
blogs, online citizen journalism, and the like) in an attempt to halt declining
circulation figures. Apart from the tabloids, South African newspapers showed a
general but moderate decline in circulation over the past couple of years, with
only a few seeing a moderate increase (Taylor and Milne 2006).[7]

While mainstream newspapers have made interesting forays into new technology,[8] the new tabloid newspapers have come to dominate the country's print-

media market with hardly any recourse to new technologies.[9] The pattern in South Africa is similar to the situation in other African countries, where "old" media (mostly radio, due to high illiteracy rates and low circulation and advertising revenues) still dominate (Beckett and Kyrke-Smith 2007, 24, 45). The popularity of tabloids also has a precedent in other countries on the continent, such as Nigeria, Uganda, and Zimbabwe (Mabweazara 2006; Beckett and Kyrke-Smith 2007, 55), and although there were precursors to tabloids in South Africa (which will be discussed in chapter 3), the country has not seen such a meteoric rise in circulation before, even considering its relatively strong and sophisticated print-media industry. The *Daily Sun,* the country's biggest newspaper, is aimed at the Black[10] working class, or the "man in the blue overall,"[11] as its publisher Deon du Plessis somewhat patronizingly describes the typical reader (pers. comm., February 1, 2007). Two shop-window mannequins dressed in blue overalls reside at the paper's Johannesburg offices, apparently to remind the editorial staff of their constituency.

In terms of formatting and approach to stories, the South African tabloids draw on features borrowed mostly from British tabloids (ibid., 25). The South African versions too contain celebrity news and gossip, sensational human-interest stories, and scandals. Froneman (ibid., 26–27) gives the following as typical features of tabloid news:

- *Strong visuals.* Big, bold headlines and a combination of upper case, underlined, and italic text. Two of the South African tabloids, the *Daily Sun* and *Son,* also use a red background on their mastheads, similar to the British "red-top" tabloids like the *Sun* or *News of the World.*
- *Snappy headlines.* The British tabloid press is especially renowned for using puns in its headlines; the South African papers do this to a lesser extent, according to the national editor of *Son,* Ingo Capraro (pers. comm. 2007), because their readers are less likely to understand the word play. Across the bottom of the front page, the *Daily Sun* does run a humorous, rhyming strapline that refers to an inside story (e.g., "Use a bud to clean your ear, then you will hear clearly, dear! P38," July 16, 2008, or "It's black and pale and has a big tail—it's a male killer whale! P42," July 14, 2008), and occasionally headlines will use word play, like when *Cape Son* reported on a racist incident in a family restaurant and used the headline "Beef over Race Row" (January 29, 2007) or when the *Daily Voice* (which probably follows the British format more closely than any other South African tabloid; see chapter 3) chose the headlines "Stoned" and "Rock 'n Rol" [*sic*] to report on mob violence in a Cape Town township, where two alleged robbers were attacked by a crowd hurling a "massive rock" at them (February 26, 2007).
- *Sex and sensation.* Critics of the tabloids (like Froneman 2006, 26) refer to the "trivial" celebrity news, sexual innuendo, and scandals that form the backbone of tabloid news. The scantily clad or topless "page-three girl," a well-known feature of British tabloids, also features in some of the South

African tabloids (but not the *Daily Sun*) and has become one of the main objects of criticism against these papers.

• *Sports and TV*. Entertainment news forms an important part of tabloid content, and this is indeed the case in South Africa. Snippets from showbiz, both local and international, as well as television program schedules and sports fixtures, analysis, and commentary are standard features. Not all South African tabloids pay equal attention to celebrities, however, and although the *Son* has a daily two-page spread of celebrity news, other tabloids, like *Daily Sun,* focus more on "hard news" like crime or human-interest features, often describing an individual's hardship or triumph over adversity. To argue that entertainment news forms the bulk of content in the South African tabloids would be misleading, since the emphasis in these papers (as also clearly spelled out by editorial policy; see chapter 7) is on covering news of interest to local communities regarding their everyday lives. This may include experiences of racism, accusations of misconduct or corruption by authorities in the community (like teachers or clergy), crime stories or courtroom dramas relating to the communities served by these papers, personal testimonies of victims of crime, and accidents or accusations of government ineptitude. What sets the South African tabloids, especially the *Daily Sun,* apart from their British counterparts, is their reports of supernatural occurrences, often attributed to witchcraft (e.g., "I'm married to a BIG, evil snake!," *Daily Sun,* July 14, 2008; "Evil beast outwits inyanga! [traditional healer]," *Daily Sun,* December 18, 2007). While tabloids in the United States such as the *National Enquirer* also include farfetched stories and claims of alien visitations, the reports in the South African tabloids are different: they are usually not written in the same tongue-in-cheek manner, but in a more credulous tone. The reasons for this controversial approach to stories about the supernatural will be discussed in chapter 6.

Because of the conditions of poverty in which many tabloid readers live, the majority of South African tabloid stories relate to readers' daily struggles for survival, attempts to achieve recognition in society (for instance, the daily accounts in the *Daily Sun* of people's difficulties in obtaining identity documents from the Department of Home Affairs), or outrage against the government's lack of provision of basic services and infrastructure. As chapter 7 will discuss in more detail, tabloid editors know that sports and entertainment news make their papers attractive to people who need some light relief from their daily chores and struggles. But to claim that light relief is used to "provide diversion to the masses" (ibid., 26) is a misleading description of South African tabloids if by this it is meant that light, insubstantial news stories form the bulk of the country's tabloid content. In fact, tabloids often make for quite depressing and distressing reading (which often traumatizes tabloid journalists who are exposed to news of crime, poverty, and violence on a daily basis, as chapter 7 will discuss) because of their consistent and uncompromising coverage of news concerning the poor and working class, who mostly fall off the radar of the mainstream or are viewed from a distant vantage point by the mainstream press.

- *Informal, easy-to-read text.* As Froneman (ibid.) indicates, tabloid stories are often short, and sentences and paragraphs are also kept short to facilitate readability. Yet it is not only tabloids that are cutting down on story length and relying on visual elements to ease readers' entry into stories—recent years have seen a marked shift in South Africa's mainstream "quality" press toward shorter articles and more visual presentations of news.

- *Populist politics.* According to Froneman (ibid.), tabloid newspapers "often shun hard politics, except when a political figure is involved in some real or fabricated scandal." The personalization of politics is indeed a common tabloid approach,[12] but this does not mean that political coverage in tabloids is not influential—the British *Sun* famously claimed in a front-page headline that "It's the Sun wot [*sic*] won it" after backing the victorious Conservative party in the 1992 election, and observers have also attributed the Labour party election victory in 1997 to the *Sun*'s switching allegiance and supporting Tony Blair. While the South African tabloids also tend to eschew formal politics, they have covered key political moments like the succession battle between former president Thabo Mbeki and his successor Jacob Zuma. The more important political influence of the South African tabloids might, however, be seen in their coverage of everyday issues that have political implications, like their readers' frustration at the lack of basic infrastructure or poor service by government departments. This "politics of the everyday" will be discussed in more detail in chapter 5.

- *Tips on getting on with life.* Topics such as dieting, family planning, careers, and relationships form a central part of tabloid coverage in Britain (ibid., 27). Self-help advice forms a big part of South African tabloid content—tips and information are provided on topics ranging from health to legal matters, from raising children to buying a first house, from relationships to growing your own vegetables. The type of information provided also relates to the changes that South African society has undergone and the aspirations to social mobility among the tabloids' readers. These aspects will be discussed in more detail in chapter 2.

The *Daily Sun* and other tabloids—*Son, Daily Voice,* and *Sunday Sun*—have created a mass readership out of the poor and working-class (although upwardly mobile) Black majority of the country that had hitherto been largely out of the focus of the post-apartheid mainstream press, apart from township freesheets distributed by big conglomerates, while newspapers like *City Press* and *Sowetan* were primarily aimed at a middle-class black readership (this excludes the much smaller community newspapers, or papers in indigenous languages, like *Isolezwe* and *Ilanga,* that have also shown growth in circulation over recent years—see Bloom 2005). While aiming at a racially defined audience is in keeping with the still highly segmented media market in South Africa, the tabloids went against the grain of commercial logic, which would prefer an audience in a higher Living Standards Measurement (LSM) category (a tool used by South African media planners to find an audience niche attractive to advertisers) than that of the working poor. But it should also be clear that the decision to target the poor and the working class was not an altruistic decision, but a commercial one based on the lucrative potential of a new market to be tapped. After all, Du Plessis told the *Wall Street Journal* that the emergence of a Black middle class in post-apartheid South Africa is "the beginning stirrings of what [the United States] was in the 1950s . . . There are great fortunes to be made" (Wessel 2007). These "fortunes" are to be made from an upwardly mobile Black working class and growing Black middle class.

> Despite persistent poverty, AIDS and violent crime that mar South Africa's economy, the change in government, steady economic growth and urbanization are yielding a growing number of Black households with middle-class incomes or aspirations to join the middle class. Back in 1990, the total income of the 10% of South Africans who are White exceeded the incomes of the 45% who are Black. (The remainder are deemed colored or Indian.) Since 2001, however, the collective income of Blacks has exceeded the income of the White minority. (ibid.)

The tabloids have also impacted the circulation of other papers, notably the *Sowetan*,[13] whose circulation figures took a nose-dive after the 2001 introduction of the country's first tabloid, the *Sunday Sun,* but especially after the 2002 introduction of the *Daily Sun* (Taylor and Milne 2006). Within its first year, the *Daily Sun* grew its circulation by 228 percent.[14] The phenomenal commercial success of this tabloid was partly blamed for the huge circulation losses at the *Sowetan* and was seen as a reason for the appointment of a new editor to restructure the *Sowetan* and *Sunday World* (by also including "tabloid" elements) and to try to reverse their circulation losses.[15]

In the wake of the *Daily Sun*'s success, other tabloid newspapers followed. An Afrikaans-language weekly tabloid, *Kaapse Son* (Cape Sun), was launched in the Western Cape province in 2003 and published by the same media house, Naspers. Aimed at both the Coloured and White Afrikaans working classes (Koopman, pers. comm., 2005), its popularity soon became evident and it changed from a weekly to a daily in 2005. From 2006 to 2007, it launched a series of regional editions outside the Western Cape, published weekly and titled simply *Son* (Bizcommunity 2007). (Two of these, the Gauteng and Free State editions, were closed in February 2008 because of a "combination of market-related factors" [Media24 2008], leaving only the Western and Eastern Cape editions.) Naspers' rival company, the Irish-owned multi-national Independent News & Media Group PLC, replied by launching an English-language tabloid, the *Daily Voice,* in the same region in 2005. Providing much the same fare (its tagline is "Sex, Scandal, Skinner [gossip], Sport"), it challenged the *Son* head-on by using colloquial language, among other things (Penstone 2005) and by publishing one of its three editions in a hybrid between Afrikaans and English (Brophy 2007). Naspers again fired back by launching an English-language version of *Son* in 2006.[16]

Figure 2.1. The front page of the (now discontinued) English-language edition of *Son*. The headline uses an Afrikaans expression to declare: "We are fed up."

Figure 2.2. The front page of the Afrikaans edition of *Daily Voice*. The headline reads: "I am seven years old and I do Tik (methamphetamine). My aunty gives it to me. Help me."

In addition to these daily tabloids are two Sunday tabloids, the *Sunday Sun* and *Sondag*. These are also in the Naspers stable, owned by its subsidiary, Media24, and published by RCP Media. *Sunday Sun* was the first tabloid to be published in the country and is also aimed at a Black market. *Sunday Sun* competes with the *Sowetan's* Sunday edition, *Sunday World* (circulation 203,460).[17] *Sondag* in turn provides a lighter alternative to its sister paper *Rapport*, which is strongly focused on political issues, especially as they concern White Afrikaners. Despite a solid performance (a circulation of 43,464 for *Sondag* in January–March 2008,[18] and 202,524 for *Sunday Sun*), these two tabloids have not had the same impact nor created the same level of controversy as their daily counterparts.

One could safely say that the arrival of the new tabloid newspapers has changed the media landscape in post-apartheid South Africa irrevocably. In a new democracy, they have drawn readers from the majority of the population who were previously on the margins of the print-media sphere. The arrival of the South African tabloids is significant not only because of their impact on the journalism profession and media market in the country, but because their genesis and growth are linked to the country's changing socio-political context since the demise of formal apartheid in the 1990s. Democratization changed the regulatory as well as professional normative regime under which the media operated, weakened the old ideological positions to which media houses were tied, and opened new markets for big media conglomerates. South Africa re-entered the globalized media sphere, which meant that influences from abroad were more easily incorporated into local media (this aspect will be discussed in more detail in the next chapter), and that global media conglomerates such as the Independent Group made their presence felt in the South African media industry (for example, by establishing a tabloid, the *Daily Voice*). Other salient factors underlying the rise of tabloids can be summarized as follows:

The Demise of Alternative Media

A vacuum had been created by the demise of anti-apartheid alternative media, which used to cater to the concerns and interests of the Black majority in their struggle against apartheid (Switzer 1997; Switzer and Adhikari 2000) but saw their funding dwindling with the advent of democracy.[19] In the early nineties, the alternative papers largely disappeared or were taken up into the mainstream (e.g., the current *Mail and Guardian,* which developed from the alternative paper *Weekly Mail*). Other newspapers that catered to the Black market, like *Sowetan* or *City Press,* focused more on middle-class Black readers. By pointing to the demise of the erstwhile alternative media, it is not suggested that the new tabloid media should be considered alternative media in the sense that the term was used in the apartheid era (this description would fit a social-movement publication like the Treatment Action Campaign's *Equal Treatment*). Tabloid media certainly cannot be described as alternative media if that definition pertains to media produced by "individuals, or by small, non-hierarchical collectives" that "seek not profit but to represent particular interest groups" (Franklin et al. 2005,

14). In fact, although there is some difference of opinion of whether alternative media is just the more politicized version of its "respectable twin," the "quality press," but essentially still aimed at the same middle-class, affluent, and educated readership (Glynn 2000, 6; Fiske 1992, 74; Franklin et al. 2005, 14), tabloid media is usually seen as part of a third journalistic form that falls outside of both the "quality" and "alternative" designations.

Viewing the tabloid audience only in market terms, however, would neglect the tabloids' contribution to the restoration of a civic presence for neglected sections of the population. Although not "alternative" in the usual sense of the term, in some respects the tabloids might be telling the type of stories that Anton Harber (2002) expected new alternative journalisms in democratic society to tell:

> So where are our alternative voices of today? Let me hasten to say that we would not be looking for the same voice as before. Great journalism would [no] longer, I believe, be defined by defiance and bravery—as it had to be during the years of repression, when getting something said was often more important than how one said it; courage will be required, yes, the courage to swim against the tide, to probe uncomfortable wounds; it is now about telling stories which get under the skin of this complex and difficult country; it is about material which—through careful research and thoughtful compilation—leads us to understandings which are not apparent on the surface; it is about writing which makes us think more carefully about this country and its people.

Although tabloids do "probe uncomfortable wounds" and tell "stories which get under the skin of this complex and difficult country," as Harber wanted new alternative media to do, some would argue that their commercial nature and sensational approach often lead to a reduction of broader political and social issues to the micro, individual level without having a real political edge. While social movements like the shack-dwellers' organization, Abahlali baseMjondolo, have criticized the mainstream media for not giving them a voice (Abahlali baseMjondolo bakuAsh Road, June 24, 2008; also see the motto at the front of this book), other movements have come to regard tabloids as counter-productive for putting the concerns of the poor on the public agenda. Dale McKinley (pers. comm. 2008),[20] spokesperson of the Anti-Privatization Forum, a social movement working to resist neoliberal policies its adherents perceive as worsening the historical legacies of apartheid under which the country's poor still suffer, believes that no media outlet in the country pays adequate attention to stories "that come out of poor communities." He laments the disappearance of the erstwhile alternative anti-apartheid press and the failure of the SABC to play the role of public broadcaster due to its increasingly commercial motives—"that has been a huge loss in terms of being able to communicate things that are not hooked into market-related mechanisms." McKinley does not see the tabloids as having stepped into the gap left by the alternative media, describing the *Daily Sun* as a "reactionary rag":

> What it does is it takes what a bourgeois tabloid in London would do and takes it down to the local level. It sensationalizes poor people's lives as well. "Man has sex with goat," you know, this kind of thing. OK they occasionally have a couple of good

pieces. They were the ones that fomented a lot of alien hate around xenophobia . . .
They know that a headline "Man has sex with goat" will sell. What won't sell is a
headline that actually says "5000 evictions took place in the last month in Mamelodi
because people have lost their jobs."[21]

McKinley's criticism of the tabloids as not uncovering the root causes of poverty was echoed by another social-movement activist, Andile Mngxitama of the
Landless People's Movement. Mngxitama (pers. comm. 2008) argued that the
tabloids engage in a "mystification" of poverty and do not assist the reader in
making the links between the conditions under which the subjects of their stories live and broader political and policy matters. One could argue (as Glynn
2000, 10 does) that if social movements tapped into the communicative networks
provided by the tabloids and better understood the political dimensions of the
popular culture (often dominated by a sense of marginalization) the tabloids
embody, these social movements would have been able to use tabloid media more
effectively to their strategic political advantage, bringing them closer to becoming "alternative" media. (The role of tabloids in political life will be discussed in
more detail in chapter 5.)

Criticism that the new tabloids are not political enough, or that they do not
provide a sufficiently alternative perspective to that of the mainstream press,
should be taken seriously. Such criticism notwithstanding, the fact of the demise
of the alternative media in the country does go some way in highlighting the
gaps in the print-media market that provided the new tabloids with a foothold.
This is especially true if one considers the claims laid to civic rights, either im-
plicitly or explicitly, by the subjects of tabloid reports. Whether these claims are
for delivery of basic services such as housing, water, and electricity; for receiving
identity documents from the Department of Home Affairs; or for being treated
decently at state hospitals,[22] tabloids invoke the rights all citizens should be enjoying in the post-apartheid era. Such an insistence on civic rights can be seen as
the continuation of the struggle for acknowledgement and respect that the alternative media fought for. Steenveld (2006, 18) sees the tabloids as part of such
a post-apartheid restoration of citizenship by enabling readers to exercise their
social rights: "Under apartheid, a sense of self was denied along with political
and civil rights. The core of apartheid entailed dehumanizing many South Africans and rendering them invisible. Tabloids, at some level, enable a sense of visibility and voice." As Steenveld rightly continues to point out, acknowledging that
tabloids have given voice to marginalized subjects does not preclude a critical
interrogation of the terms and conditions under which such vocalization takes
place. Even if a space might be given for the subaltern to speak (Spivak 1985), that
space might be clearly circumscribed by powerful economic interests.

It is true that these tabloids are not operating independently, as did the erstwhile alternative media. Rather, they are owned by conglomerates that have identified the Black working class as a lucrative market segment. From this perspective, tabloids provided "the opportunity to service the bottom end of the media
market [that] was not exploitable before" (Rabe 2007, 28). Even while South African

tabloids arguably pay more attention to "serious" news and politics than their UK counterparts (and certainly more than the U.S. "supermarket tabloids"), their ownership by big capital in all likelihood constrains their ability to provide a radical critique of the political-economic status quo. This also explains the paradox between the critical coverage of what could be called the politics of the everyday (lack of service delivery, health care, crime) on the one hand and the celebration of consumerism and upward mobility through "lifestyle" supplements with features on cigars, wine, and partying (e.g., the *Daily Sun*'s supplement, *SunLife*) on the other. In the way that South African tabloids seem to engage in a progressive rhetoric but shy away from radical politics, they can also be seen to "borrow the people's voice" (Conboy 2008a, 115) to a large degree. Their politics remain in line with the liberal consensus of the post-apartheid democratic settlement, even if they vociferously attack the government and the establishment when the government fails to keep the promises made as part of this consensus. One could also see the tabloids' ownership by big profit-seeking conglomerates as proof that for tabloids, their poor and working-class audiences remain merely a market to be tapped. This point of view would coincide with the Habermasian notion that the public sphere has been "refeudalized" by market concerns and that consumerism is masquerading as citizenship (Glynn 2000, 15–16).

Yet for all these limitations, it would be a mistake to dismiss the tabloids out of hand for not being able to provide an alternative perspective on the news, one which differs significantly from that provided by the mainstream press. Even if they do not build on the tradition of radical critique, the tabloids could still be regarded as having stepped into the void left by the demise of the anti-apartheid alternative media in some ways. For example, as we will see in chapter 7, there is a close relationship between tabloid journalists and their readers, and despite their working within the confines of a large commercial concern, tabloid journalists for the most part see their publications as vehicles for a socially engaged type of journalism that they were not able to pursue in the mainstream press. Moreover, the tabloids open up the possibility for a counter-hegemonic discourse to emerge at the moment of consumption, when readers engage with tabloid news in such a way as to read against the grain of official narratives and dominant meanings. Even if the tabloids might seem a far cry from the critical alternative media of the apartheid era or from the Habermasian notion of a rational public sphere (a concept which in any case can be seen as a Eurocentric notion—Gunaratne 2006), they contain the potential for critical "counterknowledges" to emerge.

Shifts in Ownership and Editorial Staff, but Continued Market Logic

When South Africa embarked on the transition from a racist minority regime to a democratic government, the media were seen as central to building a new democratic culture and society. For the media to do this, they had to transform their ownership and staffing. White ownership and production of media were seen as resulting in a limited and skewed picture of social reality (see, e.g., Mandela 1994a). In terms of staffing, this situation changed as more Black journalists and editors were appointed to publications formerly edited by Whites, and a racially inclusive professional body of journalists, the South African National Editors' Forum (SANEF), was established. However, the continued commercial logic of mainstream newspapers, even as their editors and staffs changed to reflect more racial diversity,[23] continued to marginalize the experiences of the Black majority in press coverage as they sought audiences that would be attractive to advertisers. Since class and race still largely coincided in post-apartheid South Africa, this meant that these audiences were either White or belonged to a Black middle class or elite. Several critics have indicated that the print media's class base remains the same despite the restructuring of editorial staffs (Duncan 2003; Jacobs 2004).[24] The limits of the transformation in the sector have been conceded by the (then) editor of one of the arguably more progressive mainstream newspapers, the *Mail and Guardian*'s Ferial Haffajee:

> Would that I could stand here with the 10 year media dream delivered and speak to you of an institution wholly transformed. Of an institution rooted where you are—in the community, reflecting your daily struggles. One that understood unemployment as more than just an economic slogan—that investigated its causes and its fall-out. Of an institution that held to account those in power and empowered those that were not.
> Would that I could stand here and tell you about a thousand flowers blooming. About a public broadcaster that we all felt we owned—here you could go and learn the community broadcasting skills that would enable you to take your struggles out, out beyond the confines of a few streets, a couple of extensions. Would that I could, or you could, show me examples of street newspapers stuck up on corners that you could savour over a morning break coffee. But I can't tell you such a story ten years into our freedom. Like all of the country, nothing has turned out quite as planned. Freedom rarely turns out so—and the truth is good for the media as much as it is for your lives. (Haffajee 2004a)

At the level of ownership, significant shifts took place. Yet ironically, these structural shifts often resulted in an increased commercial environment for the media, as South African media re-entered a global media sphere marked by high levels of competition and profit seeking. At the advent of democracy in the early 1990s, the country's print media were largely owned and edited by Whites. The press was split along ideological lines corresponding with language and the interests of mining capital and the apartheid state respectively (Tomaselli and Dunn 2001). This picture changed when two big transactions involving so-called Black-empowerment consortiums (Johnnic [now known as Avusa] and Nail) brought some of the biggest newspaper titles under Black ownership in the 1990s. The Irish-based Independent Group gained control of a series of English-language newspaper titles, thereby opening up South African media for global competition (Tomaselli 2000c). Restructuring of the Afrikaans-language press was more limited.[25] Whereas the English-language print media have seen their control passed to a foreign company, the largest Afrikaans media conglomerate,

Naspers, only "unbundled" slightly by forming new firms and selling some of its "family silver" to Black business groups (ibid.). The concentration of ownership into essentially three big companies led to a loss of diversity among different newspaper titles, with papers in the same company syndicating content among themselves. "Global economic challenges and technological innovations" were blamed when Naspers in 2008 further restructured its print sector, threatening wide-ranging retrenchments and the further centralization of its newspaper editorial functions with the aim of eventually merging its mainstream newspapers (Makholwa 2008; De Waal 2008). The commercial pressure resulting partly from the opening up of the local media industry to global competition had "devastating" results (Harber 2002) on the local media scene. It led to "juniorization" of newsrooms, a preference for commercial imperatives in making editorial judgments, and an erosion of specialized reporting (ibid.; Jacobs 2004). These trends are often blamed for what has come to be referred to as the "tabloidization" of the mainstream print media, with more attention paid to entertainment and celebrity news, which is often taken over from wire copy produced abroad (Media Monitoring Project 2007). The shift to popular media formats had therefore already begun to take place well before the formal entry of tabloid newspapers to the market. The "tabloidization" process eventually was intensified when tabloids started to exert pressure on the sales figures of papers such as the *Sowetan* (*Financial Mail* 2004).

Even as ownership structures changed and editorial staffs became more representative of the country's racial demography, the print media after apartheid still operated according to the same logic of circulation, distribution networks, price structure, and advertising (Jacobs 2004). News values and business models employed by the "quality press" favored White and increasingly Black middle class and elites. The Black working class and underclass continued to be treated mostly as objects of news rather than as news consumers from whose perspective news events could be viewed and narrated. When issues like poverty, social delivery, HIV/AIDS, and crime formed part of the news agenda of the "quality press," more often than not these issues were presented as abstract political or economic problems rather than as the daily lived experience of the millions of poor in post-apartheid South Africa. The Media Development and Diversity Agency (MDDA), funded by levies on mainstream media companies, was established to provide assistance to independent community print media serving historically disadvantaged communities. Nevertheless, the print-media sector remained dominated by commercial interests.

For all their shortcomings and problems, the tabloids went against this dominant current by providing personalized (and often sensationalized) accounts of the effects of social ills from the perspective of those having to live them. On the occasions when growing frustration at the lack of social delivery, continued poverty and unemployment, crime, and other socio-economic problems such as drug abuse and HIV/AIDS boiled over in street protests around the country, the tabloids, especially the *Daily Sun*, seized the opportunity to capitalize on this widespread dissatisfaction. During 2007 alone there were 5,000 protests around the country objecting to the continued lack of basic services.[26] This groundswell of popular unrest was also seen as a large part of the reason for the defeat of then-president Thabo Mbeki by Jacob Zuma at the ruling African National Congress' annual national conference in 2007. Zuma was seen as a candidate with more grassroots appeal among the working class.

The *Daily Sun* conducted a campaign highlighting the failings of local government and reported on the eruption of community protests against the lack of social delivery (Du Plessis, pers. comm. 2007). In the run-up to the election of Jacob Zuma as ANC president, the *Daily Sun* ran commentary on its front page explaining how Zuma's popularity related to Thabo Mbeki's lack of leadership on social issues such as HIV/AIDS, public service inefficiency, crime, and reconstruction and development. In their coverage of popular disillusionment at the slow pace of social reform, the tabloids gave their readers a way to engage with those aspects of politics that relate to their daily lives. Instead of providing their readers with what is considered a wholesome diet of formal political coverage, tabloids offer them fare they are more familiar with—the personal, the anecdotal, and the diurnal experiences of what politics mean on a day-to-day basis. In this way, the tabloids seem to have caught on to the "alienation felt among the working classes from the formal political processes" and the "struggle fatigue" (tiredness of political rhetoric drawing on anti-apartheid struggle) among their readers, focusing on the exercise of their readers' social rights as citizens rather than their political rights as voters (Steenveld 2006, 19). The tabloids' political role will be discussed in more detail in chapter 5.

Socio-Economic Shifts

The transition from apartheid to majority rule brought about formal democracy in South Africa. Yet, certain types of rights were easier to realize than others. The new Constitution guaranteed both "first-generation" democratic rights, such as freedom from discrimination and freedom of expression, and "second-generation" rights, which include the right to food, housing, health care, education, clean water, and so on (Robins 2005, 2). While the achievement of first-generation rights is often celebrated, the second-generation rights have failed to become a reality for many South Africans (Robins 2005, 2). In fact, studies have shown that the gap between rich and poor has widened since the arrival of democracy in South Africa, with the country's Gini coefficient (a measure of inequality in a society, with 0 denoting perfect equality and 1 perfect inequality) of around 0.72 percent (in 2005/2006) making it one of the most unequal societies in the world. It is estimated that about 45 percent of the country's population lives in poverty, below the Minimum Living Level (MLL)[27] (ibid.; Terreblanche 2002; SARPN 2003; SSA 2008). We will return to the relationship between rights, citizenship, and tabloid media in chapters 5 and 6. What is relevant to an understanding of the socio-economic shifts taking place in the country and how these relate to media is that while income between population groups remains high,[28] so that class still corresponds to race overall, income inequality within an individual group was highest among Black (African) households.[29] This figure indicates that a small section of the Black population managed to increase its economic position significantly. Removal of restrictive apartheid legislation and the introduction of redistributive government policies like affirmative action and Black Economic Empowerment have created social mobility for a group of Black consumers belonging to or moving into the middle class. At the top end of this class is a new Black elite, nicknamed the "Black Diamonds" (Unilever Institute 2007). The growth of a Black middle class and elite coincided with (and is linked to) the emergence more generally of a consumer identity, especially among young South Africans who prefer to express their identities by means of conspicuous consumption rather than through the old identity categories inherited from apartheid (Alexander 2006).

These socio-economic shifts had implications for media target markets. While newspapers like the *Sowetan* and the *City Press* continued to cater to Black middle-class readers, a range of magazines (e.g., *Blaque, Black Business, Afropolitan,* and *Enterprise*) reflected the aspirations of the new Black elite and attest to the attractiveness of this market to high-end advertisers.[30] The tabloids, while aimed at a much lower-income segment of the market, picked up on this aspirational culture, and through special pages and supplements provided their readers with tips and advice on "lifestyle," home ownership, and financial matters. In this way, the tabloids engaged with this young, upwardly mobile audience and created a new advertising market in the process. While this upwardly mobile class makes up a small percentage of the Black majority, it is in the tabloids' best interest to contribute to the creation and development of such an aspirational class of readers. As commercial enterprises, tabloid papers seek to attract advertisers, and advertisers are interested in capturing readers who are in the process of redefining their social identities by means of consumption.

"People that are still not in count": South African Tabloids and Society

We have thus far seen that the South African tabloids emerged at a point in South African history where media coverage was a highly contested terrain. Their emergence can be related to a number of developments in the South African media sphere but also in society at large. How should we understand the relationship between the tabloids and South African society? Are tabloid readers the individual, consumerist subjects of postmodern entertainment media, or can tabloids construct a community? Can we understand the popularity of the South African tabloids as something more than just the result of a "race to the bottom" or a pandering to the lowest common denominator? If so, could the reason for their success also tell us something about the question with which we started this chapter—about the future of newspapers?

A common reaction to the high circulation figures of tabloids is to dismiss them as vulgar and sensational and therefore popular—"popular" here used not only to denote their mass appeal, but also marking a class distinction between "popular" and "quality" journalism which conventionally has been at the basis of normative criteria for the media's role in the public sphere (Meijer 2001). Such a view would associate tabloids with the homogenization of the public sphere rather than the diversification thereof—as Louw (2001, 48) points out with reference to the emergence of "sensationalism" as a means to attract mass audiences. Tabloids are associated with an appetite for scandal, celebrity, superficiality, lack of seriousness, and entertainment or "infotainment" rather than with serious news coverage (Hinerman 1997; Gripsrud 2000; Sparks 2000). In sum, they are seen as contributing to the depoliticization of publics and the "lowering of journalistic standards" (Curran 2003, 93). The spread of these characteristics to "quality" papers or other media platforms like television or magazines is often referred to as "tabloidization" or "dumbing down" and takes place around the world (Grabe, Zhou, and Barnett 1999; Glynn 2000; Hallin 2000; Ursell 2001; Jones 2002; Davis 2003; Bek 2004; Conboy 2005).

Counter-perspectives from scholars who work (broadly) within the cultural studies tradition like John Fiske and Elizabeth Bird (Fiske 1989; Bird 1992; Fiske 1992) have argued that tabloids undermine the high culture–low culture hierarchy, provide a voice to marginalized publics, and serve as a site for resistance against cultural hegemony. Some believe that tabloids maintain a society's dominant values and norms by showing spectacular instances where these norms are transgressed (Grabe, Zhou, and Barnett 1999, 636), while others (e.g., Conboy 2005) point out that tabloids have throughout their history contested bourgeois societal values.

Which of these two views hold true for South African tabloids? Probably both.

Looking at their content, these tabloids eschew formal political coverage, sensationalize news, and publish excessively lurid or graphic pictures (including portrayals of violence). There is a strong focus on sports and entertainment, and through the avoidance of controversial political or ethnic positioning, they ensure that as large an audience as possible is delivered to advertisers.

But the picture is contradictory and complex. These tabloids also provide a voice to the country's working-class majority, whose perspectives remain marginalized in the mainstream print media of the post-apartheid era. Stories about crime, drugs, and social problems that beset their communities are covered in-depth, extensively, and from a personalized perspective rather than as merely social pathologies marked by race and class or as formal economic and political issues; allegations of racism in the workplace or in the social sphere are treated seriously; and the daily struggles brought about by the confluence of historical inequalities and post-apartheid neoliberal economic policies are viewed from the perspective of those that have to deal with them. For instance, the evicted illegal occupants of council houses are represented as "defenceless women and children" that "had to look on yesterday as the contents of their houses were carried away under the surveillance of heavily-armed cops,"[31] rather than as lawbreakers, as they might have been in the mainstream press—if their plight even made the pages of the mainstream newspapers (which in this case it didn't). The unequal access to health care (with the poor reliant on under-resourced state hospitals and the elite having access to well-equipped private care) is foregrounded through individual accounts,[32] as is the powerlessness of individuals against the systemic incompetence that robs them of chances to better themselves, like the inability to get the correct identity document needed to apply for study or work or even to retire.[33]

While recounting individual experiences could be seen to neglect larger structural issues or formal politics, conventional reporting, with its preference for "hard facts" like statistics or policy documents, would in all probability only serve to remove formal politics even further from the daily experience of tabloid readers. The same approach goes for reports that hold government or officialdom to account. First-person accounts of police violence and incidents of racism are splashed on the front page and often continued across several inside pages.[34] These individual accounts of system failure and personally experienced prejudice are what constitute tabloid politics in the post-apartheid democracy (see chapter 5 for a more in-depth discussion of tabloid politics). This is why, on the same day in February 2007 that the *Sowetan*, the mainstream stalwart of Black journalism, announced the death of Adelaide Tambo (the wife of the former ANC president) on its front page with the headings "Mama Tambo dies" and "Nation mourns," the tabloid *Daily Sun* ran a front-page headline, "No Mercy!," on a hospital that barred patients from parking their cars, resulting in a car jacking (February 1, 2007). This focus on the politics of the everyday will be discussed further in chapter 5.

The publisher of the *Daily Sun*,[35] Deon du Plessis, ridiculed the *Sowetan's* choice of leading with the Tambo story, saying that the "collective is dead"[36] (Du Plessis, pers. comm., 2007). This view of readers as individual consumers would fit with the highly commercialized, entertainment-driven tabloid format that is central to the commodification of news globally (Thussu 2008; see also chapter 3). In the case of the South African tabloids, the shift from the collective to the individual can indeed be seen in the presence of articles, supplements, and columns that interpellate tabloid readers as consumers and facilitate their entry into the middle class. For the owners and publishers of these tabloids, this social mobility is what makes their readers attractive to advertisers. Economic news is provided in practical terms, such as "Budget and You."[37] The *Daily Sun* gives new homeowners advice in a supplement, "Sun Houses" (with the tagline "Getting a place of your own"), and the *Daily Voice* has a section called "Kwaai Cabbies" ("Cool Cabbies"—"cabbie" is a colloquial term for "car") that "keeps you up to date on motoring news."[38] The *Son* regularly publishes advice and tips on health, household, and safety matters, and has even published a self-help medical booklet for separate sale.

These consumer-oriented features remain in tension with the reports of the despair and precariousness of township life. Such are the contradictions of a society in rapid and unequal transition, and the tabloid media, as commercial entities reliant on a public caught between the legacies of the apartheid history and the promised future of consumption and progress, reflect this.

Figure 2.3. The *Sowetan* announces the death of Adelaide Tambo on its front page (see discussion on pp. 36 and 99).

Figure 2.4. The *Daily Sun*'s front page on the day the *Sowetan* ran the front-page lead on Adelaide Tambo's death (see discussion on pp. 36 and 99).

Yet for all the consumerism underpinning Du Plessis' declaration that the collective is dead, the tabloids have managed to create a sense of community among their readers. Conversations with tabloid readers (see chapter 6) indicate that reading tabloids also has a socializing function. The act of reading a tabloid, sharing it with someone else, or just to be seen reading it provides social capital to tabloid readers and facilitates interaction between members of the community.

One could point to cynical commercial motives of the owners and publishers of these tabloids, but readers experience the stories they read about in tabloids as validation of their daily lived experience. While the subjects of these stories mostly enter mainstream print-media discourse as statistics or objects of news, the tabloids have created a relationship with their readers through a willingness to listen and recount "stories of working class life that manage to be both humdrum and dramatic" (Krüger 2006). One would be naïve to imagine that the tabloids see their role in altruistic or social responsibility terms. But regardless of the strong commercial imperative underlying the tabloid venture, their readers see tabloids as their advocates, often their only hope of being heard or taken seriously. In the post-apartheid society, the tabloids provide a space where dominant post-apartheid narratives of democratic progress and the "better life for all" promised by the ANC when it came to power can be contested.

The role of individual journalists and editors in maintaining this relationship of trust should not be discounted. In interviews with tabloid journalists and editors (discussed in chapter 7), they often expressed empathy with their readers and a desire to do justice to their stories. The extent of this reciprocal relationship between tabloids and their publics far exceeds that of the mainstream press, if it is to be measured in the number of letters received—figures run into several hundreds per day.[39] The *Daily Sun* ran a campaign about social delivery, for instance, asking readers to tell the paper about local government failings, and it received an overwhelming response of around ten thousand letters a month, of which the paper ran ten a day for a year (Du Plessis, pers. comm., 2007).

The *Daily Sun*'s editor, Themba Khumalo, recalls several incidents where readers preferred to call the paper instead of the police, sometimes while a crime was in the process of being committed:

Once, there I was at home, on a Friday or a Saturday, a call comes through on my cell phone—don't ask me how people get my number—and there was somebody telling me "there are criminals in the shop where I'm working." They gave me the name of the shop, I phoned it through to the editorial team working on that day, they phoned the police, and by the time we got there we got there at the same time as the police. That level of trust, if you look at that . . .

Then there was a case where the level of trust between a reader and the paper took a bloody turn:

This man came to us, the story was carried by all the mainstream newspapers the previous day, about a man that had killed his wife. He was saying yes, I killed her, but I want to tell my side of the story, and I want to hand myself over and I want you to be there, I want you to take me to the police because I trust you. . . . The man didn't trust anybody, he called us to take him to the police station, he committed suicide, the bullet went through him and it went through me here.

Perhaps indicating the machismo among the *Daily Sun*'s senior staff (Du Plessis has figurines of Conan the Barbarian adorning his desk, and he recites with a twinkle in his eye his motto: "Find the enemy, crush him, and hear the lamentations of their women!"), the *Daily Sun* had T-shirts printed with the words that Khumalo uttered upon realizing that he was hit by the ricochet bullet from the suicide victim: "Shit, I'm shot!" This was also the headline for the paper's report on the incident, which hangs in a frame against Khumalo's wall.

The editor of *Son* testifies to a similar relationship between this tabloid and its readers:

> People call us often. "Come and look, the city council is evicting us [from our homes]" or "the police are beating us" and then we go out. It's actually tragic how much pain the people we work with have to go through. And they are people that are still not in count. And they see *Son* as a way of bringing out their voice, of being heard. Often people phone us and say "we went to the police but the police didn't help us." The police are now also anti-*Son* because people come to us, we are their watchdog. Everywhere I go, I hear that people aren't saying "we are going to take you to the police" anymore, but instead "we are going to take you to *Son*." So *Son* is used as a threat. (Koopman, pers. comm. 2007)[40]

The three tabloids also each have their own regular features (Captain Voice Power, Sun Power, Mr Fixit, Son gee om) where help is provided in practical ways, from fixing leaking toilets to reuniting loved ones to handing out Easter eggs to township children. This is another way in which interactivity between the newspapers and readers is maintained in a visible and tangible way.

The level of trust that readers of South African tabloids invest in these publications sets them apart from tabloids in, for instance, the United Kingdom. Although tabloids have been seen as being "at the heart" of newspaper journalism in that country (Johansson 2007, 177), public trust in tabloids is very low. A survey in 2008 found that tabloids are trusted to tell the truth by a "miserable 10% of the nation."[41] When asked whether tabloids would be more interested in getting a story than telling the truth, 82 percent of tabloid readers in this survey agreed. The situation looks very different in South Africa, where although tabloids are often at least partly read with a pinch of salt (as we will see in chapter 6), there is a much stronger bond between tabloid readers and their papers.

What does the emergence of South African tabloids tell us about the future of newspapers, and perhaps journalism studies more generally? First, the debate about the future of newspapers—in fact, the question that led to the debate in the first place—has been dominated by dilemmas and crises experienced in the media-saturated Global North, where audiences are deserting newspapers because of a proliferating range of media-consumption choices linked to social and lifestyle changes. The ways newspapers are countering this trend—such as through convergence and interactivity—are mostly predicated on the access their readers have to new media technologies. The case of South African tabloids (and tabloids elsewhere in Africa) indicates that this situation is not universal. Newspapers are still important in the South African context, and where they are overtaken by other media, it is because of the socio-economic context (e.g., radio being preferred because of low literacy rates and affordability). Acknowledging this is not the same as viewing African newspapers as lagging behind on a universal evolutionary trajectory toward technological innovation. Change and evolution in newspaper journalism is a heterogeneous and contextually dependent process. A multi-linear, multi-perspectival view on journalism studies should be followed, with more perspectives from the Global South entering the debate.

Second, the success of South African tabloids is linked to the social and political changes taking place in the country after democratization. Their emergence and popularity cannot be reduced only to the format, style, or genre taken over from similar newspapers elsewhere, but should be considered against the political economy of the South African media landscape as well as the social and material conditions shaping the lived experience of their readers. Newspapers should be viewed within their historical, social, and material contexts, which are constantly changing and shifting. Such a contextual approach would prevent a discussion about the future of newspapers and journalism from applying the status quo in certain parts of the world universally.

Third, evaluating the South African tabloids against the emerging literature on convergent and networked journalism, they would seem to follow a conventional journalism model, where information is gathered by journalists (albeit with the help of correspondents and informants in the field), packaged according to conventional journalistic routines in the newsroom, and then disseminated to a mass audience. However, considered against the broader picture of the structural exclusions still experienced by a large section of the South African public with regard to mainstream print media, these tabloids manage to elicit from their readers a significant amount of trust and reciprocity. There is an element of interactivity between the tabloid editorial staff and the papers' readership that extends beyond the conventional one-dimensional model of news dissemination and consumption, even if this interactivity is not mediated extensively through new media technologies. In fact, if new media technologies were to be introduced into this relationship, it would perhaps broaden the divide between elite, urban-based journalists and the working-class and largely rural constituencies the tabloids serve. Bardoel and Deuze (2001) suggest that "networked journalism" results from technological, professional, and cultural changes that re-invigorate the values of civic journalism in the new media age. The South African tabloids may well fulfill some of the ideals of orientation toward the audience that civic journalism holds dear. One should, however, not push this analogy too far. Just as the interactivity created by new media technologies can seduce one to view the reader-as-consumer relationship through rose-tinted glasses without recognizing persistent inequalities and power differentials, one could romanticize the South African tabloids as well. The fact remains that they are big business ventures with an eye on profits, and that they still operate very much according to commercial logic and an editorial audience hierarchy, with the former (editorial) in control. The opportunities for feedback and user-created content remain limited.

The fourth and perhaps the most important point that the South African tabloids illustrate is that, whether a newspaper has all the technological bells and whistles, or whether it is printed on paper and passed on from hand to hand at taxi ranks and on the factory floor, interactivity takes many forms. What form it takes depends on material conditions, historical context, and social formations. And these conditions will keep changing constantly, both now and in the future.

Regardless (or perhaps because of) their huge popularity, the tabloids have not been welcomed by the journalistic establishment. They have been accused of flouting journalistic norms like objectivity and truth telling by publishing far-fetched and sensational stories, of objectifying women by publishing pictures of scantily clad or topless women, and of overstepping the boundaries of good taste through their fascination with sex. In some cases, the tabloids have also clearly flouted the media's ethical codes, which has led to widespread protest, not only from the journalistic and scholarly community, but also from the public. These issues will be discussed further in chapters 4 and 5.

Even while the South African tabloids present us with an argument for the importance of particularities and specificities of local contexts in the field of journalism studies, this should not be taken to mean they can be seen in isolation from larger global processes. South African tabloids, even in their specificity, are manifestations of a very old genre, and reflect tabloidization trends occurring across media platforms internationally. Yet, they are not mere copies of pre-existing blueprints. The future of newspapers in the era of globalization lies in a space between the local and the global. In considering these trends, we should remain mindful of these flows, contraflows (the flow of news, information, and cultural content backward and forward between nations and regions [see Thussu 2006]) and interconnections. This global/local intersection will form the focus of the next chapter.

3.   Black and White and Read All Over: Tabloids and the Glocalization of Popular Media

It is hard to miss the tabloid newspapers at newsstands, in corner shops, and on street corners in South Africa. Their mastheads are brightly colored, and the headlines, printed in big capital letters and often underlined, italicized, or with an exclamation mark adding emphasis, scream out a sensational bit of news across the whole of the front page: MURDER FOR MONEY!; THE GIRLS WHO PEE SPOONS!; *BODY IN ATTIC!; GRU-VONDS* (Horror find); TRAGEDY!; GEVANG! (Caught!).[1] Around the main story box, there are usually several teasers inviting the reader to turn to a gripping story, feature, or contest on an inside page. The visually striking cover also uses large photos.

A copy of *The Sun* in Britain looks much the same at first glance. The red-top masthead on *The Sun* or the *Daily Star* in the United Kingdom is almost identical to that of the *Daily Sun* and the *Son* in South Africa. The headlines are laid out in much the same way, with even the fonts showing a high degree of similarity. The similarity continues in the teaser boxes on the UK *Sun*'s front page, which promises exclusive photos, giveaways, or competitions; the notorious "page-three girl" in *Son;* and the middle-page celebrity spread. The Irish-owned Independent Group's South African tabloid, the *Daily Voice,* has the most distinctive layout and color scheme, although its approach to stories is arguably more sensationalist and closer to the UK and Irish tabloids. In terms of layout, presentation, and general approach to stories, similarities can also be found between South African and U.S. tabloids (which were, at the outset, modeled on British tabloids) like the *Star* (News America Publishing), the Murdoch-owned *New York Post* and its competitor the *New York Daily News* (owned by Mortimer Zuckerman), and perhaps to a lesser extent with the supermarket tabloids like *National Enquirer* and *National Examiner* (see Bird 1992 for a discussion of these). It is, however, clear from even a cursory glance at the South African tabloids, as well as from discussions with their editors, that the UK tabloids are the key source of inspiration.

There are also important differences, especially in the tabloids' subject matter and their socio-political role, which we will later explore in greater depth. But a certain kinship with the tradition of the UK tabloids cannot be denied. For many critics of the South African tabloids, finding a foreign-looking publication at their front door was not a welcome discovery. Some responses to the new tabloids were tantamount to a nationalistic rejection of what were seen as degrading foreign influences on South African journalism. Consider the reaction by Manson (2005):

> We all accept that tabloids will continue to launch and grow in this country. But instead of copying and pasting from the sick British model, why aren't local tabloid owners brave enough to embrace the spirit of our democracy? Why not accept that you can publish a tabloid without sacrificing your sense of social responsibility or the humanity of those you report on, and dare I suggest that of your writers and editors?

Guy Berger (2005a, 19), one of the tabloids' fiercest critics, also deplored the "imitation" of British tabloid style (yet he also criticizes the narrow "nationalistic focus" in South African media):

> Too much of our reporting is dull, dry and predictable—and of interest only to a bunch of middle-aged elites. Much else is trivial entertainment for dumbed-down masses, without any illuminating information. There are many—too many—mistakes and inaccuracies. Worst is the recent advent of imitating Fleet Street's tabloid-style fictionalising and sensationalism. That mix of clichéd sexuality and soccer scandal does not make for a valued model of South African journalism. Finally, the narrow, nationalistic focus in much media is an injustice to the richness of all who live in our society.

For these critics, the foreign model of tabloid journalism is a problem because the realities of South Africa demand a different model of journalism. It raises the question of whether the South African tabloids are merely British red-tops in disguise, a genre that has parachuted into a context for which their style of journalism is ill-suited, with the aim of exploiting local audiences in the service of big capital (both foreign and locally owned). This question in itself is informed by a larger debate over the role of journalism in a developing country like South Africa, and the argument that foreign media influences constitute "media imperialism." This chapter will briefly explore some of these arguments and their theoretical underpinnings by summarizing the main arguments in the literature around notions of media, globalization, and development, focusing specifically on the contrast between the notions of media imperialism and media hybridity. The globalization of the tabloid genre and the spread of "infotainment" through global media will be touched upon, including examples of tabloids elsewhere in Africa and in South African press history. Lastly, the local-global relationship in South African tabloids will be examined. In the following chapter, we will further explore the criticism South African tabloids have received from their colleagues in the South African media industry and academics in media-related fields to see how the paradigm according to which mainstream journalism is practiced in the country was transgressed by the tabloids.

Tabloid Travels: From Ballads to Infotainment

Attributing the spread of popular genres like tabloids around the world to the globalization of media can go some way in explaining why there is, at face value at least, such a similarity between the format of South African tabloids and those found in other countries. At the same time, this explanation opens up a new set of questions.

Globalization is a complex and often disputed concept. Although its widespread use as a buzzword might suggest a broad consensus over its meaning, the scholarly debate about globalization, with the various theoretical positions occupied in that debate and the vehement disagreements about what constitutes globalization, is a complex one. As Sparks (2007, 126) points out: "There is a certain banal agreement that globalization means greater interconnectedness and action at a distance, but beyond such generalities theories differ in fundamental ways." As part of the debate, the role of the media as facilitator or accelerator of globalization is often accepted, though it is not seen as central by all theorists (Rantanen 2005, 24). Some critics (e.g., Hafez 2007) even go as far as to call media globalization a "myth."

The global ubiquity of cultural goods originating in the West is a reminder of the unequal power relations in the globalization process. One might be tempted to use the form and style of South African tabloids—in many ways similar to their British counterparts—as proof of this Western dominance. Yet, simplistic notions of cultural imperialism have been refuted by scholars indicating various forms of contraflow marking the encounter between the global and the local (Thussu 2006). Attention is increasingly being paid to the heterogenizing effects of globalization (Rantanen 2005, 93), described by some (e.g., Kraidy 2002) as "hybridity." Both the homogenization and the heterogenization schools of thought have their flaws—the latter mostly because of its over-estimation of audience agency and under-estimation of Western media power; the former because it takes a homogenous nation-state as its point of departure, sees media influence as linear instead of multi-directional, and neglects audience agency (Rantanen 2005, 79, 94). Globalization theorists have also been taken to task for their perceived failure to provide empirical grounding for concepts like "hybridization" or "glocalization" (Hafez 2007, 14). Robertson (1997, 25) proposes the latter term to mean that the global and the local are not pitted against each other, but are interconnected forces.

The relationship between the local and the global in the production, distribution, and consumption of media has been the topic of a long-standing debate that is likely to continue for years to come. Of importance for a study such as this one, which deals with a local context marked by high cultural diversity, extreme material inequality, and historically skewed distribution of symbolic power, is that national audiences are not homogenous and respond to their encounters with the global in different ways (Rantanen 2005, 95). One way of describing how the heterogenization of the global occurs in local contexts is, in Appadurai's terms (ibid., 98–99), "indigenization," whereby global media products are adapted to suit local tastes and preferences. The South African tabloids, using Western forms as a starting point but bringing in their own viewpoints, agendas, and cultural lexicon, may be seen as examples of "glocalization."

Although the nuances of these debates fall outside of the scope of the current chapter, we will touch upon the broad distinctions between different paradigms within which globalization of the media may be viewed, especially as this process relates to a developmental context like the South African one. The debate around media or cultural imperialism is particularly relevant in light of accusations that South African tabloids are uncritically copying from their UK counterparts, and that this foreign influence is detrimental for South African journalism and society.

Tabloid Travels

The process of tabloidization has been occurring on a global scale in more recent times, and the panic about the threat to journalism posed by this process is currently one of the most widespread laments in academic and journalistic debates worldwide (Conboy 2006, 207; Sparks 2000, 1 and 5). The shift toward tabloid genres in the news is seen to affect tastes and preferences regarding form, content, and presentation as well as journalistic priorities, boundaries, ethics, and techniques (Conboy 2006, 207). Among the reasons for this process, which has been seen as commencing with the introduction of commercial television in the 1950s (ibid.),[2] is the heightened competition among various media platforms as a result of the introduction of new media technologies like the internet. Because print, radio, and television are at risk of losing large parts of their audiences to new media, they are seen to be increasing their provision of entertainment in an attempt to lure back readers, listeners, and viewers (Sparks 2000, 4).

A further reason for the spread of tabloidization, one which requires some nuance in the South African context, is the commercialization of news as a result of the increasing global dominance of free-market capitalism, accelerated by the collapse of communism in 1989 and the deregulation of media markets (Conboy 2008b, 207). In a cut-throat commercialized landscape, media owners are seen to be relentlessly chasing profits and driving down journalistic standards in the process (Sparks 2000, 4). As we will discuss further in chapter 5, which considers the distinction between tabloid readers as consumers and as citizens, post-apartheid South African society has been marked by a shift toward market-led macro-economic policies as well as the spread of a pervasive consumerism on a socio-cultural level. While these trends should at least partly be attributed to policies created by the post-apartheid government (especially during Thabo Mbeki's presidency), these shifts can also be connected to global events and trends. The series of changes in global media markets set off by the fall of the Berlin Wall could also be seen to have had a ripple effect in South Africa. The demise of apartheid coincided with the fall of communism and the re-ordering of global geopolitics.[3] The fundamental political changes in the country also allowed for the de-linking of newspaper houses from the political ideologies they had espoused under apartheid, leading to a re-ordering of the South African media landscape. Most notable in terms of the influence of foreign media formats and genres was the takeover of the English-language press by the Irish Independent Group that later established its own tabloid (the *Daily Voice*) in the wake of the success of tabloids belonging to the rival Naspers conglomerate.

The new openness toward global trends and influences after years of isolation, the influx of foreign capital into the local media market, business-friendly government policies, and the "end of ideology" created a climate in post-apartheid South Africa where commercialized media could thrive. These local circumstances are important to note when viewing the emergence of South African tabloids as related to a global trend toward tabloidization. Not only can "tabloidization" mean different things in different countries, but the process is also dependent on a combination of factors relating to the media landscape, journalistic culture, and the economic and legal environment in various countries (Esser 1999, cited in Conboy 2006, 209). Thus, the process has played out differently in various international contexts (see, e.g., Conboy 2006, 209–213, Bird 1992, and Sparks 2000 for mainly the United States and Western Europe; Hallin 2000 for Mexico; Bek 2004 for Turkey; Örnebring 2008 for Sweden; and Bonner and McKay 2007 for Australia).

In Africa, the tabloid genre can be seen as one of several forms of popular culture, which includes forms like music, television, and theater. African popular culture has been seen as expression of "people's disillusion and resentment" toward officialdom (Barber 1987, 3), and, increasingly, as an emergent public space where citizenship is rehearsed and negotiated (Dolby 2006). The mere choice of such a popular style instead of a more formal one associated with officialdom can in itself be a "message of resistance" (West and Fair 1993, 105). Popular culture can also be seen as either a mediation between traditional and modern forms, or the space where the very meanings of "traditional" and "modern" can be negotiated (ibid., 107). However, it is not the medium (in this case, tabloids) that possesses inherent characteristics that determines this process, but rather its location within a "nexus of political, social, and economic relations" that determines "which communicative resources will be available to whom, and what significance will be embodied in the generative forms invoked" (ibid., 108). Because it is the people using popular forms, rather than the forms themselves, that undermines officialdom, government, and the status quo, popular media could also be used to support dominant class interests (ibid., 110). This point is important to bear in mind when considering the amount of social change that one can expect of the South African tabloids, which are owned and managed by large commercial interests seeking profit rather than social justice. Tabloids in South Africa, as a form of popular media and ultimately linked to other communicative processes in society, therefore present a terrain where the meaning of culture, development, and democracy is contested between local and global forces. As West and Fair (ibid., 112) succinctly state:

> All things taken into consideration, we must now see the terrain of communication
> in Africa for what it truly is: the locus of an intense struggle over the formulation of
> societal symbols and values, drawing upon and interpreting not only the meaning
> of the past, but the significance and direction of the world at present. And as the
> African world at present contains a vast array of media forms, each with its own
> ever-shifting position in the history of social relations, we must conclude that

contestation over the social functions and meanings of these media themselves will be an inseparable part of the struggle.

The first tabloid influences on South African print media can already be noted in the 1930s and 1940s. Although these early examples of commercial papers often had an element of sensation or populist appeal, they do not conform to the contemporary definition of tabloids (Froneman 2006, 23). The Black commercial press that developed in South Africa in the 1930s was owned by White business interests and acted to reinforce the political views of the White government. Switzer (1988) gives a detailed account of the development of this press, which could for its commercialism and de-politicized stance be seen as an early antecedent of the contemporary South African tabloids. Switzer points out that very few of the independent African journals launched in South Africa in the 1880s that had been voicing dissent against White authoritarian rule survived the Great Depression of 1929–1932. The expansion of a market for African consumers in the 1930s coincided with increased segregationist policies by the state, which included attempts to retribalize Africans. In this climate, liberal White business interests saw an opportunity to develop a Black commercial press (ibid., 352). The White-owned media conglomerate, Bantu Press, took over most of the ANC-aligned papers,[4] starting a process of depoliticizing journalism and creating a compliant African middle class (Limb 2000, 96–97).[5]

During the contemporary debates about South African tabloids, one of these Black commercial papers from the 1930s, *Bantu World,* has been compared—highly unfavorably—to the tabloids by the veteran Black journalist, editor, and current Press Ombudsman, Joe Thloloe. Thloloe, who saw tabloids as a "fad" that was "bound to disappear" (Thloloe 2004) has described the *Daily Sun* as a "patronising throwback to the *Bantu World* of the 1950s" (ibid.; Thloloe 2005). His comparison is based on what he saw as stereotypes of Blacks peddled by "white editorial directors who 'knew' the Bantu" (see chapter 4 for more details of his criticism).

Bantu World was indeed owned by White capital, and like the tabloids, it was also aimed primarily at an urban Black readership. Unlike the tabloids, however, it was more interested in the petit bourgeoisie than in the working class. *Bantu World* was a weekly paper, launched in April 1932 as part of Bantu Press (Pty.) Ltd. by Bertram F. G. Paver, a "failed farmer and advertising salesman" (Switzer 1988, 352). Shortly after its establishment, the Bantu Press (Pty.) Ltd. was taken over by the Argus Group, in which Cecil John Rhodes had bought a controlling interest in 1881. The African shareholders were bought out, and the Black journalists were removed from its board of directors (ibid.). This was part of the Argus Group's plan to counter the socialistic ideas gaining currency in the country and in neighboring Lesotho by "channel[ing] native thoughts away from politics and into safer pursuits" in its newspapers (Bourgault 1995, 160). In this project, the Argus Group gained the support of the Anglo-American corporation in the 1950s, as they shared a base in mining capital (ibid.). Bantu Press later expanded into Southern Rhodesia (Zimbabwe), Northern Rhodesia (Zambia), Nyasaland (Malawi), Basutoland (Lesotho), Swaziland, and Bechuanaland (Botswana) as part of attempts to counter demands for self-government (ibid.). Although papers in this group were staffed by Black Africans, their work was "tightly supervised" by White overseers who retained editorial control (ibid.). We will see in the last chapter of this study that these power relations between White editorial control and Black journalists are in some cases not entirely dissimilar to the relationship between ownership and production in the contemporary tabloids, and, especially in the case of the *Daily Sun,* between editors and journalists.

Insofar as its contents are concerned, *Bantu World* did show some similarities with today's tabloids as well, although its approach was aimed at upper-ranked readers rather than the masses. It focused on social events, personalities, gossip, rumor, sports, and "the occasional scandal" (Switzer 1988, 358). Advice, household hints, and etiquette tips aimed at Black women were also staple fare, but politics were avoided even if African cultural heritage was celebrated.[6] Limb (2000, 105) points out that despite its moderate political stance, *Bantu World* nevertheless exposed problems related to the everyday experience of the working class, like working conditions, low wages, inadequate housing, and long working hours in the mines.

The philosophy of self-discipline and individual enterprise, central to *Bantu World*'s editorial stance (Switzer 1988, 362), corresponds with the emphasis on individual ambition—linked with consumerism—of the *Daily Sun.* Although *Bantu World* was not a tabloid in today's sense of the word, it did pave the way for a transition from an elite to a mass readership. Other White-owned papers proceeded further along the road of popular appeal and commercialism, repackaging news, entertainment, and advertising that would appeal to a lower segment of the market (ibid., 368). Pictorial newspapers like *Umlindi we Nyanga* (The Monthly Watchman), launched in 1934 in East London, can especially be seen as the forerunners of the tabloid press (ibid., 368).

Much later, in the 1960s, the Afrikaans weekly *Landstem* was founded, and later incorporated into *Dagbreek* which in turn became the current Sunday paper *Rapport* (which also includes tabloid-style reporting alongside more "serious" news and commentary—Froneman 2006, 24). *Landstem* also followed a populist approach and contained tabloid features, although it was published in broadsheet format (Froneman 2006, 24). *Landstem* was controversial for testing the boundaries of the conservative Afrikaner mores, and was seen as a newspaper with an "intentionally low intellectual standard," according to Froneman.[7] This is how the *Landstem* was described in a promotional government publication celebrating fifty years of the White-ruled Union of South Africa:

> With the help of a group of young journalists (and people like Marilyn Monroe) Piet Beukes rustled up a paper which made the peaceful Boland sit up and take notice. Like a veldfire the paper's popularity spread to the north and today the paper's circulation is distributed comparatively evenly throughout the country. At first we struck trouble. If there was a mistake to be made, it was always we who made it. The paper contained no politics, had no printing press, and no news agency to keep it supplied with reports. Everyone considered these facts to be great stumbling blocks. But the disadvantage was turned into an advantage. Die Landstem was forced to evolve an original and entirely

new approach to journalism: we would concentrate on "the news behind the news," and add plenty of photographs. At first other papers laughed at this new-fangled idea—then they copied it. (Our First Half Century 1960, 189)

Like today's tabloids, which include features like "Sun Power" where readers receive practical help, the paper also enlisted the support of its readers to help other readers in need. It also ran competitions (like a Bible quiz, with the prize of a trip to Israel) and even arranged for a Miss South Africa contest, the winner of which was sent to represent the Union in international competitions (ibid.).

During the same period as the founding of the *Landstem,* the "racy, down-market" (Froneman 2006, 23) weekly *Post/Weekendpost* aimed at an Indian readership was established and still continues to publish more than fifty years later. On its website (www.thepost.co.za), the *Post* boasts of its proud history and its ability to "stay in touch with readers, knowing what the community is about."

The tabloid genre also found fertile ground further afield on the African continent. British tabloid culture made inroads into the continent around 1947 when Cecil King, proprietor of the British *Daily Mirror,* bought several newspapers in Nigeria, Ghana, and Sierra Leone. Although King followed a policy of Africanization by training reporters, printers and machine operators, he also introduced improvements that until then were unheard of in the African context: a rotary printing machine, photo engraving, typesetting, and typecasting plants (Bourgault 1995, 156). But more than technical prowess, the Mirror Group also brought a new journalistic culture that included

> tabloid page makeup, liberal use of illustrations and photos, human interest stories, short paragraphs and sentences—all of which were highly successful at home among the British working class. The indigenous press found itself out-competed. Circulation grew from 25,000 in 1951 to 120,000 in 1965, the highest in West Africa. (ibid.)

A detrimental effect of the foreign-owned newspapers established in West Africa after independence (both the Mirror Group and the Thompson group had interests in the region), which by the 1960s had established their distinctive "flashy" look, was that they diminished the African-controlled press. The foreign papers were biased toward private economic enterprise and had Western views on international politics. It was difficult for small, indigenous African papers to compete (ibid., 159).

In East Africa, the Nation Group introduced "new tabloid formats and exciting layouts" in Tanzania and Uganda (ibid., 164). The editorial staffs of the Nation Group's papers were initially almost exclusively White, but attempts were later made to attain a more diverse demographic representation (ibid.). Currently, there are a number of African countries with newspapers that could also be considered tabloids, such as Nigeria, Uganda, and Zimbabwe (Mabweazara 2006; Beckett and Kyrke-Smith 2007, 55). The Ugandan *Red Pepper* (available online at www.redpepper.ug) has been in operation since 2002. The paper has been particularly controversial for its practice of outing prominent gay Ugandans, since the country's legal ban against homosexuality could make gays vulnerable to attack (BBC 2006). The paper's mix of sensational news, rumors, nudity, and scandal, modeled on U.S. and European tabloids, has prompted outrage and accusations of being "un-African."[8] These controversies have led the Ugandan Media Council to order the editor, Richard Tusiime, to retract some of the stories described as "fictitious," "pornographic," and not up to "journalistic standards" or face suspension.[9]

Although the establishment of tabloids in African countries can be linked to direct influence and involvement from the British and Irish press as well as the globalization more broadly of tabloid culture, it might be possible to find similarities between contemporary tabloid culture in Africa and earlier communication patterns. If we agree with Bird (1992, 8) that tabloids (and, in fact, journalism in general) are related to much older oral cultures, it might be possible to see how the contemporary South African tabloids resonate with African oral culture.[10] Bourgault (1995, 140) has already indicated how oral culture makes its way into television in other sub-Saharan countries. The rumor, political derision, and humor found in the South African tabloids could then be viewed as a printed form of what Nyamnjoh (2005, 23) in his work on media in other African countries calls "radio trottoir" (see also Ellis 1989), an informal news network that circumvents and even undermines the mainstream media controlled by elite interests (with the difference that the South African tabloids are also owned and co-produced by elites and therefore cannot be considered to be "alternative" or "informal" media in the same way.)

But emphasizing the link between tabloid media and traditional African culture could also be misleading and potentially contribute to the essentializing and exoticizing of African culture, and given the low opinion of tabloids' moral standards, it would be a short step from there to associate African culture with immorality—a point made by critics like Press Ombudsman Joe Thloloe, to which we will return in the next chapter. It would probably be analytically more useful to explore how the emergence of tabloids in contemporary South Africa is related to the spread of popular media formats around the world and on the African continent, and in particular how the end of apartheid facilitated the opening up of South African media markets to more foreign interests and influences.

Although the democratization of South Africa accelerated the interpenetration of media markets (see Tomaselli 2000c), South Africa under apartheid was not hermetically sealed off from outside influences. Alongside its isolationism and ethnic nationalism there also existed forms of cosmopolitanism, hybridity, and internationalism, as Nixon (1994) has pointed out. Influences from abroad also provided a form of identification for many Black South African journalists and writers (including those working on *Drum* magazine in the 1950s), and enabled them to defy the static ethnic identities imposed upon them by the racist regime (ibid., 16). These ongoing cultural transmigrations notwithstanding, the South African media landscape changed considerably during the 1990s when the Irish-based Independent Group gained control of much of the country's English-language press (Tomaselli 2000c). This media group extended its influence in the South African media market by starting the *Daily Voice* in the Western Cape in 2005, but this was only after the group had rejected Deon du Plessis' proposal to launch the *Daily Sun*—he eventually took his offer to Naspers, which accepted it (Du Plessis, pers. comm. 2007).

If the influence of foreign culture on the South African media can be seen to have started long before the introduction of tabloids, so can the discourses criticizing this influence. The critics railing against the contemporary tabloids for allegedly copying a style of journalism from Britain or the United States use the same discursive apparatus that has been used in debates about "cultural imperialism." We turn now to these debates.

Fit for Context? Tabloids, Globalization, and Media Imperialism

We have seen that the tabloid genre had its origins in North America and Europe, and that a shift toward tabloid genres is occurring around the world. Does this mean that the introduction of the genre in the South African landscape should be seen as an example of "media imperialism"?

The relationship between the local and the global in media and communication has been the subject of much discussion and debate. Central to these debates is the question of how local cultures are transformed and influenced by global forces, or how local actors manage to creatively appropriate global forms and transform them to suit their needs and tastes (Kraidy and Murphy 2008, 340). This question has its roots in the debates about "media for development," in which powerful global players stood accused of engaging in a form of cultural imperialism by imposing media and communication institutions and practices on the developing world. This response, informed by a critical political economy approach, was directed at the dominant paradigm of development communication that saw indigenous, traditional forms of knowledge as an obstacle in the way of development (ibid.; Sparks 2000). The media imperialism thesis later became modified by the notion, mostly under the influence of cultural studies scholars like Stuart Hall, Ien Ang, David Morley, Tamar Liebes, and Elihu Katz, that media users constitute an "active audience" that produces meaning in the process of consumption (Kraidy and Murphy 2008, 340).

The relationships among communication, development, and global cultural influence was at the center of a dispute in the 1970s between the non-aligned states on the one hand and the U.S.-led Western powers and the Soviet bloc on the other. These "third world" states demanded the establishment of a News World Information and Communication Order (NWICO) to address global power asymmetries in the global media and communication system (Flew 2007, 201). The MacBride report commissioned by the United Nations Educational, Scientific and Cultural Organization (UNESCO) that ensued from this dispute identified a one-way traffic from the developed world at the center of global communications to the third world on its periphery. It recognized the right of countries in the developing world to maintain national sovereignty, build cultural identity, and focus communication resources on developmental goals (ibid.; see Vincent, Nordenstreng, and Traber 1999 for a retrospective and update on these debates). These recommendations were seen by the developed countries, led by the United States, as an attempt to restrict the free flow of information and undermine Western notions of freedom of speech (Flew 2007, 202), and NWICO thus met its demise. The topic of access to the global information society was again put on the agenda at the two World Summits on the Information Society (WSIS), although these meetings took place under different global geopolitical circumstances and differed in key structural and institutional aspects (ibid., 202–203).

With regard to South African media history in particular, the arguments around "cultural imperialism" took an ironic twist when they were appropriated by the ruling National Party during the apartheid era to resist the introduction of television into the country. Television was seen as an evil influence "leading to dangerous liberalistic tendencies," in the words of Dr. Albert Hertzog, cabinet minister for media affairs (cited in Nixon 1994, 45), and kept out of the country until 1976. This "most drastic act of cultural protectionism" (ibid., 43) is an example of how cultural imperialism not only relates to contestations between powerful and weak states, but also between various cultural formations within the state itself (ibid., 44). The apartheid regime reinvented national and ethnic cultures in an attempt to prevent foreign influence from fragmenting national cohesion, which in turn depended on internal domination (ibid.). As such, the National Party government appropriated the leftist critique of cultural imperialism for oppressive ends, a move which (along with other developments) raised questions about the dominant theoretical understandings of cultural imperialism (ibid., 47).

When critics today reject tabloid newspapers as a foreign influence with a potentially detrimental effect on the nation's fragile cohesion, they are therefore not the first to use the argument of cultural imperialism in the context of South African nation building. This is not to suggest, of course, that the criticism of tabloid excesses is on par with the apartheid regime's abuse of culture for political expediency. It does, however, indicate how the South African media has been seen over the years as pivotal to the construction of South African nationalism—even if the media in both the case of television and tabloids have been seen as potentially erosive rather than constitutive of national unity, as Benedict Anderson would have it (ibid., 44). South African history also alerts us to the fact that critiques of cultural imperialism are not always progressive in nature.

While the tropes of the media imperialism critique still surface from time to time in the tabloid debates, there are other—arguably more fruitful—ways of thinking about foreign influences in local media and about the tensions and asymmetrical distribution of power in the contemporary globalized media landscape. Although the advent of democracy in 1994 has brought about fundamental and wide-ranging shifts in South African society and the relations between South Africa, other African countries, and the global community, it would be a mistake to see the birth of the "new South Africa" as a complete rupture with the past. Alexander (2006, 20) suggests, rightly, that continuities exist between older social formations of the nation-state and its capitalist underpinnings and contemporary patterns of globalization. Alexander's point (ibid., 21) that South Africa, as a middle-income country with the largest economy in Africa, provides a vantage point midway between Northern optimism and Afro-pessimism can therefore fruitfully be applied to the media in post-apartheid South Africa as well.

Both the optimistic and pessimistic views of the impact of globalization on South African society have been noted (ibid., 13–14). On the one hand there have been those critics (e.g., Nuttall and Michael 2000) who have emphasized the fluidity of identity across boundaries of race and class; on the other, those critics who have pointed to the persistence of political identities based on ethnicity and the continuing impact of material conditions on the refashioning of identities (Wasserman and Jacobs 2003). It would also be possible to view the relationship between the local and the global in the new South African tabloids from both these perspectives.

Any examination of the relationship between the local and the global in South African tabloids should consider contrasting influences: on the one hand, transnational flows of media formats and genres, and on the other the specific local context that shaped them. It would consider how the democratization of the country has opened the possibility of social mobility for a larger section of the population which stimulates consumption of media, but also the persisting severe inequalities that exclude the poor from elite media discourse. It would also examine both the new opportunities that have opened up for new media outlets to emerge and the large media conglomerates that remain best positioned to take these up.

As such, political-economic approaches to global media which are attentive to ownership patterns and to the structures of capital underpinning global media remain important to supplement cultural studies approaches that emphasize hybridity and transnational cultural flows such as the work of Appadurai (1996).[11] Furthermore, when studying media products like the South African tabloids, which might seem at first glance to be a local manifestation of a generic global genre, the complexity of the local–global relationship demands a nuanced and textured approach. Kraidy and Murphy (2008) suggest a translocal approach that seeks to understand global media within "pervasive global-historical dynamics" in which communication plays a role. These include economic policies like global neoliberalism and political forces like the dynamics of "democratization" as well as socio-cultural trends like consumer capitalism, the rise of transnational media companies, and global migration. Such an approach, they suggest (ibid., 343), would build on the anthropologist Clifford Geertz's (1973) method of "thick description," and would avoid foregrounding either the local or the global dimension of global media and diminishing the other member of the pair.

In practical terms, a "thick description" approach to South African tabloid newspapers would first mean examining the various economic, political, and cultural dimensions of these papers as societal phenomena within a given historical moment. This multi-dimensional examination of tabloids is akin to the one that this book attempts to follow. A translocal approach would move away from the case-study approach to global media that provide "comparative interpretations of the particularities of this or that community within the global sphere" (ibid., 345). Instead of viewing local media as particular examples of a globally dominant (and therefore most likely Northern) blueprint, a translocal approach would encourage comparisons between different "local" media, or South–South studies, such as comparisons between tabloids in different parts of the developing world or in different African countries. Such an approach would be suited to the contemporary South African media landscape in which the demands of a particular local context are negotiated by media institutions underpinned by transnational capital, within genres and formats that have been appropriated and adapted from global genres. This complex mix of local and global influences and forces requires a more intricate understanding than the center–periphery model of cultural imperialism can provide. To understand of how these various influences and factors play out in the news production process, it could be useful to gauge editors' and journalists' opinions on where they position themselves between the local and the global.

Between the Local and the Global: Where do the Editors and Journalists See Themselves?

As mentioned at the beginning of this chapter, the layout and design of the South African tabloids has been influenced by the British "red tops." The extent and form of this influence differs from tabloid to tabloid. The British influence is perhaps most evident in *Son,* which uses similar colors, fonts, and design elements to the UK *Sun.* The production editor at *Son,* Keith Allen (pers. comm. 2007), acknowledges this influence. He says he was asked to design something "close to the UK tabloids" and admits looking to the *Sun* "for inspiration." He refers to the paper as a "soap opera in print" with a specific design formula: "A big strong headline for the lead story, with a subheading that qualifies the headline. It must be 'picture-driven,' the central story must have a photo. The second lead just gets one headline, but is still picture-driven."

While he sets the design style of the UK tabloids as a norm, he does not think this style has been achieved yet:

> The emerging tabloid market in SA is not yet at the stage of doing really good UK-style tabloid journalism. In the UK they achieve a consistency of design and quality. We have not yet achieved that at *Son.* From a design point of view the Afrikaans tabloids are learning the method of the British tabloids. In terms of storytelling *Son* has achieved, but the design style can still be improved. In SA we do use more color than in the UK—we've got a top-notch blue laser German printing press that can get good quality color. In the UK, tabloids are more black and white and grainy. The market in the UK is also different—everyone speaks English, [and there is a] higher rate of literacy. So UK headline writers can think up puns. In SA some puns go over the readers' heads.

But despite the strong British influence on the *Son,* Allen believes that the paper has become a South African product—aided in part by continuous reader feedback by means of focus groups.

While the *Son* resembles the UK *Sun* typographically, the *Daily Voice* is the closest to the British tabloids in terms of content. The *Voice* often uses puns in its headlines,[12] includes irreverent humor in its stories and does not shy away from explicit depictions of violence or lurid contents. The editor, Karl Brophy, agrees:

> I think we definitely are [closer to the UK tabloids than the *Son* or *Daily Sun*], [in terms of] our presentation . . . the way we present news. . . . We are doing stories bigger than the *Kaapse Son,* for instance 14 stories a day on the Dina [Rodriguez, a Cape Town woman who hired killers to murder her ex-boyfriend's baby daughter,] case. I was amazed when I came here how little thought is given to big stories that everyone wanted to consume—a page lead and that's it. If it's good, people would want to consume it, and they would want to consume everything. We are certainly much more like the English and the Irish tabloids than the *Daily Sun* and the *Kaapse Son.* (pers. comm. 2007)

The publisher of the *Kaapse Son*, Ingo Capraro, spent time in London in the mid-1990s as Naspers' representative in Britain. He sees the British tabloid model as a "universal model," with cultural affinities between South African and British culture as a result of colonial history adding to the applicability of the British model (pers. comm. 2007):

> We are closer to the British than any other nation. The people at whom my paper is aimed, and this includes the Coloured readers, are very British in many respects. This (cultural affinity) astounded me when I first went to England. And the Brits do it well, they've been doing tabloids for 120 years. So that is my model.

To strengthen this British influence in the *Son,* Capraro brought in two consultants from the United Kingdom to give advice on layout and approach, and also to hone the journalistic skills of its journalists, including teaching them skills such as "doorstepping" (interviews without prior arrangement, usually used only as a last resort by mainstream media) (ibid.).[13] Some of the advice they received was to balance the hard news of violence, suffering, and disillusionment with which their readers are familiar with humorous and entertaining escapist fare. This led to a stronger focus on celebrity news, including a middle-page spread devoted to showbiz gossip.

One of these consultants, Charlie Bain, had worked on the London-based *Daily Mirror* and *Daily Mail,* and immediately recognized the British format in the *Son,* which had "a lot of the hallmarks" of the British tabloids he was familiar with (pers. comm. 2007). The *Son* was, however, "a lot softer than we are" because the South African tabloids were still "learning the art." While keeping within the ethical rules was important, Bain thought that South African tabloids could still cover stories in more depth and research them more. As far as layout is concerned, he did not envisage a "radical redesign," but encouraged a simplified design. The biggest difference, according to him, was the high levels of violence in South Africa compared to the United Kingdom, the reporting of which had to be balanced with light relief in order not to depress tabloid readers.

The general manager of the *Daily Sun,* Fergus Sampson, sees the importance of localization in terms of readers' identities:

> You cannot model a newspaper on another newspaper. A newspaper is alive, it's like a live person. People react emotionally to it, they allow it into their homes. They would say I am a *Burger* person, or I am a *Daily Sun* person. It has to be modeled on the character of your readership.

Ferguson does, however, admit to borrowing extensively from other countries, notably those in the South like Brazil and Thailand, as far as the "key business issues" like pricing, promotion, availability, and marketing are concerned.

Deon du Plessis agrees that the British format would not work particularly well in South Africa:

> We looked at the Brit papers, but we're not as combative as they are about politicians. You can't do that here. We don't like them, but hell, to do what the Brits do there to ANC politicians—you can't do that here, it's too raw still here. Girls, you can't do girls. It's embarrassing. We've never done that, our readers feel uncomfortable. It's very different. Although we also do a lot of soccer. I think there's an African narrative here, it's longer in parts. The Brits don't write like this. They were born out of paper shortage. The whole thing of tight writing, it's very admirable, but we don't do that. Puns, we don't do puns.
>
> We don't do celebrities so much. We don't joke about things. Things are in collapse here, it's not in collapse in Britain. This is collapsing. We want to help them [our readers]. We have jokes, but we want to help him [the reader], because things are just not right here. The hospitals are disastrous. Medical services are collapsing. We're not totally serious, but we're irritable. The hopes of 1994 have been pissed on.

South African tabloids exemplify the complex and multi-leveled ways in which the global, national, and local intersect in transnational media formats. These intersections and exchanges should not merely be seen in terms of a benevolent multi-culturalism where globalization has brought about cultural mixing, but as a space where hierarchies are undermined; orthodox, globalized notions of professionalism are challenged; and a global format is adapted to engage both popular cultural forces as well as market interests. The contradictions inherent in this process are part of the complexity which this book explores.

The criticism this chapter has focused on, namely that the South African tabloids uncritically copied journalistic models from overseas that were not well suited for the demands and challenges of a young democracy, is just one of the barrage of accusations directed against the South African tabloids. In the next chapter we will look at these criticisms in more detail to find out what they say about the country's journalistic paradigm.

4.   Not Really Newspapers: Tabloids and the South African Journalistic Paradigm

In the previous chapter, we tracked the history of the tabloid genre and associated concepts such as "tabloidization" and "sensationalism." It emerged that the sensationalism with which tabloids have been associated has been seen as a threat to journalism in various contexts around the world for more than a century and a half. During this time, dichotomies have been set up to contrast "proper," rational news with the emotionalism and sensationalism of popular formats (Grabe, Zhou, and Barnett 2001, 637). These binaries include entertainment vs. information, analysis vs. dramatization, infotainment vs. edutainment, human interest vs. public affairs, situational vs. timeless issues, soft vs. hard news, opinion vs. fact, and unexpected events vs. issue coverage. The debate following the introduction of new tabloid newspapers to the South African market was also characterized by many of these dichotomies. While the moral panic around tabloid newspapers and the perceived decline of journalistic standards is an ongoing global discourse,[1] the criticism against the South African tabloids has also sometimes stemmed from a particular normative view of the role of the media in a democratic, post-apartheid South Africa.

This chapter will review the debates that followed the introduction of tabloids to South Africa and convey the main tropes of the discourse, with special attention to the contrast between tabloid journalism and the mainstream press paradigm and how this contrast has been used to sustain the distribution of cultural capital in favor of the mainstream press.

Since the introduction of the first tabloid to the South African market in 2001, and seemingly increasing with each subsequent entrant into this burgeoning market, debates about tabloids' role, the reasons for their success, their potential, and their ethics (or lack thereof) have been raging in the popular press.[2] The fact that these debates largely took place in the pages of the mainstream press might suggest that tabloids were viewed as posing a danger to the image of journalism in the eyes of the public, and therefore had to be dealt with within the domain of the popular press. By playing host to contributors—often journalism professors—who derided the tabloids, the mainstream press could re-establish credibility in its own way of doing things. By pointing fingers at the new tabloids, critics often lost sight of the incremental steps that the mainstream press had been taking toward tabloid style.[3] A key issue in these debates was the responsibility of the tabloids—and of the media at large—to contribute to a democratic society. As discussed in the previous chapter, the foreign influences evident in the South African tabloids were seen as undermining the development of a homegrown media that could meet democratic and developmental challenges.

The responses to the new tabloids are interesting not only for what they tell us about the tabloids as such—since similar criticisms have been voiced in "tabloidization" debates around the world—but for what they tell us about the normative frameworks that the mainstream press employs and the way it positions itself rhetorically within the discourse of democracy. What may emerge from these debates is a picture of the paradigm within which the mainstream press in South Africa operates, and its willingness to examine its own value framework, journalistic routines, and socio-political positioning.

In the debates about tabloids, the norms and assumptions of the mainstream press manifested in a process that could be referred to as "paradigm repair," whereby in debating and rejecting the journalistic excesses of the tabloids, a discourse is developed that serves to repair the image of an occupation in trouble. The tabloid debate gave the mainstream South African print media, which since democratization had been undergoing significant shifts and repositioning (as described in chapter 1), the opportunity to redefine its own practices, values, and responsibilities. Although it would be going too far to suggest that the tabloids provided a foil for the mainstream press to intentionally deflect criticism, it should be borne in mind that the image of the South African mainstream press had been severely tarnished by two inquiries (the Human Rights Commission's investigation into racism in the media and the Truth and Reconciliation Commission's hearings on the media) into their role under apartheid and thereafter. Around the time of the emergence of the tabloids, the mainstream press also suffered from several ethical lapses (Haffajee 2004b). The emergence of the tabloids could potentially have provided the opportunity for a wide-ranging debate into the mediated public sphere in post-apartheid South Africa, or spurred a self-reflective questioning of dominant value frameworks and journalistic routines. Instead, it became clear that the mainstream press would reiterate its position and solidify the performance indicators against which it measures its success.

Background

The print-media landscape in post-1994 South Africa has been an increasingly commercialized one, with stiff competition among market players locally and globally.[4] While editorial staffs have become more racially representative, the continued commercial logic of especially the print media meant that the "quality press" remained by and large aimed at lucrative audiences, with voices of the poor largely absent (cf. Jacobs 2004). Because of the correlation between wealth and race established by apartheid (which remained largely intact after apartheid despite the creation of a wealthy Black elite through "Black empowerment" policies and the emergence of a Black middle class),[5] print media had been catering to a predominantly White and small Black elite audience which would be attractive to high-end advertisers.

While the new tabloids challenged the existing journalistic paradigm with their sensationalist and brash style and their focus on news of interest to poor communities, they also went against the prevailing newspaper business model. After the Irish-owned Independent Group turned down Deon du Plessis' pitch for a new tabloid, the conglomerate Naspers bought into the idea and put the paper on the market at the cheap cover price of R1. This price undercut the *Daily Sun*'s closest rival, the *Sowetan,* and its sister publication, *Sunday World,* aimed at a Black middle class. This led to an accusation by Saki Macozoma, chairman of the Black-empowerment consortium Nail, who then controlled New Africa Publications, the owners of the *Sowetan,*[6] that Naspers engaged in "uncompetitive behaviour."[7] The phenomenal commercial success of this tabloid was partly blamed for the huge circulation losses at the *Sowetan.*

Criticism, Paradigm Repair, and Normative Maintenance

Since their inception, the South African tabloids have been subjected to constant—and often bitter—criticism from mainstream media commentators.[8] In turn, tabloid publishers and editors have used public platforms and newspaper columns to defend their publications and articulate their journalistic visions.[9] At times, the exchanges between academics and tabloid publishers and editors has taken the form of virulent attacks. One such exchange took place when Guy Berger, in his speech as convenor judge at the Mondi Shanduka Newspaper Journalism awards in 2005, referred to tabloids as "junk-journalism" and advised that the awards should steer well clear of them (Berger 2005b). In his response, one-time *Daily Voice* news editor Raymond Joseph dismissed Berger's speech as a "hissy fit" by a "learned prof."[10]

While Berger remained an outspoken critic of the tabloids,[11] the journalistic climate changed gradually in subsequent years. At its Annual General Meeting in Cape Town in July 2005, The South African National Editors' Forum (SANEF) held a vigorous debate on whether tabloid editors should be welcomed into the fold of this professional body. Some editors were disinclined to grant membership to tabloid editors, while others spoke in support of how tabloids rekindled a relationship with their communities, but eventually it was determined that tabloid editors could also be members of SANEF. Ferial Haffajee, a former chair of SANEF and then-editor of the *Mail and Guardian,* acknowledges (pers. comm. 2007) that the tone of the 2005 debate was "exclusionary," but also points out that the climate in SANEF has been "swinging" in subsequent years as a result of internal differences of opinion. She adds that SANEF alone was not to blame for the stand-off, as there was "no great rush from the tabloids to join SANEF." Du Plessis (pers. comm. 2007), for example, is indeed not interested in participating in SANEF's activities, because the organization "really isn't part of my game plan anymore" (ibid.):

No, we're not a member of SANEF, Themba [Khumalo, the editor] doesn't go. You know, I don't mind, but it's not like anything like that drives me anymore. I'm now in my mid-50s, I've really done that whole corporate journalism thing, there's no vanities left about that. I'm very interested in taking the paper to 600,000 on an average, that's the driver. The rest is really extraneous. . . . I think they [SANEF] got stranded in the mid-90s, they missed the boat in the early 2000s, because these older papers have to—and I don't envy them—take with them an older audience which they had before, I don't have that problem. Our whole audience is new, and we can deal with one type of person.

The regional editor of *Son,* Andrew Koopman, as well as the tabloid's national editor, Ingo Capraro, are non-participating members of SANEF. Koopman (pers. comm. 2007) also notes a change in attitude among mainstream journalists' attitudes toward tabloids:

I belong to SANEF but I don't go to the meetings. I think they are now starting to respect us more. In the beginning we were told we did "gutter journalism," but we have scooped them so often that they reluctantly look down on us. Some people will have that perception, but I think most of them now see us as their equal. Often journalists from *Die Burger* phone our journalists to get contacts of ideas for stories. I think the respect is returning. There are some individuals that look down on tabloids, but we are getting respect.

Yet this respect is diluted. SANEF's eventual welcoming gesture was counterbalanced, in a "two-handed, and potentially contradictory" way by a reaffirmation of the organization's commitment to "journalistic integrity, tolerance and accountability" which reflected the tension between different positions in the organization.[12] Three years later, in 2008, the climate has changed so much that a new category for tabloid journalism was created at the Mondi Shanduka Newspaper Journalism awards over which Berger was still presiding. Ironically, no winner was appointed because the tabloid entries were apparently seen as too closely resembling mainstream journalism. "There are a great many bold, innovative and entertaining pages every day in the tabloid press, but they were not among the entries, which were dominated by hard news reporting or feature writing of a kind that was not specific to popular journalism," Berger was quoted as saying.[13] Tensions between mainstream and tabloid journalists are likely to remain a feature of the journalistic environment in South Africa, as they have been in journalistic debates around the world where the mainstream media often makes a scapegoat of popular culture (Scharrer, Weidman, and Bissell 2003). At the same time, it is important not to see the various positions in these debates as intractable, but as part of an ongoing negotiation and redefinition of the media's role in a transitional democracy. As the changing place of tabloid journalism within the Mondi Shanduka awards indicates, attitudes toward tabloid journalism are bound to remain in flux. This process of professional redefinition (which does not always mean a shift in professional identity, but often the opposite—namely, a reaffirmation of existing positions) is likely to intensify as the definition of journalism changes globally in response to technological innovation, the rise of citizen journalism, and increased commercial pressure on print media.

Because the criticism directed against tabloids indicates the defining lines of professional journalism in post-apartheid South Africa, as well as the normative framework within which this journalism is cast, it is worth taking a closer look at the main areas of criticism and how these were articulated. The bulk of the criticism can be grouped into two main categories: the perceived low quality of journalism practiced by these publications, and concerns about the lack of ethical standards guiding the actions of tabloid journalists.

Quality of Journalism

A central question in examining the effect of the emergence of new tabloids on South Africa's mainstream journalistic paradigm is whether the acknowledgement of tabloids as legitimate newspapers succeeds in turning the mainstream press's gaze upon itself. The (albeit reluctant) acceptance of tabloids into the journalistic fold by the establishment might suggest a certain openness to different journalistic styles and approaches. At the same time, such acceptance could serve to reaffirm that the dominant journalistic paradigm is the most suitable for meeting the challenges of journalism in the young democracy. It could also banish tabloids into a popular-journalism ghetto without taking seriously the challenge they pose to mainstream journalism in the country.

In her capacity as then-chair of SANEF, Ferial Haffajee [pers. comm. 2007], was positive about the potential rejuvenation that tabloids could bring to the country's journalism, saying,

> Tabloids have been on the SANEF agenda for the last couple of years because it is most interesting what is happening in SA journalism. There has been a complete shakeup. Tabloids are the big media story. . . . They encourage a reading public, they act as a watchdog, and they keep power on its toes. We in the mainstream media have a lot to learn! Maybe they can also learn from our codes and ethics etc.

Berger seems less amenable to tabloid influence,[14] and maintains that the dominant paradigm is the one to be followed by popular newspapers. He holds up the example of the *Sowetan* as a paper that wants to follow a popular approach but remained "at root . . . factual." The *Sowetan* in fact has been the one paper in the country that has been most clearly deserted by its readers in favor of the new tabloid the *Daily Sun* because it had turned its attention away from "the grassroots" to the "more affluent readers."[15] Berger invokes the democratic role of journalism in South Africa when he slams tabloids as being "a country away from credible journalism." For him, tabloid writing is "the stuff of cheap fiction," its "crass archetypal narratives" falling short of "at least some of the basics of journalism." "The problem," he says, "is that some tabloidism gives a bad name to this genre of journalism as a whole."[16] These comments are clearly aimed at upholding existing journalistic practices as the standard against which tabloid journalism should be measured in an attempt to stave off the decline of standards through "tabloidization." The question arises whether the only way for tabloids to attain this benchmark—which remains unchanged and does not acknowledge any challenge from the tabloids to its own professional practices and identity—would be to cease being tabloids altogether.

In an attack on tabloids in the mainstream newspaper *Beeld*, Froneman spends considerable attention on the issue of definition. "We have to understand what tabloid journalism is; who the tabloids are; where it comes from; how it influences us all; and how we can respond to it."[17]

He defines the characteristics of tabloid journalism in terms of content and presentation, but also criticizes tabloids' neglect of serious news in favor of the sensational and foresees the superficialization of public discourse. Significant in the context of self-reflexivity as a characteristic of paradigm repair is his appeal to readers as well as journalists to "urgently reflect" on these issues. For Froneman, therefore, mainstream journalism is largely defined in terms of its gravity and depth. While he acknowledges that elements of tabloid journalism can also be found in mainstream Sunday newspapers or magazines like *Huisgenoot/You* and *People,* he dichotomizes between journalism that wants to entertain and journalism that wants to inform.

While Rabe (2005) concentrates on ethical issues, she couples ethical standards (the decline of which has been seen as one of the main detrimental effects tabloids could have on journalism) with journalistic quality, stating, "Responsible journalism is good journalism. Good journalism is responsible journalism." The implication is that if tabloids fall short of the standards of "responsible journalism," they lose any journalistic merit they might have laid claim to: "Tabloids—and the . . . tabloidisation of the media—are the antithesis of good journalism" (ibid.). In this criticism, ethical norms are used as tools to define the occupation of journalism,[18] and the implication is that adherence to a set of professional criteria for ethical behavior define what good journalism is. The problem with such a definition is that it fails to spell out which aspects of tabloid journalism are merely characteristics of the tabloid genre, having to do with taste and preference, and which have fundamentally ethical implications. While genre-specific aspects like sensationalism, melodrama, and brash presentation might fly in the face of mainstream journalism's claims to distance and "balance" (ibid.), it is debatable whether these characteristics are by definition unethical.

Ethical issues with tabloids more clearly come into play in cases such as the lack of source verification. Anton Harber quips, " 'I need another source to verify the snake-rape story,' is not something one hears in a good tabloid newsroom."[19] In these cases it becomes more difficult to decide whether stories about rapes committed by snakes or gorillas actually mislead their readers (thus overstepping an ethical line),[20] or whether they are so clearly fictional as to be understood by their readers as fantasy and diversion, which only makes up a part of tabloids' overall offering (see chapter 6 for a discussion of reader responses). The complexity of these questions around ethics and genre notwithstanding, the criticism of South African tabloids has for the most part centered around journalistic ethics.

Ethics

The strongest criticism leveled against tabloids in popular debates is that of unethical behavior. This behavior often pertains to issues of gender, sexual orientation, homophobia, and xenophobia—in other words, issues of stereotyping and representation. In April 2005, one particular case of reporting that had been seen as homophobic led to intense debate about tabloid media's potentially deleterious influence on society, and it eventually resulted in the adoption of an ethical code by the tabloid *Son*.

In this case, the *Son* published harmful allegations against a gay minister in the conservative Dutch Reformed church, Laurie Gaum, made by his ex-partner, psychologist Douw Wessels. Wessels accused Gaum of promiscuity and supplied the tabloid with risqué photographs that he knew would get Gaum into trouble with the church, which condemns homosexual practice. As such, this leaking of photographs should have been seen as an attempt at character assassination by a lover scorned, and should have made *Son* wary of using the pictures. The publication of the pictures caused uproar in the church, and Wessels later committed suicide.[21] The incident led to heated debate, in especially the Afrikaans media, where the debate pertained to whether the breach of Gaum's privacy was justified in order to expose the hypocrisy of the church (Gaum's father was a senior member of the church). Some critics also seemed to suggest a link between the tabloid reports and the suicide, or at least the metaphorical death of reputation. Rabe (2005) wrote, "[E]ven tabloids should subscribe to certain 'tabloid' codes of conduct, although this may sound like an oxymoron. Otherwise, they might just carry on with a license to kill." Berger, in his reaction to the same series of articles, criticized tabloids for too easily equating what the public is interested in with what is in "the public interest," saying that tabloids are "in the entertainment market and not in the information market."[22] While he is critical of tabloids' failure to adhere to the ethical code for the print-media industry set by the Press Ombudsman, he did not support Rabe's call for a separate code for tabloids. Berger invoked the liberal democratic view of the media as a "watchdog," and acknowledged that in this role, "it may be wrong to write off a paper like the *Daily Sun* in its entirety."[23]

This debate followed similar criticisms of unethical conduct that had been made earlier. Anton Harber,[24] while acknowledging the positive potential of tabloids, lamented:

> At the same time, one can't help feeling queasy when one looks at these papers, with their gory crime pictures, their fascination with superstition and bestiality ("I was raped by a snake") and their capacity to sail as close to the wind as possible on the worst populist sentiments, like xenophobia and homophobia. Recently, the *Daily Sun* spread across its front page—for all the world, including children, to see—the most sickening and degrading photograph of a pile of bodies after a Soweto family murder.

In Froneman's earlier criticisms of tabloids,[25] he also bemoaned the banality and triviality of tabloid content, calling it "low-level shock journalism" that affects readers' rights on a fundamental level. He saw the world created by tabloids as one where "everything is allowed," where "half truths are more than enough," and feared the long-term damage the tabloids might do to people's "sense of decency."

That worries about the detrimental social influence of tabloids can sometimes become a paternalistic concern on the part of elites is suggested by Joe Thloloe, himself a vigorous critic of the tabloids, in his capacity as Press Ombudsman (pers. comm. 2008):

> It's very seldom that I get a complaint against the tabloids from the target market—complaints that you do get will be complaints from outside that target market. Someone will be saying "my domestic was reading this paper and I looked over her shoulder and I was shocked to see what she was reading." But it's never the domestic who actually complains. I've taken time out to ask people who read these publications why don't you complain about what is in the publications. And they say of course we know what they are, we take them for what they are, for us it's just fun that's the end of the story. So there's absolutely no reason why we should be coming to complain to you because we think these are just fun publications.

In response to the severe criticism it received for its perceived lack of ethics, the Cape Town-based *Son* adopted the ethical code of its "quality press" stablemate, *Die Burger* (although changing it slightly). The debate about the perceived ethical misconduct of tabloids, however, continued seemingly unabated (for instance at a SANEF council meeting panel discussion in Cape Town in February 2007 with the title "Tabloids: Are we true to the public trust?" and a special journal issue by the NGO Genderlinks in June 2007).

A question that has not been addressed sufficiently in these debates is whether the mainstream press has also been guilty of the sins it accuses tabloids of. For instance, two of the biggest Sunday newspapers, the *Sunday Times* and the *Sunday Independent,* have in 2008 and 2009 been the focus of inquiries into inaccurate and libelous reporting. The former appointed an independent panel to review the paper's policies and structures in an attempt to avoid repeat mistakes and bad judgment calls. Similarly, the adoption of what was, in essence, a mainstream ethical code by *Son* in an attempt to silence its critics from the "quality" press and academia seems to suggest that the critical debate around tabloids has been focused largely on getting the tabloids to conform to the normative frameworks agreed upon among mainstream media outlets. The dubious ethical conduct by tabloids was therefore used more to re-establish the existing professional boundaries of journalism in the country rather than to examine the journalistic culture in the country more broadly. Let us now look at how these professional boundaries were set out.

Professional Boundaries

In the reactions to tabloid journalism cited above, familiar dichotomies were drawn up between ethical and non-ethical journalism, information and entertainment, and high level and low level journalism, with tabloids consistently being placed at the negative end of the binary. In this debate, little attention was paid to whether mainstream journalism also peddled entertainment, sensational event-based journalism, superficial analysis, or biased news coverage.[26] Instead, the status quo of mainstream journalism has largely been taken as the defining standard of journalism. The recurring objections against the brash and sensational approach of tabloids and their perceived lack of detachment and factuality refer back to the elitist view that oral and visual cultures are inferior to the literate, high culture of social elites (Glynn 2000, 21 with reference to Walter Ong's work). "Quality journalism" is most often associated with textual rather than oral communication patterns (e.g., the use of colloquialisms); with rational debate rather than emotion, spectacle, or ritual; with the "'hard', masculine, news" rather than the "feminised realm of emotion and intimate life" (Johansson 2007, 40).[27] As we know from Bourdieu (1984; see also Glenn and Knaggs's use [2008] of field theory to explain the criticism against South African tabloids), such distinctions of taste have the function of ordering society and creating cultural capital. As Glynn (2000, 21) points out:

> The public (and private) demonstration of one's capacity for detachment and distantiation in cultural consumption is among the primary practices through which the socially powerful create and display a sense of their own cultural superiority vis-à-vis the weak.
>
> Consequently the place of visual images in journalism has long been a subject of controversy, since many perceive, in the directness and immediacy of images, a threat to the pseudoscientific objectivity of official news work.

When such distinctions of taste are used (and often confused with or used alongside legitimate ethical considerations) to adjudicate on inclusion or exclusion from professional journalistic organizations, questions around the social function of professionalization arise. While frequently trumpeted as a check and balance against the abuse of media power, the professionalization of journalism is also often viewed in critical terms.[28] Allen (2005) refers to the process of professionalization as "corporate rationalization" that "establishes an elite, technocratic press that is more concerned with social control than promoting discursive forms of democracy." Professionalization in the South African context occurs through the adoption of a set of hallmarks identified by Garman (2005) as follows:

> Knowing what is and isn't "news"; crafting this "news" into a "story"—a peculiarly, medium-specific, constrained format which demands not only training but lots of practice to master; and a tone of address which aims the information at the audience a particular media channel imagines itself to be speaking to/writing for. There is also a moral claim to be disinterested and dispassionate and to be working on behalf of the public, a claim known as "objectivity," which gives the operation of journalism a moral imperative that can be wielded to weed out particular types of knowledge the journalist or editor considers too high-brow, unfamiliar, arcane or partisan or even irrational/dangerous for their readers/audiences. As a result news journalists operate not simply as conduits who disseminate information but as specialists who decide what information is public-worthy and who then shape it into particular forms for dissemination. . . . This means that journalists can police a set of boundaries around

their domain and protect their autonomy as specialists in particular knowledge areas and practices.

The debate around tabloids during the past few years can indeed be seen to have functioned as a form of this boundary policing which Garman describes. The criticism of the tabloids in the end boiled down to the question of whether they can even adhere to the definition of journalism. The heading of Berger's column on tabloids (*Mail and Guardian*, December 8, 2004) says it succinctly: "Headline-grabbing tabloids: are they journalism?"[29]

The tabloids have been perceived as transgressing some of the central defining characteristics of the journalistic orthodoxy—the notions of "objectivity" (or "factual" reporting); truth, accuracy, and balance; and the facilitation of rational deliberation in the public sphere. When tabloids overstep these boundaries, they threaten the dominant journalistic paradigm. This could either lead to a thorough investigation into the paradigm itself, or a process of "paradigm repair" (Berkowitz 2000, 128) in order to re-establish the hegemony of the dominant professional value system. The latter process entails identifying the culprit(s), castigating them or ostracizing them from the community,[30] and offering a public explanation of the wrongdoing (ibid., 127). This creates a ritual of self-reflexivity that allows for a limited critique, but is usually aimed at the expulsion of individual wrongdoers from the professional community rather than a thorough introspection of the profession itself and the paradigm upon which it builds its reputation (ibid., 128):

> In all, paradigm repair becomes a way for the media institution to justify its existence within its current system of practice. . . . [N]ews paradigms tend toward the hegemonic within a profession; a member of the profession must follow the routines of the paradigm in order to be seen as a member in good standing.

The ongoing debates at SANEF about the standing of tabloid journalism can be seen at least partly as performing this function of paradigm repair. While the rejection of tabloids has not been unanimous throughout the professional community of South African journalists, the dominant opinion did place them on a lower rung on the professional hierarchy than, for instance, "quality" newspapers, which are seen as "dumbing down" when they dare to incorporate the techniques of popular journalism.

The vehemence with which the dominant professional paradigm was reasserted can be related to the recent and significant shifts and reconstructions that the professional identity of journalists in South Africa has undergone as part of the transition to democracy. The (re-)establishment of a professional identity for journalists came as the result of considerable efforts that were seen to be under threat from the new upstarts. This renegotiated identity also has a political dimension, which in turn explains why much of the critique against tabloids was on the basis of the tabloids undermining the democratic role of journalism—SANEF itself came into being in 1996 as a new organization that aimed to cross the divide between Black and White journalists in the country. These two groups had been polarized along political and ideological lines, as Barratt (2006, 4) describes:

From two polarised groups—the Black Editor's Forum (BEF) and the Conference of Editors (CoE)—SANEF was formed in October 1996. BEF members were politicised, inclusive and had strong Black consciousness or Africanist approaches, while CoE members were mostly white liberals or apartheid supporters in an exclusive, non-political club of English and Afrikaans newspaper editors.

Thus, when Joe Thloloe, erstwhile chairperson of the BEF and president of the Union of Black Journalists, vehemently criticizes tabloids because they remind him of earlier publications which in his view were contemptuous of their Black readers,[31] his criticism could also be seen against the background of the struggle for professional recognition for Black journalists. Thloloe explains this connection as follows (pers. comm. 2008):

> If you look at *Bantu World* of the 1950s, 1960s essentially the mix was quite simple: it was soccer, it was crime, it was witch stories and lots of sex. That was the formula at the time. Now when I look at a publication that says "a tokoloshe [mischievous, dwarf-like mythical figure] sleeps with me every night," for me it's a throwback to that time. It was a huge struggle by Black journalists to move away from that type of journalism. . . . After all these years of struggle to say Black journalists can hold their own against any other journalist in the world we now have this throwback to that period which we tried so hard to eradicate.

Thloloe's criticism of tabloids might, however, be read as a more wide-ranging lament about the direction that journalism in the country has taken. In response to a question whether, in his experience as the Press Ombudsman, he would single out tabloids for unethical behavior, he responded:

> Even the supposedly serious publications are trying to complete with the tabloids on circulation figures, and therefore even dumbing down the broadsheets to the point that you wonder what is the difference between tabloids and broadsheets. So the quality of our journalism hasn't matched the new freedoms that we are supposed to be having. No, [I won't single out tabloids] as the main culprits. All I was pointing out is that we haven't consciously sat down to say what is the role of the media in a transforming society. I won't single the tabloids out—the problems I see range from tabloids to broadsheets. . . . [Y]ou will find that the more serious publications commit much more serious blunders, simply because they are trying to exploit the freedoms that we have, and they are trying to push against the limit. So it becomes easier to defame people, easier to hide behind anonymous sources, etc. etc. So the problems I am talking about are right across the board, it's not a case of saying that the tabloids are more irresponsible than the broadsheets are.

So while Thloloe has criticized tabloids for now fulfilling the dream of a democratic journalism, this criticism turns out, upon further investigation, to be part of a wider disillusionment with post-apartheid journalism. But most of the criticism of tabloids did not take this wide view, instead trying to protect the existing journalistic paradigm from the tabloid influence. Such paradigm repair becomes problematic when it prevents a critical look at the existing way of doing things by deflecting criticism onto deviants. While this process has international precedents,[32] the policing of professional boundaries in the South African context can also be seen against the background of local changes to the journalistic environ-ment. These include shifts in the demographic representation of editorial staff and the formation of a professional body, as mentioned previously.

Paradigm repair in South African journalism should be understood against the background of the shift toward professional self-regulation of the media that accompanied the transition to democracy. After apartheid, the media moved from an era of strict legal control to an era of operating on the basis of profes-sional ethics and of constitutional guarantees of freedom of speech. This shift demanded that media institutions develop ethical codes that would fit with the new order, whereas before they defined their conduct in terms of the prevailing laws and their resistance or complicity to the apartheid regime (cf. Froneman 1994). In countries moving from an authoritarian regime to a liberalized, market-oriented media system, the system of self-regulation is potentially an important mechanism to ensure press accountability. In this respect, the situa-tion in South Africa after apartheid was similar to those in other parts of Africa. For instance, when the "second wave of democracy" caused post-colonial one-party regimes in West Africa to relax their grip on the media (Frère 2007), the organization of journalists into professional bodies guided by ethical codes has helped to protect them against harassment, improved their working conditions, and increased social responsibility (ibid., 43). Whatever criticism one might have against the ways such organizations operate, or the way professionalization can impose limits on participation in the mediated public sphere, one must acknowl-edge that a system of self-regulation is vastly preferable to an environment where the media are controlled, threatened, or curtailed by government.

But self-regulation does present problems, including the lack of sanction or legal status and the challenge of how to generate sustainable income, retain cred-ibility, and avoid political interference, as has been the case in several African countries (ibid.). Around the same time that tabloids burst onto the scene in South Africa, it also became clear that this system of self-regulation in the new democracy was not operating as flawlessly as hoped. There were a number of setbacks in this new normative environment, among them inadequate knowl-edge of and training in media ethics (as came to light in a skills audit commis-sioned by SANEF; see De Beer and Steyn 2002) and a range of ethical scandals,[33] culminating in 2003, which has been termed the "annus horribilis" of post-apartheid journalism (Haffajee 2004b). These scandals led to a campaign by SANEF of getting "back to basics" in an attempt to repair the profession's image and improve journalistic standards. While SANEF has engaged in a campaign to address the lack of ethical skills among journalists and to reflect upon the breaches of ethical conduct among its members, the tabloids have given the professional community an opportunity to point a finger to culprits outside the fold rather than fundamentally interrogating the validity of the dominant paradigm itself. Finding scapegoats in the tabloids might have served to defuse some of the criti-cism that would otherwise have been directed at the respectable mainstream.[34]

The poor record of media professionals in upholding the ethical codes that had been decided upon within this self-regulatory framework was a superficial manifestation of a much deeper malaise. Conflicts between the media and government about the media's role in post-apartheid society (see Wasserman and De Beer 2005), along with increased commercial pressures on the news media,[35] indicated deep-seated differences of opinion about the media's role in post-apartheid South Africa. It has become clear that issues such as press freedom and the public's right to know were interpreted through different value systems (Shepperson and Tomaselli 2002, 283). At the core of the debates about the media's role in post-apartheid democracy are two conflicting normative frameworks for the media: a classic liberal-democratic perspective and a developmental/post-colonial perspective (see McQuail 2000).[36] These two positions do not form a clear dichotomy—they sometimes overlap and other perspectives co-exist with them. However, in the meta-discourse about the media's role in post-apartheid South Africa, these two views have come to dominate the debate and have become associated largely with the media and government's perspectives.

In positing ideal roles for the media, both these normative views are somewhat out of step with new postmodern perspectives on the role of the media in contemporary societies in the developed world. As Fourie (2007, 203) points out, postmodern capitalist societies are saturated by a wide range of media, which often takes the form of entertainment rather than information, and there are increasing possibilities for audiences from a diverse range of cultures and backgrounds to participate in media production. These factors resulted in a fragmented, diverse, pluralized, and highly mediated society that makes it difficult to prescribe norms for the media.

In South Africa, however, normative debates about the media have only begun fairly recently with the democratization of the country in 1994. Under apartheid, the media were tightly controlled with an intricate set of laws protecting the apartheid state from media criticism. For the most part (excluding the alternative media and some English-language newspapers), the media were complicit with the state, or at least offered only a limited critique (some would argue, within the confinement of the myriad laws relating to media matters). In the post-apartheid dispensation, a self-regulatory system for the media was agreed upon, which made it incumbent upon the media to reflect upon their role in the new democracy and to draw up ethical codes according to which their standards can be judged. A Press Ombudsman and a Broadcasting Complaints Commission were set up to deal with the public's complaints. In addition, the work of NGO media-watchdog organizations such as the Media Monitoring Project, the Freedom of Expression Institute, and Genderlinks kept normative issues for the media on the public agenda (see Fourie 2008).

From these debates, two main perspectives emerged. The liberal-democratic perspective was mostly the one shared by the professional journalistic fraternity. Values such as independence, objectivity, and truth telling formed the bedrock of the mainstream media's ethical codes. The way these values have been articulated in post-apartheid professional media circles resonates strongly with Western ethical codes (see Wasserman 2006a). This reliance on Western models was partly the result of the country's historical connection to Europe and especially the United Kingdom, and the influence of globalization on South Africa, which after apartheid opened up to outside cultural influences after years of isolation. Another part of the reason could be that during the apartheid years, the emphasis in the South African media fell on ways to circumvent the authoritarian rule of law rather than on developing an indigenous form of ethics.

The media also formed part of a larger neoliberal discourse of free-market values and minimal government intervention that became dominant in the postapartheid society. As has been the case in other transitional societies (Josephi 2008), the increased commercialization of journalism did not eliminate state attempts to intervene. Consequently, values like individual liberty and freedom also underpinned the new media ethical codes. On many occasions, the media clashed with the new government, while the government also made its influence felt, especially in the public broadcaster, the SABC. But this commercialization did not necessarily contribute to a broadening of the deliberative public sphere commensurate with pre-democratic expectations, either, since access to the media was still unequal.

Coupled with conflicting normative frameworks for the media was an apparent decline in the public's trust in the mainstream media (Fourie 2005). Fourie (ibid.) points to an anomaly that may help to explain the rampant popularity of a medium like the tabloids, even in the face of severe criticism from their detractors:

> [D]espite the enormous growth of the media as an industry, the majority of people (under normal circumstances) tend to see, experience, and enjoy the media as a disposable but non-essential product. They see it mainly as entertainment and diversion. Yet, the media itself, journalists, social critics, moralists, intellectuals and journalism and media academics, take themselves and the media very seriously. They see and defend it as a pillar of democracy, as indispensable for information, development and education, be it through news, campaigns or entertainment.

If this preference for the media as primarily an entertainment product is widespread, then South African audiences and media commentators (proclaiming the centrality of the media for democratic participation) seem seriously out of sync. But although mainstream newspapers (and other media) might deny it, the commercial pressures brought to bear on them have led to an increased popularization, as pointed out by Thloloe (2008).

In the next chapter, the allegation that the media's penchant for sensation and entertainment limits democratic deliberation will be examined by considering the South African tabloids' potential political role. That tabloids provide entertainment does not necessarily mean that entertainment is the *only* gratification sought by the readers turning to them in droves. The popularity of tabloids might at least in part be attributed to readers' sense of alienation from and loss of trust in the mainstream media. These feelings of alienation and mistrust might be a better starting point to question media performance in general than focusing on individual transgressions. The question needs to be asked whether the communities that are now flocking to tabloids were adequately consulted when the dominant professional frameworks were drawn up. This does not mean that tabloids should get off scot-free for their often ruthless tactics and for the harm they may cause in the process of producing their distinctive form of news. However, a distinction should be made between the values that are fundamental to the good in the *broader* society (and not only the elite served by "quality" mainstream broadsheets) and questions of style, genre, or taste. If tabloids may provide an impetus for journalists to go "back to basics," this self-reflexive turn should involve more than the performance of entrenched journalistic rituals which result in a reaffirmation of existing practices. If basics for the post-apartheid media are at stake, they are the basic values of the development of a broadly inclusive democratic public sphere, the transformation of society and the redress of inequalities.

Warning Lights

In the discussion thus far in this chapter, it has been suggested that the popularity of the tabloids points to certain failures or shortcomings of the main-stream paradigm of journalism in South Africa. Conversely, it has been argued that the heated debates over whether tabloids should be allowed to carry the badge of professional journalism are an attempt to deny the problems inherent in the dominant paradigm by focusing attention on the wrongdoings of a journalis-tic Other (Örnebring and Jönsson 2004). So, if one accepts that the unprece-dented appeal of tabloids might also be the result of certain failures of the main-stream media: How exactly did tabloids do better? On which journalistic aspects might tabloids have compelled a rethinking of the dominant normative frames? A clearer picture of audience preferences for tabloids can only be obtained by speaking to tabloid readers (which we will do in chapter 6). However, some pre-liminary observations can be made (see also Wasserman 2006a).

The liberal-democratic view of independence and neutrality currently un-derpins South African media ethical frameworks.[37] This perspective hampers the media's role when judged by how well they promote and develop the politi-cal, civil, and social aspects of citizenship (Steenveld 2004, 95) since it sets the ideal role for the media as being neutral conduits for information and precludes an active involvement in social change. Moreover, it views independence pre-dominantly in terms of the media's relation to government, while its position within networks of economic power is left largely unexamined, or is limited to immediate issues, such as conflicts of interest or payment for articles, unless in the "public interest" (Press Ombudsman 2004). Audience reaction against this limited understanding of independence and (perceived dishonest) claims to neutrality might have been underestimated. Perhaps the tabloids' highly per-sonalized, overtly subjective approach to news, can—as Larry Strelitz (2005) has pointed out—be seen as an "oppositional reading" (in Hall's terms) against the mainstream rhetorical strategies of objectivity.[38] Ward (2004, 3) shows how the concept of objectivity has developed historically (more so in the United States than in Europe and elsewhere; see Schudson [2005, 32]) as a rhetorical appeal by journalists to "establish, maintain or enhance their own credibility and that of their publications," that is, to maintain or repair the journalistic paradigm. However, the traditional notion of objectivity, he asserts (2004, 4), is in trouble and needs to be reformulated, because it "is indefensible philosophically, weakened by criticism inside and outside of journalism" and embraced by "fewer and fewer journalists." In the South African context, Strelitz's (2005) suggestion that tabloids may be read in terms of Bakhtin's notion of the carnival, namely as a means of resistance against authority, provides a useful perspective. Whether the Bakhtinian polyphony of lesser-heard voices finding an outlet in tabloids will have a more substantial political impact than a subversion of the dominant order is a question that will be touched upon again in the next chapter. The more subjective and sensationalist approach to news events offered by tabloids—which is seen as a transgression of the dominant norm of cool distance and neutrality—may be supporting a popular disregard for authority. This stance, Bloom suggests,[39] has contributed to the success of the tabloids: "What it's also clearly about is turning South Africa's traditional newspaper model on its head, getting buy-in from a reader who instinctively rejects the voice of authority found in conventional titles. Western or old school media values count for squat in this new world."

According to the professional normative framework guiding South African journalism, the media's primary obligation is the surveillance of state power. This orthodox "independent watchdog" or "Fourth Estate" role, articulated over and over in post-apartheid media debates, means that appeals to the media for more active involvement in transformation or development are met with resistance. Such appeals are either framed in terms of governmental interference and interpreted as pressure to tone down criticism, or as inconsequential "sunshine journalism."[40] The possibility that a more developmentally oriented journalism could also be critical of a government that does not fulfill its responsibility in this regard (see Ogan 1982) is often left out of the equation. Approaches such as public journalism, aimed at effecting social change, are usually frowned upon.[41]

Part of tabloids' success might stem from their taking the opposite stance, namely getting involved in the communities they serve and striving toward developmental goals. While such developmental aims might at first seem contradictory to the tabloids' relentless commercialism, tabloid publishers might consider efforts to create greater social mobility among their readers an investment in a readership that would be even more attractive to advertisers. The *Daily Sun,* for instance, has a regular feature called "SunDefender" where a legal expert provides free legal advice; an advice page called "Sun Solutions"; features promoting education as well as providing snippets aimed at improving readers' general knowledge; and a regular page, "Looking at Africa," with news from the rest of the continent. It is these types of self-help and general-knowledge information that led Addison (2003b) to view tabloids as empowering for communities. However, in a study of coverage of HIV/AIDS issues by Sunday newspapers, Swanepoel (2005) found that copy related to this topic was mostly sourced elsewhere, and coverage was superficial and approached the issue from the sensationalistic angle of risk and transfer (e.g., promiscuity, rape, etc.), thereby increasing stigma. The potentially empowering role that the tabloids could have played on this important developmental issue has, according to Swanepoel, been squandered. This reiterates Harber's point that although these tabloids claim to conform to some notion of social responsibility, and although they portray themselves as representing community issues, they display a "total absence of politics and most serious public issues like HIV/AIDS."[42]

The *Daily Sun*'s publisher, Deon du Plessis, has indicated that the lack of community involvement by the mainstream print media provided him with a marketing niche, made possible by the new democratic environment, that wasn't recognized by the Independent Group, to whom he first pitched his idea:[43] "I don't think they saw as clearly as we did that the country had changed," he said. "They were foreign." But while Du Plessis claims to be committed to "the man in the blue overall" and to reporting about "people nobody ever heard of,"[44] this stance does not necessarily reflect political or societal commitment outside of commercial interests. This is suggested by comments in which Du Plessis describes the democratization of the country in terms of just another business opportunity and his racially defined audience as a marketing niche, without acknowledging the structural imbalances underlying the country's racially segmented media market and the problematic aspect of his paper being located in a multi-national conglomerate (Du Plessis 2005):

> One of the many happy spinoffs of 1994—the beginning of SA's Great Chance to re-invent itself, was that the so-called Black market evaporated. There is no such thing. The fact is there are MANY markets in the so-called Black market. It WAS there, this Black market thing, while apartheid was there. Resistance to apartheid united most Black people . . . its destruction was a great goal, a unifyer of purpose. But with apartheid out of the way the market behaved as markets should . . . it split into pieces . . . pieces resting on new rules . . . like income, for instance. . . . [W]hat used to be the impenetrable, often sullen, often violent townships 10 years ago have become the most vibrant market in the country today.

Against this ahistorical view of townships (which bore the brunt of apartheid policing and state violence), it is not surprising to find Du Plessis describing news as "a commodity" (ibid.). To its credit, however, the *Daily Sun* does often seem more concerned with the plight of people in poor communities than do *Son* and *Daily Voice* for instance, where the emphasis seem to fall more on "sex, skinner and sport" (sex, gossip, and sport), to quote the latter's tagline. Referring to the controversial "page-three girl" in *Son*, Bloom points out this difference:[45] "Where *Son* and *Daily Sun* do differ is on page three. Du Plessis opens his paper and points to a head-and-shoulders shot of a township mother mourning the loss of her children. 'There's our page three girl,' he says." Although the *Daily Sun* avoids the crude gender stereotyping of a page-three girl and even embarked on a campaign against gender violence called "Charter for a Man" in 2007, its gender representation has been shown (Dewa 2008) to remain informed by patriarchal notions of masculinity and femininity. This is an example of the conservative social politics of the tabloids.

Apart from its fare of gossip, celebrity news, and salacious pictures, the Cape Town-based tabloid *Son* does also focus on communities, often localized in its regional issues (two of which closed down in 2008). It also has correspondents in rural towns and assesses readers' opinions through focus groups (Koopman, pers. comm. 2005). The editor of the *Son* describes its content as "educational" by focusing on and exposing "drugs, prostitution, [and] corruption" (ibid.), and considers the paper "a community newspaper, just on a bigger scale" (pers. comm. 2007).

Invoking the resistance to apartheid by alternative media, Capraro (2005) has stated that *Son* would have fared even better under apartheid, "had the successive totalitarian National Party governments allowed it to be published." Comparing *Son* to newspapers that were censored under apartheid is rather rich, considering that Naspers, the publisher of the *Son,* was directly linked to the ruling party during apartheid (see Beukes 1992, 487–488). Now, however, Capraro celebrates the seemingly diverse readership of the tabloid and its disregard for moral guardians:[46]

> *Son* tells the story as it happens. Not in the language of the *taalstryders, dominees* and those longing for the days of political and cultural Afrikaner domination, but the way our readers speak. Our lingo is a "seamless" Afrikaans—the language of any race and colour. The Cape editions speak a mixture of Capey and northern suburbs Afrikaans. In the other editions, we also use the local Sefrikan vernacular. Yuppies make up an important part of our northern readership.

Another interesting aspect of *Son*'s self-styled educational role is its publication venture "Son-boeke,"[47] which are booklets with, for example, health tips (e.g., *Dokter jouself gesond* ["Doctor yourself healthy" or "Treat yourself"]).

Evaluating the success or sincerity of tabloids' community involvement often yields paradoxical results. While they often seem directly involved in community campaigns and putting community issues on the agenda (more about this in the next chapter), these communities are also often seen as lucrative markets rather than publics. Nevertheless, the tabloids have highlighted the importance of revisiting dominant normative concepts such as "impartiality" and the need for inscribing community involvement and a commitment to societal transformation into normative frameworks for the post-apartheid media. This has been recognized by Andrew Gill, publisher of the *Sowetan* and *Sunday World,* both papers whose circulation has been severely impacted by the *Daily Sun*'s success.[48] Gill acknowledges that the *Sowetan* and *Sunday World* had "no longer [been] covering relevant issues in a relevant way. . . . We had a strong voice in the community, and we've gone back to that as a basic principle."

While the tabloids have often been chastised for transgressing the ethical codes agreed upon by the mainstream media—concerns which are often valid and should be taken seriously—they have been adhering to an ethical imperative of giving voice to the marginalized. The tabloids' preference for taking a stance and getting involved in the communities they serve above the more orthodox position of neutrality and distance, will be discussed in more detail in the next chapter when tabloid editors speak about the relationship between the tabloids and their readers.

Another shortcoming of current dominant normative frameworks is that while the concept of the "public interest" is often invoked as a guiding principle for the media, this concept remains vague and has not been defined adequately in terms of the inequalities regarding access to the media in a developing country. Nor have the relations between "public interest" and "nation-building" been adequately dissected in the context of South Africa as a transitional democracy. The media often use it rhetorically in exceptionalist terms, such as to justify otherwise questionable behavior like the invasion of a public figure's privacy. While some of these claims are indeed valid from a free-press standpoint, the concept itself is very seldom opened up for rigorous analysis. For instance, the impact of (mostly racially defined) market segmentation and its link to material inequalities and societal polarizations inherited from apartheid is not considered when the "public" is described in vague or homogenous terms. This results in contesting claims made by the media and the democratically elected government about stewardship of citizens' interests. Without examining the power exerted by market forces in delimiting the opportunities for democratic participation, the concept of "public interest" is in danger of becoming a façade for sectoral interests. If claims are correct that tabloids have provided media access to sections of the community that were excluded before (as opposed to luring them away from other publications),[49] the tabloids might contribute to a broadening of what passes for "the public" in South African media. The next chapters will discuss in more detail how tabloids have broadened newspapers' readerships and created an alternative public sphere and how this is experienced by tabloid readers. Although South African tabloids claim to define the market in terms of class rather than race (Capraro 2005; Du Plessis 2005), these categories still largely overlap. While these reasons are partly related to content, the allure of tabloids' cheap cover price should not be discounted.[50]

A more productive way of understanding the concept of the "public interest" in normative frameworks would be to relate it to the imperative of broadening the public sphere to include those sections of the population who, up until recently, have been absent or marginalized from mainstream media debates—especially in the print media. However, unless readers are truly represented in tabloid content, their perspectives taken seriously, and they are given an opportunity to participate in the creation of content, the large numbers of new readers cannot automatically be seen as a broadening of a participatory public sphere. They may then remain consumers of rather than actors in tabloid content.

The dominant interpretation of the post-apartheid constitution's guarantees of media freedom seem to be rooted in an individualistic understanding of human rights, where media freedom is linked to the rights and duties of individuals (cf. Johnson and Jacobs 2004). As a result of being informed by liberal ethics and the assumptions of individualism and universality, the dominant normative framework does not incorporate a specific focus on African cultural values and as a result sets up media ethical discourses for a confrontation with emerging (and often state-sponsored) discourses on African identity. Ostensibly, tabloids do take an African cultural perspective—but to what extent stories on witchcraft, superstition, or miracle cures can serve to further essentialize the imposed ethnicities of apartheid rather than acknowledge the ways in which African identities are constantly in flux, remains a question that needs further investigation. It is in this regard that Thloloe's comments on the stereotyping of Black readerships as given to base instincts and superstition have their strongest persuasive power. The construction and often reification of African (and, in the context of the Western Cape tabloids, "Coloured") identities in the tabloids might help explain why middle-class Black and Coloured readers interviewed for the audience study discussed in chapter 6 expressed suspicion or dislike of tabloids. To these respondents, the tabloids are seen to interpellate Black and Coloured readers in terms reminiscent of older identity categories which they have either left behind on the road to a modern, middle-class, suburban lifestyle or which they associate with the stereotypical and fixed identity categories that underpinned the cultural logic of apartheid. By constantly reporting on crime, violence, and poverty, tabloid reportage could reinforce stereotypical associations of the Black body with social pathologies. Through the constant portrayal of the Black body as problematic, disrespected, or violated, tabloid coverage might in fact support an essentialist and perjorative view of African subjects instead of undermining White or Western prejudice. While tabloids attempt to introduce African cultural meanings into a Western-dominated media discourse, these attempts can be examined critically for whether they have fallen afoul of the reductionism and essentialism that Tomaselli (2003) pointed out in other contexts.

For normative media ethics to be about more than the routine enforcement of existing guidelines, rituals, and professional standards, critiques should go beyond the surface manifestations of media phenomena. If debates about media ethics in South Africa are to assist the transformation of journalism and the media industry, they should also address larger, structural issues. For the debate about tabloids to contribute to a thorough re-examination of the South African media environment, the following points should be taken into account:

- The debate about tabloids should move beyond the professional ritual of paradigm repair. The emergence and unprecedented success of tabloids provides an opportunity not only to investigate transgressions of the current hegemonic standards of professionalism, but to interrogate those standards themselves. It provides an occasion to critically examine the dominant normative frameworks of the media in an attempt to find out why they are not broadly accepted and how they could be revised.
- There is a need for proper audience ethnography of tabloids to establish what uses and gratifications these audiences derive from tabloids that they do not find in mainstream newspapers. Chapter 6 will explain the reasons behind audience preferences for tabloids and why these audiences have either deserted or never felt at home in mainstream print media.

- Simplistic binaries between mainstream media and tabloid media should be avoided. Although the terms "tabloid media" and "mainstream media" are contrasted in this book, the implication is not that there are no overlaps between their respective styles and approaches.

  Tabloids should not be homogenized—the differences in style, content, and emphasis among them should be acknowledged. The danger inherent in creating dichotomies (such as professional vs. unprofessional; information vs. entertainment; "quality" vs. popular) between mainstream media and tabloid media is that it relegates tabloid media to the position of a journalistic Other (Örnebring and Jönsson 2004). Caught up in such a binary, it becomes difficult, if not impossible, to recognize the positive and negative aspects of tabloids, because they remain the deficient and inferior Other. This also puts mainstream press in such a position of power that criticism is directed outward only, instead of inward as well.

- Taking tabloids seriously does not mean that everything they do should be condoned. There have been too many examples of South African tabloids engaging in despicable journalism. Nor does it mean that market success should be taken as a normative standard of what journalism in a transitional democracy should be about. Here again there are examples of how South African tabloids have attained popularity through pandering to popular prejudices expressed in the form of, for instance, homo- or xenophobia. One should therefore be careful in assessing which aspects of tabloid journalism should be taken as serious challenges to current normative frameworks and which should be rejected.

- Alternative approaches must be found of viewing tabloids other than from existing, entrenched professional standards perspectives—especially when these professional standards are upheld by a patronizing, knee-jerk morality. Nor should tabloids be granted a place in the sun from the assumption of superiority that tabloids are a type of "kids menu" from which readers will "grow up" to start appreciating mainstream fare. There should be an acknowledgment of the difference in genre that does not necessarily imply a hierarchy. Rather, the debate should be concerned with the effects tabloids could have on the existing, extremely commercialized media environment. Could tabloids contribute to a broader public sphere, or are they following the example of the mainstream media (albeit more overtly and spectacularly) in limiting public participation by turning readers into spectators rather than participants?

- The debate about tabloids and mainstream media should also contain a critical political-economic focus. All South African tabloids belong to commercial conglomerates, so it could be expected that profitability would be higher on their publishers' agenda than increased public deliberation. The support of conglomerates for tabloids is also important when drawing conclusions on the basis of the high popularity of tabloids. The fact that tabloids can sell (especially initially, when breaking into the market) at a cheap price because they are cross-subsidized by other products in the same media group should also be factored in when trying to account for tabloids' popularity. Readers may buy tabloids partly because they are cheap, and not only because they provide desired content. Glib and overly easy inferences between content and audience preference should therefore be avoided.

The emergence of tabloids has created an important opportunity for the South African mainstream press to critically engage in introspection and self-criticism. This, however, should be done in a rigorous and uncompromising fashion, and not only performed as a ritual of professional self-reflexivity. Though there is much to find fault with in the South African tabloids, if the only response to them is to ensure the maintenance or repair of dominant professional frameworks, an important opportunity to renegotiate the journalistic "paradigm-in-process" (Berger 2008) will be lost. If nothing else, tabloids should remind the mainstream South African media that large sections of the South African public are feeling left out. In this regard, the remarks made by Emery and Emery about the penny press in nineteenth-century United States are uncannily appropriate (albeit in a somewhat patronizing manner) for the South African context today (cited in Örnebring and Jönsson 2004, 288):

> Whenever a mass of people has been neglected too long by the established organs of communication, agencies eventually have been devised to supply that want. Invariably the sophisticated reader greets this press of the masses with scorn because the content of such a press is likely to be elemental and emotional. Such scorn is not always deserved.

In the next chapter, we will look in more detail at the criticism that the tabloids undermined the country's fragile new democracy, and we will consider what political role tabloids can play in the transitional South African society.

5. The Revolution Will Be Printed: Tabloids, Citizenship, and Democratic Politics in Post-Apartheid South Africa

Drugs. Prostitution. Corruption.
We don't do politics—but we do politicians.

—*son, marketing presentation, 2004*

From the discussion thus far, one could safely say that the arrival of the new tabloid newspapers has changed the media landscape in post-apartheid South Africa irrevocably. Emerging within the first decade after the end of apartheid, these papers are at least temporally linked to the country's democratization process. It was argued in the first two chapters that these links extend beyond the temporal, but that the emergence of these papers can also be related to shifts occurring in broader society, culture, and the media sphere during this transitional period. But, as discussed in the previous chapter, these tabloids also met with strong opposition and criticism from the mainstream press, media commentators, and journalism educators for contravening the professional and ethical standards of the country's journalistic establishment. We concluded that the tabloids, while not above criticism, were so controversial in large part because they posed a challenge to the existing journalistic paradigm. Their sensationalist, no-holds-barred, opinionated approach flies in the face of journalistic conventions such as "objectivity," neutrality, and social responsibility—or dominant interpretations of these values, at least. Their choice of and approach to stories do not conform to the dominant notion of veracity that sees "truth" as based on value-free facts. Tabloids often appeal to a cultural and social imaginary that lies outside of the experiential horizon of the elite audiences served by mainstream commercial media. Because they transgress the boundaries of conventional journalism, they are seen to pose a danger to journalistic standards of professionalism and ethics.

While the criticism against tabloids largely has to do with their perceived transgression of the ethical standards of good journalism and the blot this has left on the reputation of the profession, some critics have explicitly accused the tabloids of undermining the role the media were supposed to be playing in a fledgling democratic society. One commentator (Manson 2005) compared the local tabloids to their British counterparts and concluded that their reporting style was against the values of the new South African democracy (see chapter 3).

Another critic (Froneman) sees the world created by tabloids as one where "everything is allowed," where "half truths are more than enough."[1] Froneman reiterates the point made by Berger (2005b), who accused tabloids of being "not really newspapers" because "they play in the entertainment market rather than prosecute the business of information," pointing out that tabloids often ignore important political news, such as the 2005 elections in Zimbabwe. Froneman's main argument, however, is a moral one, in which he deplores the long-term damage the tabloids might do to people's "sense of decency."

A significant part of the criticism against tabloids has been based on the assumption that media in post-apartheid South Africa should play a role in strengthening and broadening the country's democratic culture. Critics of the tabloids contended that they neglect to play this political role, and that in some instances they even act *contrary* to the new democratic culture. This chapter will first examine some of these criticisms in more detail, then offer alternative perspectives on the democratic roles that South African tabloids could fulfill. These roles become clear when the tabloids are evaluated within a combined political-economy and cultural studies perspective.[2] A view of the political economy of the South African media within which the tabloids operate (which has already been alluded to in chapters 1 and 2) gives us a critical understanding of the limitations of the mainstream, elite print media to provide a space for politically relevant discourses for the majority of poor and working-class audiences. A cultural approach, on the other hand—from which tabloids' political relevance will be approached in this chapter and will be extended in the following chapter when focus-group interviews with tabloid readers are analyzed—would examine how tabloids provide a space where readers can actively make meaning from tabloid content and use this meaning to claim their places as citizens in a democratic society.

A "crisis for democracy"?

In a marketing presentation in 2004, the Cape Town tabloid *Son* summed up its editorial mission as follows: "Drugs. Prostitution. Corruption. We don't do politics—but we do politicians."

This motto seems to reflect the celebrity approach to politics for which tabloid newspapers (and, increasingly, other media formats) are often criticized. This approach sees individual personalities as more attractive than policy issues, and more substantial political issues appear on the media radar only when they can be sensationalized (Sparks 2000). Sparks describes tabloid content as characteristically paying "relatively little attention to politics, economics, and society and relatively much to diversions like sports, scandal, and popular entertainment." International literature suggests that tabloids seldom deviate from this formula for content, and if political positions are taken up, it is done though the range of devices available to tabloid journalists (Tulloch 2007, 50). Exceptions to this rule do occur—for instance, the publication of a petition protesting the invasion of Iraq on the front page of the UK tabloid the *Daily Mirror* in 2003, or extra-textual protests like marching, projecting an anti-war slogan against the Houses of Parliament, or infiltrating a nuclear power station (ibid.). The deployment of celebrities in campaigns and the use of stunts, parody, cartoons, and similar popular devices are often seen as signs of a conflation of the bourgeois public sphere with the realm of entertainment, displacing the Habermasian space for political deliberation enabling rational political choice (ibid., 57–58).

For these reasons, tabloids are often seen as constituting a "crisis for democracy" (Sparks 2000) or a "depoliticization" of the public because less attention is given to the "serious" news seen as necessary for the well-being of democratic society, like politics, economics, and social issues, while more is given to what are seen as diversions—namely sports, scandal, and entertainment (ibid.). This leads to the "lowering of journalistic standards" (Curran 2003, 92–93). This kind of "moral panic" (Cohen 1973) in reaction to "tabloidization" is by no means specific to the South African situation. Gripsrud (2000) points out that such alarmist responses have been voiced "ever since the birth of the modern press," and sees the term "tabloidization" itself as "a tabloid term, more of a journalistic buzzword than a scholarly concept" (ibid.). Sparks (2000) has pointed to the "heated, and often ill-informed" debate about the "rise of the tabloid" in American journalism, although this phenomenon also occurs elsewhere in the world:

> At first glance South African tabloid editors seem to have internalized some of these accusations about their papers' tendency to provide entertainment rather than serious political content.
>
> The *Son*'s description of itself as a paper that does not "do politics" is echoed, in stronger terms even, by the publisher of the *Daily Sun,* Deon du Plessis. Du Plessis sees politics as relatively unimportant to the success of his paper, even ascribing its popularity to the fact that the paper launched at a time "when people were less political" (Froneman 2006). According to Du Plessis, the editorial team at the *Daily Sun* sensed they "were talking to the sons and daughters of the revolution. . . . They were off the barricades and into improving their lives." (ibid.)

This downplaying of political debate was not welcomed in a society keenly aware of the importance of fostering a new democratic culture. The overwhelming consensus among the journalistic establishment was that the media in post-apartheid South Africa should function as creators of social cohesion, educating the citizenry about their democratic responsibilities and acting as watchdogs against government excesses. The huge market that the tabloids had at their disposal seemed to place them in an ideal position to play this political role. By appearing to eschew this role, they invited the rage of their critics. They were accused not only of neglecting their democratic responsibility by not paying enough—or proper—attention to politics, but also of infringing on the democratic rights of the citizenry by peddling sensationalist news and perpetuating stereotypes.

One such critic (ibid.) refers to the *Daily Sun*'s approach as "sunny" and "nonpolitical." He sees their shunning of "hard politics" in favor of a personalized approach as one of the central characteristics of the South African tabloids (ibid., 26). Harber pointed out the tabloids' "total absence of politics and most serious public issues like HIV/AIDS, their salacious, celebrity-driven tone, and the fact that they are all owned by one company: Media24 (. . .), rapidly becoming the 94-pound gorilla of our newspaper industry."[3] Harber's observation regarding the conglomeration of the South African newspaper industry is a valid criticism of its structure—this concentration limits the range of political perspectives available in the media. A later arrival on the tabloid scene, the Cape Town–based *Daily Voice*, is also owned by a big conglomerate—Naspers' rival, the Independent Group. Harber's criticism of the *Daily Sun*'s neglect of "politics and most serious public issues" is similar to Froneman's, although in a subsequent article, he tempered his critique with a measure of optimism:[4]

> Some would argue that the main function of the tabloids is to distract ordinary people from the bigger political and social issues—and that is why they contain almost no government or party-political reporting. But this, I suspect, will change in time, as with the British tabloids. These papers—with their influence on millions of voters—will become politically more important.

Harber might be referring to the increasingly important role that tabloids like *The Sun* in the United Kingdom played in the Blair/ New Labour era.[5] Although tabloid journalism is commonly seen as providing a stage for politicians as personalized figures rather than as political representatives, often fitting political archetypes (Van Zoonen 2000), cases have been noted (Tulloch 2007) where tabloids have taken an explicitly political stance on an issue.

In some cases, tabloids' political stance might not be articulated in terms of party politics, but nonetheless relates to an issue with significant political impact. One such issue is nationalism and xenophobia. UK tabloids have often been criticized for their nationalistic and xenophobic discourses, and rightwing politics in general, that include racial and ethnic stereotyping (Curran 2003, 13; Conboy 2005; Pickering 2008).[6] South African tabloids have also been criticized for reactionary coverage (Jacobs 2004). The South African Media Monitoring Project (MMP) has been very critical of various aspects of the tabloids, leading to several complaints being made to the Press Ombudsman and the Human Rights Commission against the tabloids and a petition against the *Daily Voice* for what it considered indecent coverage of a child-pornography ring (Media Monitoring Project 2007b). The MMP has also criticized tabloids for what they saw as their xenophobic reporting and disregard of human rights. When xenophobic violence swept across the country in May 2008, the MMP laid an official complaint with the national Press Ombudsman against the *Daily Sun,* phrasing its objections as follows:

Tabloidisation of the news has been increasing for a number of years in South Africa, and is often typified by dramatic, personal and in many instances mythical reporting. While tabloids have introduced newspapers to millions of new readers, and some provide informative content on the inner pages, often the reporting in some of these tabloids is not only sensationalist in nature, lacking context and leading with shocking visuals and inflammatory headlines, but they are also blatantly sexist and frequently xenophobic. As a result journalistic practices of ethical conduct are sometimes sidelined by such tabloids. This leads to lower-quality news and less regard for human rights.

Coverage of race in the context of the tabloids is particularly problematic. Focused, clear and informative media coverage of race issues is particularly important in South Africa, given our history of racial segregation. The media have the ability to perpetuate and challenge stereotypes in South Africa. It is therefore particularly troubling to see coverage by media of race lacking this socio-historical context, as it often tends to support and perpetuates stereotypes. Some media are actively xenophobic, creating stereotypes of people from the rest of Africa which are dangerous, offensive and harmful. (ibid.)

From this criticism it is clear that the attack on tabloids extends beyond moralistic objections to political concerns. Another media watchdog, the Freedom of Expression Institute (FXI), has called tabloids the "biggest problem facing the media industry" in the country. Part of its criticism echoes the more general complaints of sensationalism and gossip discussed in the previous chapter, but it also accused tabloids of "depoliticizing" their readership "instead of empowering them" and shifting attention away from "important issues such as transformation."[7]

According to the FXI, the tabloids "exploited the poor and their living conditions and denied them the extended freedom to express their class conditions":

> In the era when the working class is faced with unemployment, cutoffs in services such as water and electricity, and a lack of delivery of basic rights such as education, housing and health facilities, it is critical that there should exist media that are able to highlight some of these challenges in an accessible and yet intelligible manner and not simply in patronising terms. (Derby 2005)

What is interesting about the FXI's criticism is that it employs a broader definition of democratic politics than those critics demanding more attention to "hard politics," like the crisis in Zimbabwe (Froneman 2006) or "serious public issues" like HIV/AIDS,[8] by including issues affecting readers on a local and community level, like social delivery. The question not raised is whether the mainstream print media adequately pay attention to matters of importance to the poor, or whether tabloids are measured by a standard that the mainstream press is not. The objections voiced by social-movement activists that tabloids sensationalize the lives of the poor is also relevant here.

This chapter examines whether the concerns regarding tabloids' political relevance as pointed out by these critics remain valid when the political functions of the press are seen more broadly than coverage of party political debates or formal political processes.

Politics by Other Means

Even if it is acknowledged that tabloids generally avoid "serious" political news of the kind found in mainstream newspapers, it has been argued that they could still play a democratic political role in other respects.[9] Tabloids' defendants have pointed out that popular journalism contributes to a democratic public sphere by undermining the social hierarchy which allows the elite to dominate mediated debate (see Fiske 1989, 103ff.; also Sparks 2000, 5). Tabloids provide an alternative view of reality not found in official, "quality" news. Through sensation and excess, popular texts like tabloids question the dominant social standards and point to the "excessive failure of the normal" (Fiske 1989, 116). As such, tabloids can be read as having political impact, even if not in the form associated with the rational public sphere of official media.

As "ritual forms of communication," tabloids "reproduce and instill in all [their] members a sense of community and identity, of shared conditions, values, understandings and so on" (Gripsrud 2000, 285, 295). Tabloid journalism can therefore "provide the audience with existential and moral help, and support in the daily struggles to cope with an everyday life marked by the uncertainties characteristic of modernity" (ibid., 297). Tabloids view their audiences as human beings first and not only as citizens—but the tabloid notion of citizenship includes more than political, because democracy for Gripsund (ibid.) includes

> cultural life; various forms of reflection on existential matters or "the human condition"; the formation, maintenance, deconstruction, and reformation of identities; and so on.

From this point of view, the melodramatic tabloid approach to news provides a "bottom-up" perspective (ibid.) on daily life that helps audiences make sense of a world that often seems to defy the cool distance of rational explanations or dominant value frameworks. This is especially the case in contemporary media-saturated societies, where popular culture is increasingly central to political communication (Van Zoonen 2000, 6). Especially relevant for the South African context is the view that popular culture can function as a form of political practice when used as such by citizens who are excluded from the traditional social and political channels (ibid., 13). The South African tabloids speak to the section of the population bearing the brunt of the legacies of apartheid. The material conditions they live under and their disadvantages in terms of literacy and education levels diminish their access to political debate in the public sphere. Popular media broadens the bourgeois public sphere by validating a more diverse spectrum of topics and styles considered worthy of public discussion (Van Zoonen 2000).

Costera Meijer (2001, 191) shares this view and points to the ways popular media (in her case, sitcoms, talk shows, and other narrative television formats) can "reveal, exemplify, or reflect the ways in which a democratic culture is operating." Popular media could also act as a disciplinary discourse that instructs publics on how to be good and loyal subjects of the state. To this one could add, with a view to the celebration of consumerism by the South African tabloids aimed at the socially mobile Black market, how to be a good consumer in the marketplace. Meijer (ibid., 194) argues for the "revaluation of the journalistic and civic significance of everyday life," since for most people citizenship means the most in relation to their everyday lives and interactions with family, friends, institutions, and such.

Sparks (2000, 28), however, points to the limitations of tabloid discourse for political participation, arguing that tabloids do not necessarily cultivate familiarity with the core issues of politics:

> It is not simply that tabloids and tabloidization constitute a threat to an existing democracy; rather they make its practical functioning an impossibility because they are unable to provide the audience with the kinds of knowledge that are essential to the exercise of their rights as citizens.

The question about the influence of tabloids on democracy is an important one to ask, since, as Gripsrud (2000, 288) points out, the expansion of a particular form of popular journalism "affects cultural, political, and public life in general, not just a set of journalistic formats." While the impact of new developments such as the South African tabloids on the framework for journalistic practice provides us with an interesting insight into the journalistic paradigm(s) of a country (as discussed in the previous chapter), it is also important to assess whether these new papers can be "resources for active and informed citizenship" (ibid., 292).

Can the South African tabloids be considered to play a political role in this sense? Perhaps, but this political role should be broadly defined. Taking the above discussion of the international academic literature about tabloids' political role as a point of departure, and contextualizing this literature against the background of the debates about South African tabloids, several potential political roles for South African tabloids could be identified:

1. Tabloids can play a political role by providing an alternative public sphere.
2. Tabloids can resist the exclusion of certain groups from mediated public discourse and contribute to "media citizenship."
3. Tabloids can assist their readers in coping with life in a democratic society.
4. Tabloids can foster democracy by keeping the powerful accountable.
5. Tabloids can provide their readers with guidance in terms of participating in formal political processes.
6. Tabloids can also play a negative political role by engaging in reactionary politics. This includes xenophobic and other stereotypical attitudes, as well as the individualization and sensationalizing of popular disillusionment to the point of defining tension and resistance.

Let us look in more detail at how the South African tabloids address each of these areas, and therefore what their contribution to democratic public life in South Africa could be.

Tabloids as an Alternative Public Sphere

Critics of tabloids see them as lacking the quality of democratic debate and having a negative impact on the rational public sphere (Sparks 2000, 24) These criticisms flow from a Habermasian notion of the rational public sphere as the terrain where public opinion can be formed outside of state or commercial pressures, a notion with its roots in liberal democratic theory and the philosophical legacies of the Enlightenment (Glynn 2000, 15; see Glenn and Knaggs 2008 for a similar argument in relation to South African tabloids). It has, however, been argued by several scholars that the notion of the public sphere can be modified and transformed to be more heterogeneous and contestatory, and not dependent on rational debate (Örnebring 2004; Glynn 2000, 17 cites Livingstone and Lunt 1994 in this regard but himself doubts the benefits of retaining the concept). As Johansson (2007, 169) points out, even within the Habermasian view, accessibility to the public sphere is a key requirement for debates about citizenship and democracy to have broader validity. In this respect, tabloids are contributing to a widening of the public sphere by making it more accessible to more people. Popular journalism can also contribute to an *alternative* public sphere because its discourse takes place somewhere other than the mainstream, because it has other participants, other issues are addressed, and tabloid debates take a different form than those in mainstream journalism (Örnebring and Jönsson 2004, 286).

Tabloids can be seen to contribute to an alternative public sphere when they provide ordinary people with the opportunity to tell their stories and bring the struggles of their everyday lives into the public arena (Örnebring 2006, 862). This is also done through "addressing readers as equals" and letting them speak in the newspaper through *vox populi*-type articles and introducing issues that would previously not have been raised in public discourse (ibid., 864 and 866). Hermes (2006, 28–29) sees the broadening of what we understand as the "public sphere" as an urgent project, since citizenship currently is "elsewhere." She argues for a more "cultural understanding" of the public sphere than the dominant view of the public sphere as predominantly shaped by news media acting as "democracy's watchdog." If her reference to popular media and entertainment is applied to tabloids, these papers should be taken seriously as a site for the shaping of public opinion and the building of identities. In this realm, sensation and emotion are also valid experiences. Popular culture can also make people "feel they belong," allow people to dream about their ideal society, and blur the borders between the public and the private more than any other institution and for more people across different ages, genders, and ethnicities (ibid., 37–38). Viewed from this perspective, Hermes argues that popular culture (which for our discussion includes media like tabloids) can even be considered among the most democratic and inclusive domains of contemporary society, even while it is shaped by commercial interests. These insights about the popular dimensions of political culture have direct bearing on the South African tabloids. By broadening the media landscape to include audiences who often do not recognize themselves in the mainstream print-media discourse, tabloid media can create an alternative public sphere where citizenship and democratic politics are debated and negotiated on other terms.

This alternative public sphere is, however, highly commercialized, which is not to say that the mainstream print media are free from commercial interests. However, in the case of tabloid media, this commercialism is often more brash and more visible. Du Plessis (pers. comm. 2007) acknowledges the commercial benefits of providing his readers with an alternative to the mainstream:

> It's a very desirable market, and we're dominating it by far. More and more big-time advertisers, ranging from cell phones to money loans to cars, want to be there, because this is where the money is. So it's a very happy confluence.

The editor of the *Daily Voice,* Karl Brophy (pers. comm. 2007), emphasizes his newspaper's role as providing a media sphere for members of the working class that they cannot find elsewhere. He sees the paper as "embedded" in the community, and refers to stories aimed at preventing child abuse as examples of their orientation toward issues of interest to the community. For him, the key difference between his tabloid and the mainstream press is the perspective from which stories are covered. For the *Daily Voice,* events in the townships and working-class suburbs are not distant conflicts that only enter the news discourse when there are spikes of conflict, tragedy, or disaster, but their readers' everyday lived reality, demanding an ongoing engagement:

> One of the reasons we're accepted so readily in communities around Cape Town is that in the past, newspapers would go into townships every now and again and then present it in a way as if they are writing for their *own* readership about how these people live. What we're doing is we're going in there every day and we say this is how you live, and they know it is how they live because they see it every day. And that is why we are more trusted than *Die Burger* or *Cape Times.* [They do] stories on shack fires now and then, but these papers haven't been there for the past couple of months while more people have died.
>
> Our readers are massively loyal, because we are there every day, and we go out to them when they call.
>
> We get a massive amount of phone calls.

Brophy also highlights a campaign against the "Bush of Evil," a thicket in the Coloured township of Delft near Cape Town, where children and women had been raped and murdered.[10] The tabloid accused the then-mayor of Cape Town, Nomaindia Mfeketo, of having "blood on her hands" until she agreed to have the bush cut down.

Brophy's view of the relationship between the tabloids and their publics is echoed by the editor of *Son,* Andrew Koopman (pers. comm. 2007):

> What we try to do is write for the ordinary people—their suffering and their joys. We give people unique news, news that *Die Burger* might not take seriously. We are a community paper, just on a bigger scale. We really try to tell ordinary people's stories. People can come and sit here and tell us something happened, and we will pay attention to them. At *Die Burger* they won't even give those people a hearing. We try to give them news that they won't find on television or [in] another paper.

This community involvement for *Son*'s relationship with the public sometimes extends to active and visible involvement in the community:[11]

> We sponsor a Klopse[12] group who are involved in the community and keep children off the streets. They are anti-tik [tik is the street name for the drug methamphetamine],[13] they wear our colors and participated in the Green Point march, and we give them posters, etc. It is publicity for us, but in this way we also support the community. . . . The other day I reminded the staff, remember, we are a newspaper. We get so many requests for sponsorships, and we don't have the money. We won't organize a tik march ourselves, but if people are having a march we will provide them with newspaper posters saying, for instance, "stop drug abuse." You will also see at court cases, people outside the court waving *Son* posters. *Son* was the first newspaper that wrote about tik, and other newspapers jumped on the bandwagon. I also told the staff the other day that we should make a habit of publishing the telephone number of a helpline— drug-abuse hotline, rape, child abuse. This is a service we can provide, that other newspapers won't do, but we can do that because we are not a conventional paper. (ibid.)

Of course, the commercial benefits of brand visibility in association with campaigns that enjoy strong community support would not be lost from sight by tabloid editors, and mainstream South African newspapers also often use public events like festivals as marketing opportunities (Botma 2006). However, the kind of issues supported through reportage or by actively participating in campaigns differ both in perspective and scope from those covered by mainstream print journalism. The trust vested in tabloids by their readers also seems to suggest a more reciprocal relationship than merely one predicated on marketing and sponsorship. This relationship does not, however, extend to engaging in activism or including reader-produced content in the way civic journalism attempted to engage the public in a "joint venture with the press" (Buller 2007, 28), and in that regard control remains with the editorial staff. Given the South African context, where large sections of the public historically experienced the mainstream print media as remote and even antagonistic to their daily experiences, the participation in public campaigns probably not only contributes to restoring the image of the press in the eyes of the public, but also interpellates their audiences as participants in public life by appealing to issues they experience daily. In return, tabloids are called upon by their readers to provide legitimacy and authority to their causes by attaching their names to them. This is political work, but not in the sense that it has come to be expected of mainstream commercial print media.

Although it is clear that the tabloids create an alternative mediated public sphere, a caveat is needed. While issues like gangsterism, drug use, and related social ills that pertain to the daily lives of tabloid publics are dealt with more extensively and from a different approach than in the mainstream print media, the moral authority implicit in the outrage articulated in these stories mostly remains that of the establishment and the state, often linked to class. When, for instance, a story on drug use on the Cape Flats is headlined on the front page with a sensational human interest angle, members of the community, who would not typically be seen as authoritative sources for mainstream news, will get an opportunity to speak to the issue through direct quotes and interviews. However, the story might still be framed by a concluding quote from a voice of authority from an official institution or the state, and helpline numbers are also provided as a means to rectify deviant behavior provided the first step is taken by the individual. This framing can be seen to act as a disciplinary measure through which popular journalism train publics to become citizens loyal to the state and the market (as mentioned with reference to Meijer [2001] earlier).

An example of this can be found in the March 23, 2007, *Son,* in which the focus fell on cell phone chat software about which a moral panic had developed in the country. The program, MXit (developed in South Africa), is a free instant-messaging software application that allows users to chat in chat rooms, share photos, and so on. Fears arose that MXit would allow minors to download pornography and enable sexual predators to contact minors. Parents also complained that their children became socially maladjusted as a result of spending hours in chat rooms and that they neglected school homework. In this particular issue, the front page of the paper carried the headline "MXit craze mucks up marriages," with a super-headline "Chatters Addicted" and a text box "Cell-phone whoring a new worry." The moral outrage over broken marriages supposedly caused by this new technology indicates a socially conservative morality centered on family values, and the way the story is presented underscores this value framework. The front-page story is elaborated upon in a spread on pages four and five of the paper, where, in several separate but linked stories, victims of marital infidelity speak out about their ordeals. Through these interviews, the tabloid public is lent a voice to articulate their everyday experiences through the prism of the story already framed by the tabloid.

Significant in terms of the class perspective in this particular example is the reference to the intruder in the marriage, who is first identified as someone from Lenasia near Johannesburg (i.e., from a province other than the tabloid's Cape Town readership), and second—and more importantly—the intruder is described as "poor man" who "doesn't have any money." In the Afrikaans edition, this identification was especially strong, where the man was labeled an "armgat" (poor-ass) in the block headline. In the story itself, extensive mention is made of the estranged husband's disbelief that his wife preferred someone else even after he had spent a lot of money on her:[14]

> Over Christmas, Abdul decided to spoil Shanaaz, by letting her beautify the house to her heart's content. The shopping list included a new lounge suite, bathroom, swimming pool and children's room. It cost R15 000 to decorate the swimming area. "I designed the place the way any woman would want it to be. There's a 2006 Yaris standing outside. It belongs to her, but she left it behind," he says. Abdul can't understand how his wife could give up everything for a man who doesn't have any money.

The story continues on the next page, where a further testimonial appears along with an "expert" view on compulsive sexual behavior by one Dr. Elna McIntosh, a Johannesburg sexologist.

Stories like this could lead one to conclude that the public sphere created by the tabloids is "alternative" more in appearance than in substance. A political-economic perspective on the positioning of the tabloid public in relation to authoritative establishment discourses linked to class would perhaps see this as a consequence of the location of these tabloids in big commercial media conglomerates. Yet the positioning of tabloid publics as citizens is not a predictable or unilinear process of interpellation by authority. While tabloid narratives do in some cases act as disciplinary discourses serving as surveillance measures to ensure tabloid publics are "good citizens," this process also works the other way around. In focus-group discussions with tabloid readers, participants recounted how they used tabloid stories on ongoing court cases (like the popular Dina Rodrigues case) as a way to exercise surveillance over public institutions, in this case the court, to ensure that it is functioning properly. These audience responses will be discussed further in the next chapter. Clearly, one of the political functions of tabloids is to create an alternative space where readers can validate their identities as citizens, engage in debate, and confront social, political, and economic hierarchies even through emotional and sensational narratives.

Media Citizenship

Cultural studies approaches to journalism emphasize the role that audiences play in making meaning, rather than seeing knowledge as being transmitted to a mass audience by mass media. This scholarship mostly supports the view that media texts have minimal effects, and audiences are influenced by other social and cultural factors as they actively interpret polysemic and often contradictory media texts (Davis 2003, 671). Even this view, Davis suggests, is becoming outdated as audiences consume less political news and become increasingly niched, fragmented, and more interested in general information, sport, and entertainment (ibid.). The result may be that, as far as political communication in mainstream journalism is concerned, elites are "simultaneously the main sources, main targets and some of the most influenced recipients of news," which means that the mass of consumer-citizens are excluded from the negotiations and decision-making in mainstream news media (ibid., 673). It is with the aim of bridging this divide between the "knowledge class" and ordinary people that the notion of "media citizenship" has been proposed (Hermes 2006, 33 citing Hartley 1998, 58–59).

One of the arguments for the positive potential of tabloids is that they provide readers that are excluded from dominant discourses and social processes with the pleasure of seeing the establishment's norms subverted, undermined, or satirized. This is the point of view of John Fiske (1989, 117), for whom the existence of tabloids should be read as an index of the "extent of dissatisfaction in a society, particularly among those who feel powerless to change their situation" (ibid.). By exceeding what is otherwise considered "normal," tabloid narratives render societal norms visible so that they "lose their status as natural common sense, and are brought out into the open agenda," turning these norms "back on themselves" (ibid., 114). The disjuncture between the everyday lives of tabloid readers and dominant explanations of "common sense"—that is, the failure of mainstream discourses of science, politics, and culture—explains, according to Fiske, the popular demand for this type of publication. In the South African case, this disjuncture between formal politics and the lived experience of tabloid readers is predicated not only on the legacy of the historical exclusion of the majority of South Africans from the democratic community of citizens, but on continued economic exclusion and marginalization. While tabloid readers have since 1994 been legally included in the citizenry of the new democracy, their living conditions still prevent most of them from enjoying the full benefits of democracy. This fissure between the democratic and development imperatives of government has also been at the heart of the split in the ANC between the camps of former president Thabo Mbeki and his successor, Jacob Zuma (Pillay 2008). The "media citizenship" offered by tabloids provides an alternative to the dominant political discourses built on a notion of citizenship that does not represent the everyday realities of those for whom democracy has not improved their lives.

The distance between "democracy" and "development" (ibid.) often expresses itself as apathy, ridicule, or mocking. West and Fair (1993, 104), referring to development theater in Tanzania, invoke Bakhtin's work (e.g., Bakhtin 1968) on the carnival to suggest that "laughter, frivolity, and the carnivalesque open up an 'unofficial' discursive space from which the 'official' world may be ridiculed and resistance sustained." This frivolity, they note, resonates with the tone of voice in South African tabloids, where the disjuncture between official discourse and the daily lives of tabloid readers leads to a pleasurable skepticism which involves the formerly oppressed in a public contestation over meaning. Strelitz and Steenveld (2005, 267, citing Fiske 1991, 48) remark in this regard:

> One of its most characteristic tones of voice is that of a sceptical laughter which offers the pleasures of disbelief, the pleasures of not being taken in. This popular pleasure of "seeing through" them (whoever constitutes the powerful *them* of the moment) is the historical result of centuries of subordination which the people have not allowed to develop into subjection.

The same function can be fulfilled through rumor and gossip, the "radio trottoir" in African societies that was mentioned in chapter 3 (Ellis, 1989; Nyamnjoh 2005, 23). Rumors are politically significant, Glynn (2000, 12) argues, because they express popular suspicion of socio-cultural hegemony. Entertainment and pleasure could serve to draw historically subordinated publics into the realm of the political in a way that formal political debates are unable to. Strelitz and Steenveld (2005, 266) suggest that the rise of South African tabloids ten years after democracy could be a sign of both "the alienation felt amongst the working classes from the formal political processes in the country" and "struggle fatigue," which would lead media users to prefer entertainment to serious news. The preference of South African tabloids for stories related to people's everyday hardships rather than news about formal political processes (although these do get covered from time to time, as we will see later) suggests that "politics" in the tabloid context is understood as the power dimensions of everyday life rather than the policies, procedures, and rituals associated with the formal political sphere.

While democratization in South Africa meant the achievement of "first generation" human rights (freedom from discrimination and equality on the basis of race, gender, sexual orientation, religion, etc.), the socio-economic rights that citizens in a democracy are entitled to have failed to materialize for the majority of South Africans (Robins 2005, 2). Rights to food, water, housing, health care, and social security remain ideals, enshrined in the Constitution, which have not been realized for huge swathes of the population (ibid.).[15] These are the people the editor of *Son,* Andrew Koopman (pers. comm. 2007), refers to as "still not in count." For those that still feel like second-class citizens in a new democracy, recourse to a media outlet that seems to listen to them and take them seriously seems like a more viable recourse than a government that seems aloof and distant. This corroborates Sparks' (2000, 9) remarks about tabloids in another context—namely, that tabloids provide ways in which "news can be rescued from irrelevance to the lives of the mass of people who would otherwise reject it entirely."

This is not to say that the South African tabloids are produced with democratic inclusivity as their intended priority. As Strelitz and Steenveld (2005, 268) warn, these tabloids are driven by commercial agendas and the hunt for profits "gained precisely from those very people who were not regarded [by big conglomerates] as significant enough to constitute a viable 'market segment.'" It is obvious that the tabloids, belonging to big commercial interests, have profit as their primary objective. While Themba Khumalo, editor of the *Daily Sun,* might publicly (Khumalo 2007) present his publication as contributing to a democratic debate that can benefit from a diversity of outlets, saying "More voices, more news platforms and more channels of opinion can only be good for our young democracy. The revolution, as they say, will not be televised—IT WILL BE PRINTED!," he admits in personal communication (2007) to a fierce competitive attitude in the commercial media market, which casts his concern to keep readers interested in a different light:

> [I]f you see people chasing you, no matter if you're leading the race by a 1000 kilometers, if you say "now I'm going to take it easy and take a walk in a park," they might cover that 1,000 kilometers. It never stops. You've got to keep running. Like a shark—I've been told it never stops, once it stops, it drowns. You've got to smell the blood, and see the prey. You've got to excite the reader. The reader is king. If they're not going to be talking about *Daily Sun* in a tavern in Umlazi, in their home somewhere in Polokwane, a factory in Alberton and Vanderbijlpark—why are you doing it? It's one of the greatest challenges of keeping people from going out of the paper—stay there, stay there. From the first to the last page we're trying to make it as exciting as we possibly can.

But the contradiction between the South African tabloids' ruthless commerciality and their strong ties with the community—reciprocated by intensely loyal readers—is part of the ironies of these papers' position in post-apartheid South Africa. It is not sufficient to view this relationship as merely exploitative, nor is it justified to compare it with alternative, community, or developmental media.

The fact that these tabloids are "clearly and obviously not part of any revolution-ary praxis" does not mean that they are politically insignificant (Glynn 2000, 10). A more critical perspective would lead one to ask questions about how these new voices will contribute to democratic politics in a media landscape marked by unequal opportunities to exercise the right to freedom of expression. Even if the producers of tabloid journalism are interested primarily in commercial gain (al-though profit seeking is not necessarily as important a motive for tabloid jour-nalists as it is for their papers' proprietors), tabloid audiences have their own reasons for consuming this type of journalism (ibid.). To understand these rea-sons and their implications for political life in South Africa, we have to examine the political dimension of tabloid readers' everyday lives.

Coping with Everyday Life

It has been noted above that the South African tabloids broaden the medi-ated public sphere by including publics that had hitherto been marginalized in the print media on the grounds that they are not financially lucrative. From the per-spective of critical political economy, it might be argued that these tabloids in effect also exploit a mass audience for profit, and that they represent falling standards journalism because of their crass sensationalism. This view on tabloids has long been opposed by an approach to popular journalism that allows for agency on the side of audiences. This cultural studies approach, associated with exponents like John Fiske and John Hartley, sees tabloids as "both liberating and inclusive, as en-couraging skepticism and rebellion against authoritarian systems" (Johansson 2007, 42). It could be argued (as Graeme Turner does, see ibid.) that the binary op-position between these approaches is unnecessary and that ways could be found to incorporate both these critical perspectives when examining tabloids.

When evaluating the ways South African tabloid audiences can create politi-cal meaning, a political-economic perspective on the structural limits of this meaning-making process remains important. Yet political-economic arguments, even when they are optimistic about the creation of a new market for newspaper readers, do not always account for the ways audiences employ these media in their everyday lives. While these uses might not be overtly "political," tabloids can be "used as a resource for political knowledge" and establish a "framework for political events and processes" (ibid., 155) in the way they construct a view of the world, and in the way they are read by their publics. Even content that seems to be mere entertainment or diversion can have implications for the way that tabloid readers view the world and position themselves in democratic life. Jo-hansson (ibid., 165) refers to this impact on politics by tabloid discourse as the "politics of the non-political."

In the South African context, the coverage of issues that have a bearing on readers' everyday lives can be political in the sense that it can assist readers in finding their way in a transitional society which has seen tremendous and rapid changes in recent years. In a society marked by severe inequality, cultural dis-courses promising an escape from poverty are bound to be attractive. The type of lifestyle guidance tabloids provide their readers with can also interpellate them as consumers to whom products can be sold or whose tastes can be nurtured to suit advertisers' marketing strategies. Consequently, this type of non-political news can be read as political in various ways—as an ostensibly apolitical focus on everyday life that makes sense to readers who feel disconnected from formal politics, or exactly as a political discourse that obscures its orientation toward free-market, liberal, individualist ideology, or as an empowering discourse that enables readers to position themselves as citizens within a new democracy.

Although the coverage of non-political news may have political implications, the *Daily Sun* constructs its reader as someone who has moved beyond politics. Deon du Plessis (pers. comm. 2007) describes the typical reader of the *Daily Sun* at the time of the launch of the paper as follows:

> He [the reader] was then 28, settling in with a partner (we did not really care about her in the beginning), they had a young kid, just born, maybe two, maybe three, he's had a background of in the early 90s of directives, ranging from Boipatong to Sebokeng, street committees, and to his relief it was over. He was allowed to embrace education, he was on his way as an individual, he was a family man, we never had the opportunity to do before, and now—in 2007—him and his partner now represents, by any measure, the biggest chunk of money in the country.

The *Daily Sun* aims to cash in on this "chunk of money" in search of social mobility by, among other things, publishing a weekly supplement called *Sun Life,* which "says 'you're on your way baby', and it talks about things—coffees, wines, stuff like that. The (reader's) kid is also 8 or 9 now, so they are worrying about schools. Schools are a massive issue" (ibid.).

Khumalo also sees the paper's role as encouraging social mobility:

> Stories of empowerment, hence you will see supplements like *Sun Money, Sun Life.* People are asking where am I going? Celebrating women who would otherwise not be celebrated in a serious business magazine. Celebrating those little victories of people, you're saying to people yes, we're together, we see what you've done and we know what you've gone through, so let us celebrate it. Let us tell your story that will inspire other people to move on. These are not stories that come from the major corporate bedrooms, these are stories about ordinary South Africans, things that ordinary people dream about. For instance, the story about a youngster who didn't think he would stand a chance to get a job, didn't have a good Matric [school-leaver's diploma], and he decided, "look, I'll polish people's shoes, I'll clean their takkies [sneakers] when they get home from work and they'll pay me." And his business has grown. We always tell people that is how big companies are born, they start small.

The *Daily Sun* makes no bones about what can be seen as a neoliberal, individualist view of social change. Its general manager, Fergus Sampson, describes (pers. comm. 2007) the *Daily Sun*'s "central message" as "It's your life, take control now. You can make it work. Only you can make it work. Don't wait for handouts, don't ask anybody for anything. Get up in the morning and go get it." The similar consumption-oriented guidance provided by the *Sunday Sun* is described by its publisher, Mike Vink, as a "service" (pers. comm.):

We provide a lot of advice—how do you buy a house, a car, how do you draw up a last will and testament, how do you draw up a business plan. Our audience research shows us there is a big hunger for these type of stories, you cannot do enough of them. And it is a hell of a service you are providing.

While upward mobility is clearly an important determinant of the *Daily Sun* and *Sunday Sun*'s news values, the editor of the Cape Town tabloid, the *Daily Voice,* claims to not consider upward mobility in its news selection and presentation. Karl Brophy ascribes the popularity of this tabloid less to aspiration than to "cultural" factors, and while its "humor sometimes attracts more upper-class readers," its focus falls squarely on the working class on the Cape Flats—a largely poor area of Cape Town whose "Coloured" inhabitants were forcibly moved there during apartheid. Brophy is nonchalant about the direction of social change in his readership, saying, "If we catch them on the upper curve or downward curve it doesn't really matter. [It's] [n]ot much of a concern."

This is then also one of the ironies or paradoxes that complicate a view of the political role the South African tabloids play. While they champion the cause of the "man in the blue overall" in protesting against lack of service delivery, poor living conditions, and government failures, they do so in neoliberal terms. The "man in the blue overall" is positioned as an individual rather than as a member of a group; his struggles are seen—as is neoliberalism's wont—in terms of the present rather than in terms of history and power relations. The tabloids need to perform a balancing act in this regard: while appealing to their readers as a previously disadvantaged and still currently marginalized *group* with rightful claims to political and economic redress (and selling them as a socially mobile group to advertisers), their underpinning commercial ideology demands that they also position these readers as *individuals* whose social progress depends on their mastery of the codes of a fragmented, individualized consumer society.[16] Ultimately, the tabloids are interested in him as a consumer. In the next chapter, we will look in more detail at how tabloids readers have responded to this construction of them, and how tabloids contribute to their negotiation of everyday life.

This construction of the reader as an individual rather than as part of a political collective has implications for the tabloids' content and approach to stories. By choosing to construct their readers as individuals, and by fostering consumerist attitudes through the celebration of upward mobility, the South African tabloids can indeed be seen as contributing to a process of depoliticization. If tabloid readers are constructed as individual consumers within whose power it lies to change their own circumstances, it is highly unlikely that the tabloids will ever provide thorough-going criticism of the structural factors which contribute to their readers' social positioning. Tabloid readers are unlikely to ever be encouraged to question macro-economic policy or to participate in social-movement activism or industrial action because tabloid readers are seen as individuals who have to "take control" and not "wait for handouts." Yet even if they are constructed as consumers rather than as political actors in the public sphere, this does not completely evacuate the political from tabloid discourse.

As Conboy (2008b, 51) points out in relation to tabloids in Britain, political debate in the popular press is framed by "contemporary patterns of consumption and identity." When, as in the South African case, the factors impeding on the social mobility of tabloid readers to exercise their freedom of choice within this neoliberal discourse are related to structural factors like social and economic policy or lack of delivery on the part of national and local authorities, the possibility exists that even this discourse of consumption and individual choice may take on a political or public dimension. Within the discourse of individual mobility and consumption-linked identities, when occurring within a postcolonial, transitional context in which the dreams of modernity co-exist with demands by the formerly colonized to be recognized as citizens, popular journalism might retain a space for political claims—even if these are articulated in terms of consumption and social mobility. For example, tabloid outrage over the conditions of life in informal settlements might be framed in terms of its impact on individuals, yet it retains a political dimension when this outrage is directed at politicians or government officials. Tabloid reports celebrating individual successes might be presented as personalized, human-interest stories that still manage to frame the political from the perspective of highly personalized experiences (for instance, the story of a couple who could get married only after the *Daily Sun* intervened and arranged for the Department of Home Affairs to issue a correct identity document for the bride after her five-year struggle to have her gender indicated correctly on the document—"Maria's Dream Comes True!," *Daily Sun,* July 21, 2008). The opposite can also be the case, however, when individual experiences are used to reject attempts to collective political action. The inconveniences and hardships experienced by readers in their everyday lives can be framed to counter collective claims to social justice or redistribution of economic resources and instead reinforce the discourse of consumerism. An example of this type of reporting is when readers are encouraged to blame power failures on those who make illegal electricity connections in townships (which includes social movements like the Soweto Electricity Crisis Committee who resist the privatization of basic services) instead of seeing this illegal consumer action as a political response to the developmental failures of the post-apartheid government.[17]

But even if a political dimension can be rescued from the individualized, consumerist discourse of popular culture, this does not necessarily qualify these publications as vehicles for alternative politics. The blame for this shift from politicized members of a collective to consuming individuals cannot be laid at the tabloids' door alone. This tabloid discourse can be seen to form part of a broader depoliticizing shift in South African society since the end of apartheid. Van Kessel (2007) describes how the anti-apartheid activists she interviewed "harboured contradictory expectations about post-apartheid society":

> On the one hand, there was the Marxist-inspired ideal of an egalitarian society in which the state would provide. On the other hand, comrades aspired to inherit the seductive world of White South Africa, with its comfortable houses, manicured gardens, flashy cars and modern gadgets. They wanted to undo the apartheid state while simultaneously inheriting white privilege.

Ashforth (2005, 29), in his study of life in Soweto, also points to the steady decline of political symbolism as a means of providing social cohesion, and its replacement by an all-encompassing consumerism. Even as they experienced extreme hardship and the "better life for all" that had been promised by the ANC in the first democratic election seemed to slip further into the distance, consumption, rather than politics, became the central characteristic of community life in Soweto: "In the mid- and late 1990s, the tenor of life in Soweto seemed agitated by nothing so much as the desire to go shopping, as if the political energies of the previous decade had been channeled into consumerism" (ibid., 28). This observation reminds one of the quote attributed to a former Apla cadre by Graeme Addison (2003a, 15): "South Africans went to the brink of full-out civil war in the 1980s, but decided to go shopping instead."

This shift from activism to consumerism mirrors the type of reader envisaged by Du Plessis, one that experiences "relief" at the end of the era of political ideologies. But the aspiration to a historically White consumer culture via mediated commodification is not something new to post-apartheid publications, nor are the contradictions between the affirmation or rehabilitation of subaltern Black identities and a discourse of consumption in a publication aimed at a Black readership. Rauwerda (2007, 393) has pointed out how advertisements in the well-known magazine *Drum* in the 1950s reveal desires that "are more complicated than can be expressed by referring to the publication as 'pro-African' or 'pro-Black.'" In the tensions between the advertisements and the articles in the pages of *Drum*, a desire for middle-class privileges (marked as "White" within the racial hierarchy of apartheid South Africa) and an affirmation of African Blackness operated simultaneously, Rauwerda argues. In her work on consumer magazines, Sonja Laden (1997) has suggested that consumption and desire for commodities can in themselves be indicators of "social reordering." The representation of commodity culture in the pages of the tabloids can therefore also be read as a reconfiguration in the social landscape of post-apartheid South Africa, one which is related to the political shifts that have and still are taking place in the country.

Furthermore, too rigid a dichotomy between citizen and consumer might not only be false, but also obscure other ways in which the performance of citizenship roles and political contestation take place within a context where neoliberal market discourses dominate. As Conboy (2008b, 49–50) has argued, although the celebration of consumer culture in contemporary tabloids takes place in a postmodern era marked by the absolute dominance of the commercial (as opposed to the informational and political imperatives of the press in previous eras), tabloid readers are still addressed as "interested consumers" who can win "battles against the system." Because political debate is framed by patterns of consumption and identity, tabloids retain a measure of political involvement in the "flows of everyday life" (ibid., 52).

The tabloid preference for what can be termed the "politics of the everyday" above formal political news of the kind found in mainstream newspapers can best be illustrated by an example contrasting the *Daily Sun* to the stalwart Black newspaper *Sowetan*. Under a previous editor, Aggrey Klaaste, the *Sowetan* had a slogan printed on the masthead: "building the nation." Even though the *Sowetan* was adversely affected by the entrance of the *Daily Sun* and had to adopt a more popular approach in an attempt to reverse a sharp decline in circulation, the contrast between this view of its readers as part of a collective and the *Daily Sun's* view of its readers as atomized individuals within a broadly neoliberal sensibility became evident in the way the two papers dealt with the passing of a former ANC president's wife, Adelaide Tambo. Her husband, Oliver, who passed away in 1993, was a lifelong friend of Nelson Mandela and an icon of the struggle. The Tambo family was beloved among South Africans, and Adelaide was considered a hero of the anti-apartheid struggle in her own right. As a result of spending many years abroad during apartheid, she earned the role of "a mother to the liberation movement in exile" (BBC 2007; see also Mandela 1994b, 601). Locally and internationally, the media reported her death as a historical event. The day after Tambo died, the *Sowetan* ran a full front page announcing "Mama Tambo dies" with a super-headline "Nation mourns" and a large photograph of Tambo against a black background. In addition to the front-page story, a full-page obituary was published on page six. On the same day, the tabloid *Daily Sun* ran a front page headline "No Mercy!" with a story on a hospital that barred patients from parking their cars, resulting in a car hijacking.[18] This story theme continued on page two with other stories on "Hospital horrors." The *Daily Sun's* other front-page story of the day was on the opening of Oprah Winfrey's new school near Johannesburg. A 38-year-old mother and seller of the *Daily Sun,* Elizabeth Wanyane, told how her 12-year-old daughter, Mpho, was accepted at Oprah's school. Elizabeth cried: "I know that Mpho will come out tops and take us out of poverty" (see pictures pp. 37 and 38).[19]

While part of the explanation for the *Daily Sun* having left out the Mama Tambo story had to do with their printing deadline (earlier than *Sowetan*—they did include a small snippet on page 3 in subsequent editions), Du Plessis admitted that they would "never have it on the front page," claiming that their readers prefer stories that concern them directly, rather than big political issues. For Du Plessis, the *Sowetan* "just does not get it": "[t]he collective is dead" (pers. comm. 2007).

> [T]he *Sowetan's* treatment of it, with the subheading "Nation mourns" involuntarily takes you back to 1978. . . . "A nation mourns"? Mmmmm. People are sad, maybe. Some people. But [for] the guys on the shop floor in Alberton this morning, the Oprah story, that's big stuff. Cause if he could get his kid into Oprah's school, wow.

Du Plessis's comments neatly frame the *Daily Sun's* view of the new social and political climate in the country, where collective struggles to gain political ground belong to the past and have been surpassed by an individual negotiation of the precarious conditions of everyday life, made bearable by the aspiration to a middle-class lifestyle built on consumption, individual progress, and conspicuous success.

The political dimension of the everyday hassles in a transitional democracy can be illustrated by something as basic as being in possession of an identity document (or simply "ID" or "ID book"). This document is a crucial prerequisite for signing contracts (e.g., when opening a bank account, seeking employment, enrolling in school, and applying for services like a telephone line or cell phone account). An ID (or sworn affidavit) is also required to access government services—importantly, those aimed at poverty alleviation, like social grants to support children living in poor households—or to apply for a driver's license. Crucially, in terms of the citizenship roles discussed here, it is also needed to vote in elections. Because of bureaucratic incompetence, bungling, and lack of resources, the department of Home Affairs has become notorious for its inability to provide applicants with identity documents.[20] The struggles its readers experience in this regard have become a daily feature in the *Daily Sun*. A column titled "Home Affairs Horrors" recounts readers' struggles, in many cases lasting for years, to obtain ID books. A reader participating in a focus group in the rural town of Makhado in Limpopo saw these stories in terms of the tabloids' civic mediation role: "The *Daily Sun* addresses issues like the home affairs department, struggles to get ID books. The *Daily Sun* mediates between people and the government."

This campaign for ID books has high symbolic value as it insists on the acknowledgment of tabloid readers' status as citizens, quite literally as people that have names, faces, and a birthright to membership in the civic community. That these identities are individual rather than group rights is perhaps no coincidence in the light of the fact that the tabloid addresses its readers in terms of a neoliberal politics of consumerism and individualism rather than in the language of social justice and communal redress. The emphasis on citizenship also took a negative turn when tabloids contributed to xenophobic sentiment, as will be discussed later.

The way that tabloids acknowledge the political importance of their readers' everyday struggles has a bearing on the role that they can play in democratic life. Having constructed their readers as citizens whose daily lives matter, tabloids are in a position to challenge authority on their behalf and to claim their democratic rights.

Keeping the Powerful Accountable

Popular journalism often "harbors a disrespect for authorities" (Gripsrud 2000, 298), and in this regard it can be seen to play the role of watchdog usually associated with mainstream journalism in the liberal democratic tradition. We have already discussed the way tabloids undermine societal hierarchies through the use of emotional language, a personalized approach to stories, and irreverent humor—the "skeptical laughter." The typical irreverent tabloid approach can do more than satirize and undermine—it can also be a weapon against corruption, scandals, or other issues of political and social importance. In other words, the humorous approach typical of tabloids stories does not mean that it cannot at the same time have a serious objective, namely to play the more direct political-watchdog role usually associated with mainstream journalism.

One difference in the way tabloids fulfill this objective compared to their mainstream counterparts is that their attacks are usually directed at a person involved with the issue rather than at the issue itself. The publisher of *Son,* Ingo Capraro, describes this as "we don't do politics, we do politicians" (pers. comm. 2007). This personalization of politics has been cause for concern among some commentators, who view it as turning politics into entertainment and, in effect, distracting audiences rather than engaging them. This approach might alternatively be understood as a way of making politics relevant to a section of society that feels left out of political processes. While such personalization might not be preferable to other ways of using the media to get people interested and involved in political participation, a mere dismissal of such an approach to politics is not useful in helping us understand the political role that tabloids can play in South African society. The tabloid perspective to politics is that of ordinariness, and it is through this perspective that they can create a foothold for tabloid audiences to engage with issues that are fundamentally political even if these are not framed in the way political stories about the powerful and rich conventionally are (cf. Lange quoted in Gripsrud 2000, 299).

Du Plessis relates, for instance, how his paper ran stories of dissatisfaction with local government, culminating in the protest actions at Harrismith and Khutsong (pers. comm. 2007). He points out that the humorous tone of his tabloid's reporting should not be mistaken for a flippant attitude. They are serious in their criticism of the policies and decisions that have lead to the dismal living conditions experienced by their readers: "We're not totally serious, but we're irritable. The hopes of 1994 have been pissed on. So that's one of the other reasons why we keep politicians in this country at an arm's length." Du Plessis' point of keeping politicians at an arm's length illustrates the sense of mistrust toward politicians and formal political processes while at the same time holding up to the light the results of political mismanagement, abuse of power, and policies poorly conceived and executed. While this aspect of tabloid reporting may be a more informal and oblique way of addressing the political concerns of their readers, the tabloids do, from time to time, provide coverage of more formal political processes.

Formal Democratic Processes and Party Politics

South African tabloids are keen to emphasize that they do not wish to burden their readers with "heavy politics," as the editor of *Son,* Andrew Koopman, put it (pers. comm. 2007). Yet although the political dimension of tabloid reporting can most clearly be seen in their approach to the politics of everyday life, from time to time they do engage in more formal political coverage. One such occasion is during local elections, around issues on the political agenda that are clearly related to the daily lived experience of tabloid readers. In the run-up to the 2006 local elections, the *Daily Sun* promised that it would be "telling the people what is relevant to them" (Felix 2006).

The paper's political reporter, Sicelo Dladla, also planned on educating voters about how the process works: "We will be educating our readers about local councils and how they run, because we have realized that a lot of these people don't really know how the local government works."

Du Plessis later looked back on this coverage as characterized by demands that local politicians improve the living conditions of the poor (pers. comm. 2007):

> During the local elections we were heavy again on stand and deliver. We took area by area and said [to the politicians] this is what you've gotta fix. It's quite graphic actually. It's horrifying when you delve into the conditions that so many people have to live in. . . . these uncovered holes that kids fall into. Now *that* is politics! You get bullshit workmen, badly directed, dig a hole and leave it. Then it rains, the water falls in and a three year old kid falls in and drowns. We've had thirty of those, and we haven't even been looking. That's politics, and we get very angry about it. We're absolutely in your face about it.

Du Plessis' point is pertinent—something as basic as covering holes in the ground at township building sites has a political dimension because it relates to the dignity that the poor are denied by those in positions of power. That this approach to the politics of daily life struck a nerve was clear from readers' responses, according to Du Plessis:

> Politics [for us] had always been as it affected the guy in the blue overall, and we had a thing that was riotously successful and that switched on a light—such as you can switch on a light in the collective brain of the Cabinet—and that was the Wall Of Shame. We invited people to write to us, daily, and tell us about the failings of local government in their area, ranging from no ambulance to no streetlight to shit in the streets to crime. We got—I never counted exactly—ten thousand letters a month. We ran ten a day for a year about this crises. And it culminated when they cut the road [from] Durban to Harrismith, on the issue of non-delivery, and that's when Mbeki started talking about this thing and called an imbizo [public meeting]. We pioneered what in our view was real politics—the guys not feeling the benefits of the undoubted revolution in 1994. There has got to be some pluses apart from happy feelings. It's not a traditional journalistic position, but we certainly box very hard for the man in the blue overall. Another example was Khutsong, the town that was taken away from [the richer province] Gauteng and stuck into Northwest [province], and the people didn't want that, because of the gerrymandering by [then Minister of Provincial and Local Government] Sydney Mufamadi for reasons that are obscure to us. So we went to back Khutsong—we took the view of the man in the blue overall and demanded explanations. So we covered that quite heavily, again from the view of the man [the mannequin in blue overalls] sitting in front of Themba's office.

Du Plessis makes no bones about the fact that he in turn is emboldened by the power of vast readership figures to make these demands on readers' behalf:

> You take the Amps [All Media Products Survey] figure of very close to 4 million people a day, that's power. But the politicians are not the boss. We're talking to the man in the blue overall. That remains the battle cry of this paper. What's good for him is good for the *Sun*.

Of course, Du Plessis' claim of speaking on behalf of the "man in the blue overall" should not be taken at face value. The complex relationship of the tabloids—as commercial newspapers forming part of huge transnational media conglomerates—with their readers, constructing them simultaneously as a marginalized section of society to whom they claim to give a voice and as a lu-crative market to be utilized for profit, has been touched upon throughout this book. This ambivalent relationship is equally true with respect to claims like Du Plessis' that the "man in the blue overall" is "boss" in terms of the political cover-age they provide. This can be taken to mean that they put issues on the news agenda that concern the poor—whose needs are often marginalized in main-stream political coverage—and/or that in their political coverage, tabloids pan-der to short-term audience tastes that would see them sensationalize certain in-cidents (for instance, a child falling into a drain) without investigating or exposing the structural factors that underlie these events (for instance, the gov-ernment policies that allow private firms to take shortcuts on building projects).

While tabloids do from time to time provide formal political coverage (ex-amples of this will be given shortly), it is not clear whether political actors take this coverage seriously. In a series of interviews with politicians and political in-termediaries from the local to the national government level, conducted in 2008 as part of an international study on political communication in new democra-cies,[21] most political actors indicated that they consider elite media—and espe-cially the weekly newspapers *Mail and Guardian* and the *Sunday Times*—as the most politically influential. Tabloids were almost throughout dismissed as trivial entertainment. However, isolated examples suggest that politicians are starting to recognize the political influence of tabloids. Du Plessis (ibid.) mentioned that only one politician came to see him at the *Daily Sun* before the 2004 elections: Patricia de Lille, leader of the Independent Democrats. *Son* publisher Capraro related (pers. comm. 2007) how the then-leader of the Democratic Alliance, Tony Leon, came to see him to complain about what he perceived as the *Son*'s "anti-DA agenda" (which Capraro denies by saying his paper is independent). *Daily Voice* editor Karl Brophy claims (pers. comm. 2007) that the (then) Demo-cratic Alliance mayor of Cape Town, Helen Zille (now premier of the Western Cape province), started ordering copies of the tabloid soon after she had been elected to office in 2006. The tabloid seems to have reciprocated this relationship by acknowledging her power as mayor, for instance through appeals like that of the columnist Nigel Pierce in 2007 for her to act against drug abuse in the city.

From the other side of the political spectrum, the chair of the social move-ment Treatment Action Campaign, Zackie Achmat, in a speech before the Pro-gressive ANC Voters' Network in Manenberg in 2007 (Achmat 2007), appealed to ANC members to write to the *Daily Voice* to demand an ANC leader in the Western Cape that promotes non-racialism. (The province has a history of voter division along racial lines, with the African constituency supporting the ANC and the "Coloured" voters supporting parties like the Democratic Alliance that are perceived to be aligned to White interests.) Two prominent—if perhaps not typical—examples of how the South African tabloids covered formal political processes could be seen in 2007 and 2008 when a hot contest for leadership of the ANC, with implications for the presidency of the country, erupted. As a prelude to the coverage that particularly the *Daily Sun* provided of these events, Du Plessis' earlier remarks (pers. comm. 2007) might prove illuminating. Du Plessis revealed that his paper had already considered openly declaring its support for Jacob Zuma after the latter's rape case in 2005, but decided against such a move:

> Now, the interesting thing with Zuma's rape charge—when we did Zuma and his court case, circulation spiked. Themba [Khumalo, the editor] then went to see him and we ran a picture of Themba and him—the great man—holding hands. We asked Zuma for his wishes for the nation, and he wrote a piece which we had on page two, saying the uncles that were the glue that kept African society together were now missing—[they're] sick, or they've left, and the young men had no guide. The second message, also strong, was that this government will not do everything for you. Stop thinking that. You've gotta go and do stuff. And then we wondered very much about Zuma. Even to the extent of saying, might the *Daily Sun* even declare for Zuma, as the next president? And of course we haven't done that, and I don't think we're going to, because I think he's run into a bit of trouble. But that's as close we've come to mainstream politics, however, this year does signal a change because it's the presidential election [for ANC president] so we've hired a bright chap who'll be looking at mainstream politics, if you like, for us this year. . . . If you ask me personally, we need a populist [for president]. The dream team in my view is Zuma with a deal with Cyril Ramaphosa, president for an agreed time. Let Zuma get his couple of years like Tony Blair. The meld of populism plus the comforting of real capital is actually . . . quite a delicate balance.

Du Plessis' justification for supporting Zuma again shows his neoliberal inclination toward individualism (recalling Zuma's remarks that the government "will not do everything for you") coupled with the interests of capital (his backing of Ramaphosa, a former politician who became a prominent businessman), dressed up as populism.[22]

Toward the end of 2007, as the succession race between Thabo Mbeki and Jacob Zuma heated up, the *Daily Sun*'s support for Zuma became more evident. Even while the paper did not explicitly "declare" for Zuma, its position was clear from its approach to reporting his election—especially when contrasted with that of other tabloids. The *Daily Sun* responded to early indications from the party's provincial structures that Jacob Zuma was leading the race for ANC president by taking a stronger political stance than had been the case before. On November 28, 2007, for instance, the paper published political commentary on its front page. Beneath a logo announcing "The *Daily Sun* says," it provided a list of areas "Where Mbeki went wrong." The paper lists Mbeki's faults as his tendency to centralize control, his indication that he was ready to serve a third term in office, the perception that he used government agencies to block Zuma from power, his aloofness, and the impression that he was more concerned about problems in other African countries than lack of service delivery in his own. "The HIV/AIDS programme, RDP [Reconstruction and Development Programme, later supplanted by the more business-friendly Growth, Employment, and Redistribution strategy (GEAR)], public service inefficiency, crime—these were the areas where many people wanted tough presidential action," the column stated.

During the time of the ANC conference, held in Polokwane in Limpopo province in December 2007, the *Daily Sun* covered the leadership battle extensively.

While ostensibly covering the election as a news event, it became clear from the coverage taken as a whole that the paper supported Zuma. The day before the election result would be announced (December 18), the paper led with a full front-page story playing up the tension with the headline "Who's the Boss?" The super-heading on the same story picked up on the apparent support for Zuma by asserting, "Mbeki loyalists take the strain in Polokwane!," while a smaller sub-heading added more suspense for good measure: "SA will only know today!" It pictured a row of "Mbeki loyalists"—Manto Tshabalala-Msimang, Frene Ginwala, Charles Ngqakula, Essop Pahad, and Mosiua Lekota—who, according to the report, were booed from the floor and "humiliated" by Zuma supporters. Below the headline, two contrasting pictures dominated the layout—a smiling, relaxed Jacob Zuma tipping his cap to supporters; next to that, a gloomy Thabo Mbeki, frowning and, according to the caption, "looking tense." The report goes on to describe this contrast: "Zuma arrived smiling and upbeat in an ANC shirt, in contrast to Mbeki, who was soberly attired and grim-faced."[23]

While Zuma was presented more favorably in the report and the accompanying pictures, the tone of the report seemed to indicate an attempt to remained factual and attain balance by including, on page two where the report continued, a picture of Mbeki "fans" showing their support. Yet read within the context of other reports on the Zuma–Mbeki leadership struggle like the one where Mbeki's litany of policy mistakes was listed, the representation of Zuma in this report as "relaxed," and the depiction and description of Mbeki as grim and "soberly attired," can be read as implying that Zuma was not only the more popular candidate, but also less aloof than Mbeki and therefore more in touch with the likely readers of the *Daily Sun*. The political coverage continued in the same issue with a report on the speech given by then-ANC secretary-general Kgalema Motlanthe, with the headline "Motlanthe warns of corruption!" (ibid.). This report was in the neutral, factual tone typical of mainstream news reports since it was not written by a *Daily Sun* reporter, but syndicated by News24.com, the online site of Naspers' mainstream publications. It relayed Motlanthe's warning that the ruling party is being "led astray" by "factionalism, patronage and vote-buying" (ibid.).

The results of the election of the party leadership did not, however, become known the following day as had been expected, and the delay meant that the *Daily Sun* had to keep the suspense going while having little new information to go on. In typical horse-race style coverage, the *Daily Sun* predicted the result on its front page: "ZUMA—but wait for it!"[24] But while the angle (an informed prediction on an election outcome) was typical of the type of election reporting one would also find in a mainstream news report, the *Daily Sun* complemented quotes from "authorities" (a political analyst from Idasa, Steven Friedman, and Patrick Craven from the trade union Cosatu) with that of a delegate offering a subtle critique of the political elite. This "one impatient delegate" was quoted as explaining the delay in vote counting as follows: "Perhaps they are still eating their supper. Maybe we will have to wait until the champagne runs out before they tell us" (ibid.). It quoted the lyrics of a song sung in support of Zuma ("Dedela abanye, iminyaka elishumi. Dedela uMsholozi")[25] without translation, a small yet significant indication of the tabloid's addressees (who would understand the Zulu lyrics). On page two the lead report was a feature-type story on the amount of food consumed at the conference, syndicated by the wire agency SAPA.[26]

When Zuma proved victorious in the leadership race, the *Daily Sun* led on its front page with an appeal to Mbeki by his brother, Moeletsi: "Make Peace Thabo!"[27] It reported on Moeletsi's wish that his brother would "hold out the olive branch to those you have offended!," including Cosatu and the Treatment Action Campaign. Although voiced via Moeletsi, the mention of these two organizations to the left of the incumbent ANC government can be seen as an indication of the newspaper's political positioning as not necessarily politically radical (especially when read against the background of Du Plessis' opinion on why Zuma would make a good president), but in tune with what is likely to be their readers' preference for Zuma's populist brand of politics. This is further suggested by a quote from the (then) ANC Youth League president, Fikile Mbalula, in the same report, in which he speculates that a Zuma-led ANC would focus on "policies which benefit the poorest of the poor" like extending the child grant beyond the age of 14.

The *Daily Sun*'s coverage of Zuma's victory also included a front-page banner report in which it recapped its earlier interview with Zuma (the one referred to by Du Plessis), with a smaller reproduction of the interview, showing the paper's editor smiling and shaking hands with Zuma. This self-referencing serves first to prove the paper's prescience in backing Zuma long before he became ANC president and second to fix a strong association between the paper and Zuma. In the (second) report, headlined "Remember what you told us, Msholozi!," Zuma is reminded of the promises he had made in the earlier interview. The report welcomes the "NEW chief" and describes him as a "very different man from Mbeki." It recalls its impression of Zuma in the earlier interview as "a man who spoke of the role of the uncles in our society"; "a man preaching self-reliance—people were their own liberators"; and "a man who was worried about his people . . . and who worried in a language everybody could understand" (ibid.). If that description suggests a politics that combines a populist flair (referring to Zuma by his clan name, "Msholozi," or calling him "chief") with the individualist, neoliberal sensibility of his predecessor ("self-reliance"), it would fit with the image that Zuma portrayed in the run-up to and early days of his ANC presidency. He wooed business leaders at home and abroad, promising he would not change the country's market-led economic program (Independent Online, January 22, 2008) while appealing to ethnic entrepreneurs across a wide spectrum, from Afrikaners (CBS News 2007; News 24 2007) to Zulu supporters brandishing t-shirts proclaiming him as "100% Zulu Boy" (Times Online 2007). This balancing act would also fit with the tension or contradiction in the *Daily Sun*'s own editorial position that simultaneously seeks to appeal to the poor and working class, yet also nurture an upwardly mobile consumer class.

In the lead report on the day Zuma's election became known, the *Daily Sun* made a list of "SunSuggestions" for Zuma that is probably the clearest articulation of the paper's political position.[28] It emphasizes local, grassroots politics (even to the point of nationalist nuances) as well as the skills required for participation in a "modern economy." The *Daily Sun*'s list of SunSuggestions is as follows (ibid.):

1. As the new leader of the party, you have to heal the wounds that have been inflicted on the ANC.
2. Stay at home more, where the REALLY important work waits to be done. People worry about their lives here—not about some faraway country.
3. Fix the State health system. Under Mbeki, it got VERY sick . . .
4. Concentrate on schools. People worry about their kids, and too many schools are dangerous disasters.
5. Fix the cops. People do not trust them. And we're ALL in danger from murderous thugs. People are taking the law into their own hands . . . that should tell Zuma EVERYTHING.
6. In addition, overhaul the system of teaching young people the technical skills needed for a modern economy. There is too much confusion, chaos and corruption there. Without skills, our nation does not stand a chance.

So we are pleading today for the new team to worry about the RIGHT things— not foreign things—and convince our people that they come first in EVERYTHING. Do that, Msholozi, and the PEOPLE's paper will be able, at last, to applaud a PEOPLE's president!

In the same issue of the paper, a profile feature on Zuma's "Dream Team" (ibid.), the newly elected top six members of the ANC,[29] provided background information on each of the top officials.

Coverage of Zuma's election was significantly less prominent in the other tabloids. On the day after the election, there was no coverage of the election in the Cape Town-based *Daily Voice*. The *Kaapse Son* only included a small snippet on page six, lifted from the website of the Afrikaans radio station *Radio Sonder Grense*, announcing that the election results for the ANC's six top posts were not available at press time. The next day, both the *Daily Voice* and the *Kaapse Son* provided coverage of Zuma's election, but to a far lesser extent than the *Daily Sun*, and without the celebratory tone.

The *Son*'s coverage focused on popular reaction to Zuma's victory, emphasizing in a sub-headline that "few were happy with the result." Coverage took the form of a *vox populi* taken from the "masses" in the "Cape Town streets" (illustrated with respondents' photos and quotes). This coverage was relegated to page six, with only a teaser on the front page announcing that readers "had their say" on the inside page. In contrast to the *Daily Sun*'s coverage, the *Son*'s report took a decidedly negative view of Zuma, stating that the paper only "after a hell of a struggle" managed to find one person that had something positive to say about him. The report also highlighted Zuma's (at the time) pending corruption charges. It mentioned the "cheers" sounded by "striking labourers" at a Cape wine farm, who "in one voice" told the reporter that "Zuma will look after us." The fact that these Zuma supporters are identified (at the very end of the report in which opposition to Zuma was emphasized) in terms of their participation in a strike is an ambivalent indication of the paper's position. Framed against the tone in which the rest of the paper reported on Zuma, and within the individualistic aspirational culture espoused by the tabloids in general, strike action is unlikely to be read as favorable. Yet, this particular strike action was covered in a supportive tone, and a telephone number for the union representing the striking workers was even provided so that readers could "help the farm workers with food parcels, or even drop off a cooldrink." In general, however, the *Son's* coverage of Zuma's election was much less favorable than that of the *Daily Sun*. Not only did it cover Zuma less extensively, but it also took a decidedly more negative position in relation to his ascendancy.

Coverage in the *Daily Voice* was even less extensive and more negative. While it did not report on the pending results the previous day, on the day the results became known, coverage in the *Daily Voice* was limited to reader responses (sent via SMS) in the "Rek jou Bek" (literally "Stretch your mouth," or "Speak Out") column on page six. Responses were on the whole very negative:

> Zuma as ANC president. What a f**king disgrace to our people. That is not a leader, but a pain in the @ss. Now our country becomes like the rest of Africa, really backward. ANC stands for African with No Common sense.
>
> What is this country coming to? Mothers neglecting their kids, scum raping the elderly, and now Jacob Zuma as ANC president. It's disgusting. Be afraid, be very afraid.
>
> How stupid to vote Zuma as president of the ANC. To the coloureds who remember the old days, get out while you can. God help us all.

The only other coverage in that day's edition of the *Daily Voice* was a short piece on page eight titled "Pres not Present," reporting on how Zuma's presidency "got off to a shaky start" after he had to cancel his first public appointment, an address to a press conference. The suggestion was that he had a hangover from his celebrations the previous evening: "But just minutes before he was supposed to speak to the nation, he cancelled, leaving many thinking he was too *babalaas* (hung over) to make his speech."[30]

The coverage of Zuma's election as ANC president tells us a number of things about the way tabloids cover formal political processes. First, it underlines the importance of not overlooking the differences among the South African tabloids and how these relate to the range of social, cultural, and political positions occupied by their readers. The contrast in political position, tone, and approach between the Cape Town-based tabloids and the *Daily Sun* in Gauteng can be explained by the differences between their readerships—the *Daily Sun* caters mostly to a Black working class, many of whom formed part of Zuma's support base of working-class Zulu-speakers and rural constituents. The *Son* and *Daily Voice* readerships, in contrast, are predominantly Coloured and were unlikely to support a candidate who was seen as overtly espousing ethnic politics. The Coloured constituency in the Western Cape has historically (most notably in the first democratic election in 1994) also shown support for historically White parties like the National Party or the Democratic Alliance (DA). At the time of Zuma's election as president of the ANC, the Western Cape province had an ANC government but a DA-led city council,[31] with continued tension between the outspoken DA mayor Helen Zille and the ANC leadership in the province. Second, the high level of reader participation that the tabloids pride themselves on is evident from the reader responses to Jacob Zuma's election. In the case of the *Daily Voice* and the *Son,* these responses were comparatively high in relation to the news reporting on the events, and constituted the bulk of the space devoted to the issue.

Third, the coverage of formal political processes at Polokwane, even in the case of the *Daily Sun* where it occupied the front pages for the days around the election, was proportionally still far outweighed by coverage of the "politics of the everyday." This is especially clear in the case of the *Daily Voice* and the *Son,* which chose to lead with crime and social-interest stories rather than coverage of Zuma's election. For instance, on December 20, the *Daily Voice* led with a front-page story on a vigilante murder,[32] which chronicled the death of a suspected thief at the hands of a group of inhabitants of the informal settlement Browns Farm in Philippi on the Cape Flats. The story, continued on page two, was accompanied by screen grabs from a cell phone video clip. These pictures (a macabre turn on the "citizen journalism" enabled by cell phone technologies) show a young man being tied up with barbed wire, getting beaten with a sjambok (whip), being revived by having water poured over him after he passed out, and then beaten again. He later died in the hospital. The vigilante murder is also the topic for the editorial comment of the day, in which a case is made for more police presence in the townships to stamp out vigilantism. Mob justice is further explained as being "fuelled by a community tired of living in fear."[33]

The *Son*'s lead story that day was about a popular singer spending the night in jail on a charge of drunken driving, but also contained its regular share of everyday politics, crime, and social issues. These included a full-page story on striking workers on a Cape wine farm, Bloemendal near Durbanville, who protested against low wages. The tabloid's orientation to the working class seems evident from this sympathetic report, even if its overall coverage of Zuma's election (which includes a supportive quote from the striking workers) clearly demonstrates a rejection of his presidency.

Zuma's election to the presidency of the party also led to the ousting of Thabo Mbeki from his position as president of the country months before the end of his term. The ANC "recalled" Mbeki after a judge found that he had acted unfairly and unjustly when he fired Zuma as deputy president after the latter's financial advisor, Schabir Shaik, was found guilty of corruption in 2005. Since the story broke unexpectedly on a Saturday (September 20, 2008), the Sunday tabloids ran strongly with it. The *Sunday Sun* announced the news boldly on its front page with a big white-on-black headline, "Out you go!"[34] The report was factual and explained the political rivalry between Zuma and Mbeki as well as the details of the judgment that had led to Mbeki's sacking. The story was given further coverage on page two, with a timeline ("Crisis Countdown") of the run-up to the clash, as well as a background story ("Mbeki: How the war was fought") about party infighting by inside sources who were "in the heart of the battle." The Afrikaans Sunday tabloid *Sondag* announced the news on its front page with a photo of

Mbeki (next to one of the movie star Charlize Theron) and the caption "Tatta-Thabo" ("Goodbye Thabo"). Appearing on page four of *Sondag*, the story was a detailed, factual account, in the style of mainstream political reporting, on the events and their implications for the party and the government. A column in more colloquial style, titled "Mbeki duik in die hek van dié SA sepie" (Mbeki bites the dust in this South African soap opera), appeared in a sidebar next to the report. Another, more analytical op-ed style column followed on the next page, in which the ANC was accused of performing an about-face on the independence of the courts.[35] The judgment by justice Nicholson was also referred to in passing in a column on the back page.[36]

The following day, the *Daily Sun* again covered the political high drama very prominently. Its series of reports throughout the paper was adorned with a logo featuring a picture of a worried Mbeki and the caption "The axing of Mbeki." The front page report (continued on page two) announced "MBEKI I will go without a fight!"[37] Similar to the background stories in the Sunday tabloids, the *Daily Sun* offered an article explaining "And How the End Came!"[38] It also had time to canvas the opinions of its readers from around the country ("Mbeki: What you say....,")[39] and even included a wire story on the concern among Zimbabwean negotiators that Mbeki might not have been able to play his role as mediator in that country's political negotiations anymore. The editor, Themba Khumalo, devoted his "Sledgehammer" column to Mbeki's ousting,[40] and in the same column highlighted Mbeki's failures with regard to HIV/AIDS (he gained international notoriety for questioning the link between HIV and AIDS and for delaying the provision of anti-retroviral drugs in the public health sector) and social delivery, resonating with the paper's earlier demands to Zuma after the latter secured the top ANC position.

As in the case of Zuma's election, the Cape Town–based *Son* again under-played the political news, choosing instead to lead with a story of a jealous husband that shot and killed his ex-wife and himself. The Mbeki story, only featured on page two, was sourced from wire copy.

The local elections, the ascendancy of Jacob Zuma to ANC presidency, and Thabo Mbeki's ousting were prominent news events. Thus, their extensive coverage in the tabloids does not necessarily mean that the tabloids would pay continuous attention to more run-of-the-mill politics. Yet, these examples show that the tabloids, contrary to popular criticism, do cover formal political processes, at least when they become big news events, albeit to varying degrees depending on their readership. The real political role these publications play in post-apartheid society should, however, be examined in terms of their coverage of the politics of the everyday.

News about formal politics still plays second fiddle to typical, dramatic tabloid fare. In a content analysis of tabloid content from January to December 2006, the media-analysis company Media Tenor found that party political issues rank high on tabloid agendas, but that "crime," "general interest," and "society" still outranked politics. Out of a total of 11,825 articles in the *Daily Sun* over the period, across 26 categories, only 892 articles (or 7.5% of the total) dealt with "politics." (This definition excludes policy issues, and focuses on articles explicitly related to party political matters.)[41] "Crime" ranked highest, with 3,311 articles (or 28%), followed by "general interest" (17%), "society" (14.5%), and "domestic issues" (9.4%). Policy issues that are ostensibly of great political (in the broad sense) interest to *Daily Sun* readers like "Education" (2.3%), "Health" (2.2%), "Transport" (1.4%), and "HIV/AIDS" (1.1%) ranked much lower. The prominence of categories like "crime" and "society" seems to suggest that the *Daily Sun,* while claiming to "take up cudgels" for the "man in the blue overall" (Du Plessis, pers. comm. 2007), still employs conventional news values when selecting stories. However, such a quantitative picture remains limited—understanding the political significance of South African tabloids requires a more qualitative approach to the perspectives and content of tabloid stories.

Reactionary Politics

Not all the political work that tabloids do is constructive. They often engage in reactionary politics, ranging from populist calls for the death penalty to be reinstated to amplifying calls for revenge by outraged community members through sensationalist coverage of justice. Tabloid treatment of women has also received criticism for being socially conservative or degrading. The feminist criticism against the tabloids' patriarchal gender politics, epitomized by the page-three girl, is well-known and perhaps the aspect for which the tabloids have received the most criticism in South Africa.[42] On several occasions, the tabloids have also received criticism for fuelling xeno- and homophobia. These concerns came under an intense spotlight in 2008, with criticism directed primarily at the *Daily Sun.* A homophobic column by Jon Qwelane in the *Sunday Sun* also led to widespread protests and complaints.

In May 2008, violent attacks against foreign nationals erupted around South Africa. More than sixty people were killed, hundreds were injured, and scores were left homeless. Following the outbreak of xenophobic violence around the country, the media watchdog Media Monitoring Project (MMP) and its partner Consortium for Refugees and Migrants in South Africa (CoRMSA) submitted a complaint with the Press Ombudsman Joe Thloloe and the South African Human Rights Commission (SAHRC) against the *Daily Sun.* This complaint followed earlier criticisms by the MMP of the tabloids' coverage of immigration. The MMP accused the tabloid of stereotyping foreign nationals as "aliens," presenting a "biased and limited" representation of government agencies, failing to "clearly condemn the violence until most of it had been contained," and failing to "offer any non-violent alternatives, or additional information to help prevent violence and to condone mob justice" (Media Monitoring Project 2008).

The MMP had a point as far as tabloid content goes. A cursory look at tabloid content makes it clear that these papers have been tapping into the widespread xenophobic attitudes in the country and amplifying them for sensational value. "Clamp-down operations" on "illegal aliens" get prominent and gleeful coverage, and foreign nationals are often glibly associated with crime. And if foreigners were the "problem," the horrific "solution" witnessed all over the country in 2008 is also not unlike the vigilante justice often uncritically depicted on the front pages of tabloids. The coverage given to the violent rage of communities lashing out against the suspected criminals in their midst often stops just short of celebration.

During the attacks in May 2008, the *Daily Sun*'s coverage was marked by the paradoxes and contradictions that can now be seen as characteristic of the South African tabloids in other respects as well. The *Daily Sun* seemed to have taken a critical stance toward the attacks in particular, but persisted in referring to foreign nationals as "aliens" and upholding the us–them distinction between South Africans and immigrants. In his editorial column ("TK's Sledgehammer"), Khumalo was unequivocal in his rejection of the attacks:

> The demons of death and destruction are high with joy as we kick, loot, slash and kill each other. *But why? Why this amount of self-hate? Why is it becoming so impossible for us to live with each [other] regardless of which country we come from?*[43]

He also uses the opportunity to criticize government for lack of leadership, with regard to both an immigration policy and the lack of progress with programs of social reconstruction and development that could alleviate the poverty that lies at the root of the conflict:

> Government cannot just cross their fingers and hope miracles will happen if there are no proper structures to look after refugees. Miracles only happen when you have a plan. In addition, we cannot underestimate the negative impact of corruption. Corruption halts progress. Very little progress has been made in reducing unemployment. Corruption in housing has made some communities very angry. The situation is becoming volatile as food prices skyrocket. Add to that the fact that there are knuckle-headed criminals who will always take advantage of explosive situations for their twisted and greedy needs. What has government done so far to make life unbearable for criminals? **ABSO-BLOODY-LUTELY NOTHING!**[44]

The paper's news reporting also attempted to personalize foreigners even though they remained "aliens." For instance, a report on the front page of the *Daily Sun* on May 19, headlined "When love turns to hate!," recounted how Nomoya Mabaso and "the man in her life, a Mozambican immigrant," who had been living in the Kanana informal settlement near Tembisa for five years, used to host parties on weekends where "[t]heir shack would be filled with happy laughter" and "[t]he neighbours knew they were always welcome." This all came to a "horrible end" when their shack "was burned down by people from the SAME NEIGHBOURHOOD which had been so happy the week before."[45] The report sympathizes with these "victims of the violence which is making SA a hell for many aliens" and makes clear that the couple "tried to fit in" with the community.

This contradiction between sympathy for victims of the violence and the persisting distinction between "us" and "them" runs through the *Daily Sun*'s other reports on the violence. A prominent report on page three of the same issue, headlined "Blood and Flames!," deplored the attacks as "the evil flames of violence,"[46] and a sub-heading announced "Aliens killed and injured as new attacks stoke flames of hatred." Yet while one sidebar to the main story reported on ANC president Jacob Zuma's reminder that foreigners assisted South Africans in their struggle against the apartheid regime, another sidebar upheld the distinction between South African and foreign nationals. This second sidebar, headlined "SA couple's shop looted and burned," informed readers that "Not all the victims of attacks across Joburg are aliens." The report quotes a couple from Tokoza whose shop had been looted and burnt as saying, "We are South Africans, we are not foreigners! What is going to happen to us now?" While the story elicits sympathy for victims of the attacks and could be read as a further criticism of the violence, it could also be seen to imply that South Africans are less deserving of violence than foreign nationals. The latter reading is supported when juxtaposed with a story on page five which reports, "SA man called an alien and thrown into jail!"[47] This type of story, in which people recount the havoc wreaked upon their lives as a result of bungles by officialdom, is a regular feature in the tabloid's pages. But on this occasion, the story further serves to criminalize foreigners (consistently called "aliens" regardless of their immigration status) and to cast South Africans in the role of victims of immigration. It tells of a "Xhosa man, Johannes Mgiqwa (27) of Tsakane, Ekurhuleni" who "has spent six nights of horror in the Lindhela [sic] Repatriation Centre, west of Joburg" because police stopped his car and told him "he looked like a Zimbabwean and threw him in jail!" The report quotes Mgiqwa's aunt, Lettie, who confirms the implication that South Africans are "hard-working" victims of an influx of Zimbabweans (who by implication are not): "It is really sad when police arrest a hard-working, honest orphan like Johannes. He is the only breadwinner in the family."[48]

In trying to understand the xenophobic tropes in tabloid reporting, these papers should again be seen not in isolation as the vile and unethical journalistic Other that much of the mainstream discourse, including that of the MMP, constructs them as, but as part of the social phenomena characterizing post-apartheid society. This xenophobia is linked to the precarious and highly strained lived experience of the poor in post-apartheid society. Consider this response from a reader in a focus-group interview conducted in the rural town of Makhado in Limpopo province:

> Zimbabweans are making trouble, they are killing people and take our jobs. Weekends after seven o'clock we don't feel free to walk around—the Zimbabweans will rob you. There is a lot of anger in the community against Zimbabweans—they are vandalizing [electric] transformers in the municipality. The *Daily Sun* does not talk about it [these problems] enough, only sometimes. There is not a lot about it in the *Daily Sun,* there should be more.

These comments, made in 2007, have an ominous ring to them when read after the spate of xenophobic attacks against foreign nationals that took place in May 2008. But they are clearly linked to the lack of security, employment, and basic services that poor communities are experiencing. In the absence of a trustful relationship with a government which they view as having failed them, they turn to tabloid newspapers to articulate their fears. This is also more or less how Du Plessis (2008), the unrepentant publisher of the *Daily Sun,* explained his newspaper's position in response to the MMP's complaint about it fueling xenophobia:

> He [the man in the blue overall]'s many things, our guy. But he IS South African. That's not to say that other kinds of people are not important . . . but from where we sit, our guy (and his partner as always) is MORE important. . . . Our views about South Africa First are clearly not wildly popular in august circles. But then in august circles they have mostly not had to fight so hard for the good things in life as our guy . . . There is a lot of talk in these not-so-mythical and elevated circles about one Africa, one brotherhood, even one GIANT brotherhood (and sisterhood!) from the windy south to the blazing sands of the distant north. In our market people are NOT so sure about all that . . . That's because it's been a struggle . . . Getting your own free-standing house, sitting on a little discretionary income for the first time ever, starting to travel a bit, getting the kid (now nine or 10) into something at least approaching an acceptable school, even buying a first car—these things have not been easy. And that's because the dice have always been loaded against our hero. In apartheid days the government didn't care. These days, though the rhetoric has changed, it STILL seems the authorities often don't care. From our guy's perspective, services have not improved . . . there are holes in the street, the cops are pretty much hit-and-miss, lots of hospitals are nasty, schools are not much better . . . and a distant national government seems to seek its friends elsewhere. That's the gap we've taken here. We have put our inky arms around our guy. We defend him from crass and often useless officialdom, we advise him on getting ahead, we provide examples of how others like him have found success, we tell him about amazing things, hopefully we enthrall him . . . we give him stuff to talk about around the urns at tea break tomorrow morning on the nation's factory floors. And, trust me on this, having struggled so hard since the days of the barricades in the early 90s when he was still a kid, our guy isn't about to give up any of his victories. He doesn't have that luxury yet.

This justification for the paper's xenophobia as being an articulation of widespread attitudes among its readers resonates with comments Du Plessis made in the BBC documentary *Black, White and Read All Over* in 2006.[49] The context is a report on a shootout in Johannesburg following an armed robbery, in which four policemen and eight robbers were shot dead:

> This is a great story here, you know, we've long held the view that organized crime here is completely out of control.
>
> Early reports that they are Zimbabweans or many of them Zimbabweans, evil doers there can come in here almost unstopped.
>
> We reflect the emotion of the guy, our reader, that he's not entirely enamored with refugees from the north.

The *Daily Sun*'s reporting on foreign nationals as "aliens" who are unwelcome in South Africa clearly tapped into a widespread xenophobic sentiment in the country. Its somewhat ambivalent response to the outbreak of xenophobia and seemingly reluctant agreement that it will refrain from using the term "alien" in future is still far from an unequivocal stance against xenophobia. One can certainly not expect that xenophobia will be one of the causes they will be campaigning against in the coming years. Although cause-and-effect links between the *Daily Sun*'s reporting and xenophobic violence should be avoided, its stance on xenophobia is clearly problematic in a country where such sentiments run high.

Yet a response aimed at preventing xenophobia in the media would have to include much more than making tabloid newspapers the scapegoats. While encouraging tabloids to desist from xenophobic representations, their critics should recognize the responsibility of all South African media to critically engage with the root causes of the xenophobic attacks, not just the articulation of the attitudes that manifest as their symptoms. The tabloids point to system failure in the country from the perspective of the grassroots: economic policies that have failed the poor, a loss of faith in the police and criminal justice system, and the demise of hope that the government and institutionalized politics will bring an end to precarious, miserable living conditions. The tabloids, for all their baying for blood, have also paid attention to the lives of the poor in a way that the mainstream newspapers and other elite media have not. The mainstream press are also not without blame in persistently linking foreign nationals with social pathologies like crime or drug use, and the nationality of arrested suspects is almost without exception provided in news reports. If the media are to be taken to task for their complicity in xenophobia—as they should be—such criticism should go beyond a moralistic denunciation of the "usual suspects" (Glenn 2008, 18) and ask more fundamental questions about the media's democratic role in one of the most unequal countries in the world.

The homophobic attitude that South African tabloids have often been accused of was demonstrated clearly by Jon Qwelane in his weekly column in the *Sunday Sun* on July 20, 2008.[50] Qwelane used the dissent in the Anglican church over its stance on homosexuality as a starting point to engage in anti-gay diatribe:

> There could be a few things I could take issue with Zimbabwean president Robert Mugabe, but his unflinching and unapologetic stance over homosexuals is definitely not among those. . . . Homosexuals and their backers will call me names, printable and not, for stating as I have always done my serious reservations about their "lifestyle and sexual preferences," but quite frankly I don't give a damn: wrong is wrong!

Qwelane went on to argue for amendments to the South African Constitution, which has been interpreted by the country's Constitutional Court as allowing same-sex marriages.[51] Qwelane, whose column was illustrated by a cartoon equating homosexuality with bestiality, said he would "pray that some day a bunch of politicians with their heads affixed firmly to their necks will muster the balls to rewrite the constitution of this country, to excise those sections which give licence to men 'marrying' other men, and ditto women."

The column was met with a furious and widespread response, ranging from Facebook pages protesting the "APPALLING homophobia in our midst" to protests outside the offices of Media24 (which owns *Sunday Sun*) in Cape Town and Johannesburg to an online petition calling for Qwelane's dismissal. The latter referenced the dismissal of David Bullard, who was fired as a *Sunday Times* columnist on account of a racist column some months before.[52] After Press Ombudsman Joe Thloloe received more than one thousand complaints about Qwelane's piece, Qwelane was found in contravention of the Press Code and ordered to apologize.[53]

The outrage at the clearly homophobic rant by Qwelane in the *Sunday Sun* was akin to the debate following the outbreaks of xenophobic violence, and could be seen as an encouraging sign that a culture of public debate about issues key to post-apartheid democracy is emerging. Criticism against homophobic coverage in the *Daily Voice* has prompted the editor, Karl Brophy, to admit having made "1 or 2 mistakes" by engaging in homophobic reporting (SANEF 2007). That these examples of unethical reporting were taken to regulatory bodies (the HRC and the Press Ombudsman) further indicates the viability and trust placed in the self-regulatory system. The responses on Facebook against Qwelane's column are an interesting example of how social networking sites are serving as vehicles of media criticism, and the public's reaction is an encouraging sign that audiences are not the passive victims of tabloid stereotypes they are often made out to be by watchdog organizations and concerned critics. The question remains, however, whether this outrage was shared by tabloid readers or whether it was made by those middle-class critics "looking over the shoulder" of tabloid readers (Thloloe, pers. comm. 2008). If the latter is the case, the complaints might not be effective in the long term in preventing xenophobic and homophobic stereotyping, as tabloids will continue to give their audiences what they want and feed into an appetite for extremism, while criticism remains a patronizing gesture.

The highly segmented nature of the country's media markets (linked in the first instance to class, but class and race remain largely intertwined in post-apartheid South Africa) might mean that such protests would not necessarily have an effect on the relevant media institutions. As a South African blogger, Sarah Britten, pointed out:[54]

> Judging by Qwelane's pre-emptive defiance in the original piece, these protests are not going to induce anything resembling contrition in the gravel-voiced journo who was once fired from 702 for offending too many of their listeners. If anything, the protests will be positioned as the posturing of a largely white elite out of touch with the readers of the *Sunday Sun*, those LSM 3 to 6 taxi drivers and hawkers, the famous blue collar man.

Unless they decide to complain to national watchdog bodies like the South African Human Rights Commission, the engagement by the public with the media might therefore also remain constrained by market forces. In the end, such protests against media might only serve as a lightning rod to defuse the brunt of criticism against tabloids, leaving them to provide their niched market with the homophobic and xenophobic content that has proved commercially successful. But from another perspective, the criticism against the tabloids' perceived homo- and xenophobia stems from an unwillingness to engage—from a comfortable position of ignorance—with the lived reality of tabloid readers that gives rise to such sentiments.

The events of May and July 2008 indicate that the role of popular journalism and the construction of citizenship and nationhood in post-apartheid South Africa is an important topic for further research.

The emergence of tabloids in South Africa is inextricably linked to the country's democratization, which not only impacted its formal political processes and construction of citizenship, but also caused social, cultural, and economic shifts. The potential democratic role that tabloids could play in the country should therefore be understood not only in terms of formal politics, but also in the way that tabloids articulate these shifts in society of which the political implications are not always immediately evident.

Tabloids, as a part of popular culture in post-apartheid South Africa, force us to redefine our understanding of the public sphere and indeed of politics itself. As Hermes (2006, 40) states, to take the realm of popular culture seriously is to "divest governmental politics of its frightening grandeur": "It is to make clear that politics is not something belonging to (informed) elite, that you need to qualify for—but is about who we are, and what we, all of us, want to make of the world we live in."

The South African tabloids are, however, fraught with ironies and contradictions, and cannot be taken at face value. What is certain is that they play a significant role in the daily lives of their readers, including serving as a sense-making resource for their readers' political outlook. In the following chapter, we will draw on conversations with South African tabloid readers to explore how this process occurs in their daily lives.

6. Truth or Trash? Understanding Tabloid Journalism and Lived Experience

The changing media landscape and the shifts taking place in post-apartheid South African society only partly explain the popularity of the new tabloid papers. These macro-shifts in industry and society provide us with a political, economic, and sociological explanation of why tabloid newspapers emerged during a given period in the history of post-apartheid South Africa; the niche that they filled in the newspaper market; and how they challenged the dominant norms and practices of the journalistic fraternity or "profession" in the country. What these approaches do not tell us is what role these tabloids play in the lives of their millions of loyal readers. Newspaper readers are not only—or perhaps not even in the first place—a "market segment" or "niche," nor can they be thought of as passive receivers of messages selected for them by a professional group of people and against whose exploitation they have to be protected. Even if the media they consume are the terrain upon which a larger contestation among historical, political, and societal forces is taking place, they are not mere pawns in this game. Newspapers form part of people's everyday routines and habits, providing entertainment and diversion at the same time as they contribute to the way readers view the world, forge their relationships with others, and fill their places as citizens in society. While a critical perspective on tabloid media should certainly include the very important larger structural factors of markets, political shifts, and professional/industry norms, a full picture of tabloid newspapers as a social phenomenon can only emerge when the relationship between the tabloids and their readers is understood.

Tabloid media content obtains its full meaning as it is consumed. In much of the debate around tabloid newspapers, critics have condemned them after judging only what they saw on the page in front of them—assuming that meaning is either intrinsic in the textual representation or over-determined by journalists and editors located in big exploitative conglomerates, with readers as passive recipients or even victims of tabloid messages. A critical reading of tabloid content and genre is no doubt important, as is an interrogation of the political economy within which these papers are located. But the cultural dimension of tabloid journalism, the "web of meanings, rituals, conventions and symbol systems" (Zelizer 2008, 88), is often lost from sight in these analyses. The role of media in culture cannot be isolated, precisely because the media establishment itself is "firmly anchored" in culture (Bird 2003, 3). Understanding tabloid journalism in this cultural sense would require a closer examination of the interrelationship among tabloid readers, tabloid media, and tabloid journalists. After having discussed the political and economic context, the tabloid genre and content, and the professional response to tabloid media in the preceding chapters, the focus now shifts to this interrelationship. In this chapter, tabloid media will be approached from the perspective of their readers, and in the next chapter the views of tabloid journalists and editors will be discussed. The aim of this study of reader responses is to explore how tabloids are related to shifting political, social, and cultural identities and to the lived experience of readers as active audiences rather than passive consumers.

Approaching Tabloids from the Perspective of Their Readers

The debate about the new tabloids in South Africa has thus far focused exclusively on issues of production, such as professional standards (or the lack thereof), ethical issues (invasion of privacy, stereotyping, gendered representations), and aspects of form and style (like melodrama, sensationalism, etc.). Critics have neglected the perspective of readers by assuming a "top-down," one-directional influence of tabloids on post-apartheid society. A focus on audience perceptions of tabloids could indicate how media use correlates with social stratification in post-apartheid society, and how these readers position themselves politically and culturally in terms of the mediated public sphere. Such an analysis of audience reading strategies should not, however, be understood in isolation from the structural conditions that shape audiences' meaning-making and that limit the range of possible meanings derived from the text (Steenveld 2006, 20–21). This relationship among experience, social position, and consumption will only become clear if tabloid audiences are (a) considered as active readers rather than passive recipients and (b) understood as diverse rather than homogenous, occupying a range of social identities within different material contexts. Because tabloid readers occupy a range of identities in their daily lives, and reading tabloids is one activity among many and one articulation of identity among others (Bird 1992, 110), contradictory and complex meanings could emerge from such an analysis. Even though a study of tabloid audiences might start by identifying them in terms of pre-conceived market segments or categories (which in the South African case, due to the persistence of historical labels, correlate largely with racial and ethnic signifiers), the researcher should remain attentive to the differences, tensions, and divergences between the perspectives of tabloid readers and the "fluid, shifting nature of 'audience'" (ibid., 111). In the study of tabloid readers' interactions with these newspapers, it should therefore not be assumed that the audience is already "out there," ready to be found or already defined in terms of existing demographic categories. While the continued relevance of racial categories in post-apartheid South Africa and their correlation with class (and therefore "market segments") suggests taking existing demographics as a starting point for analysis, the researcher should also remain attentive to the transgression or blurring of boundaries in the process of social interaction between readers and tabloids and among readers themselves. Care should be taken not to homogenize "tabloid readers" as a group, but to be aware of the differences among readerships of different tabloids and even within the readership of one tabloid. The very notion of audience has become problematic because the media do not have uniform "effects" on masses of people, as was assumed in early mass-communication research. People are active, selective, and unpredictable makers of meaning in the process of interacting with media (Bird 2003, 3).

Although neglected in the South African debate thus far, several international studies have examined tabloid content and meaning from the reader's perspective. Attention to audience interpretations of media texts has formed part of various scholarly approaches since the 1940s, when the earlier media-effects model, which assumed a direct causal link between media stimulus and audience response, was challenged by an observation of the more complex ways that social interactions influence audience reception of information. This observation has led to the emergence of early theoretical models of social interaction among an active audience, such as Lazarsfeld, Berelson, and Gaudet's (1944) two-step flow model and the uses-and-gratifications model (Biressi and Nunn 2008, 282).

International studies of tabloid audiences have largely flowed from the so-called "cultural turn" in audience studies that parted ways with earlier mass-communication audience studies in favor of a socio-cultural analysis that examined audiences in relation to broader networks of power. Areas of specific interest within this approach, associated with the Birmingham School of Cultural Studies under the leadership of Stuart Hall, were media's mode of address and the way that media audiences could identify with, oppose, or negotiate the dominant meaning of media texts (ibid., 283). Hall's influential encoding/decoding model (1970) offered a way of understanding the production of meaning in media texts as a dynamic process of negotiation in which producers and audiences are mutually implicated. David Morley's seminal *Nationwide* study (1980) related audience interpretation of media texts to social and class position, thereby locating viewing practices within a "politicized cultural map" (Nunn and Biressi, 2008, 283).

More recently, scholars such as Nick Couldry have sought to approach media from within a broad network of everyday social practices. Couldry (2004, 115) describes this approach as one that

> understands media not as texts or structures of production, but as practice . . . [T]his paradigm aims to move beyond old debates of media effects and the relative importance of political economy and audience interpretation, at the same time as moving beyond a narrow concentration on audience practices, to study the whole range of practices that are oriented towards media and the role of media in ordering other practices in the social world.

Couldry (ibid., 116) also distinguishes between an anthropological approach to media practices and the critical audience research done by scholars such as Hall, David Morley, and Ien Ang while further setting these two approaches apart from earlier traditions such as those set in experimental social sciences (studying "effects" from a behavioralist perspective), the critical Marxist approach of political economy, and semiotic analyses associated with post–World War II European structuralism and post-structuralism. Instead of siding with one of these approaches, which have often been pitted against each other in "internecine disputes" about what the appropriate theoretical approach to a study of audiences would be, Couldry proposes a new paradigm for the general study of media in social life. This paradigm would approach media more loosely and broadly within a broader social context of "action and knowledge" (ibid., 117). Couldry relates this paradigm to Bird's work, in which she does not attempt to isolate the role of media in culture, but rather views media as enmeshed within culture itself. This approach to media as cultural practice can be summarized as: "what types of things do people do in relation to media? And what types of things do people say in relation to media?" (ibid., 121). Such an approach sees media not as central to society (and then studies how people interpret or interact with media), but as part of a wide range of social practices and experiences. Instead of being the central focus of people's interactions, media *occurs within* people's relationships, experiences, and habits. Media texts are therefore only one facet of the overall social practice which is oriented toward media (ibid., 126). Spitulnik (1993) has also argued for an approach to media studies that moves beyond a consideration of media from a primarily textual point of view to one that sees the meaning of media as not only to be found in media messages, but also in media's cultural, social, and economic roles and in the everyday practices of consumption. From the media-anthropological perspective that Spitulnik proposes, a textual analysis of media will be "incomplete" without an analysis of "the culture of media production, the political economy and social history of media institutions and the various practices of media consumption that exist in any given society" (ibid., 295). As the cultural studies tradition (for instance Hall's encoding/decoding model and Morley's later adaptation thereof) has already shown, interpretations of media texts should be understood within the social and class positions of their readers, since these positions may influence the meaning derived from media texts. Because the range of social and class positions of media audiences differ, a variety of interpretations of media texts are possible. From this point of view, the criticism that tabloid content might adversely affect audience behavior ("the impact this type of pulp journalism has on society," as suggested by Rabe 2007, 29–30),[1] becomes difficult to sustain, based as it is on a prediction of a certain "media effect" by a media text on an audience conceived of as a monolithic entity. Media anthropologists suggest that a view of audiences as active interpreters of media is taken even further, to a "post-content" or "post-text" position where the production–consumption dichotomy itself is rethought (Spitulnik 1993, 298).[2]

Taking such a holistic media-anthropological approach would mean understanding the use of tabloid newspapers within a broader social context, not only as texts or messages but as points of reference in people's everyday lives. Such an approach would mean taking media seriously in terms of its important position within contemporary social life, without exaggerating that position as being necessarily central to people's experience (so as to avoid perpetuating what Couldry [2005] called the "myth of the mediated centre").

In the context of this book, such an approach would (partly, alongside a larger ethnographic study of readers' social interaction with tabloids, which falls outside the scope of this book) mean taking tabloid newspapers and their audiences seriously (as seriously as the elite press has been taken as a measure of the post-apartheid public sphere), instead of dismissing the papers out of hand as inferior journalistic products or the audiences as somehow misguided or victimized by exploitative media. Tabloids are often defined by elite journalists and readers as "the epitome of 'trash' reading," and accordingly its readers are often stereotyped or dismissed: "[i]f tabloids are trash, so are their readers" (Bird 1992, 107). This dismissal extends to the producers of tabloids, who are looked down upon by elite journalists as having betrayed their profession or sold their souls to commercial interests. South African tabloid editors and journalists, for instance, have been described as "brainless," as they "barely use cerebral matter to contemplate these matters (the perpetuation of gender stereotypes)" (Rabe 2007, 29). In other words, audiences and tabloid producers are both assumed to lack good taste and judgement, and share culpability for displaying symptoms of a "major cultural failing" (Langer cited in Biressi and Nunn 2008, 283).

In contrast, research influenced by the "cultural turn" in audience studies has focused on how audiences use meanings created by active readings in their everyday lives, and how such (often subversive or irreverent) readings can be used to engage with or challenge hegemonic cultural, social or political discourses (Biressi and Nunn 2008, 283). Tabloids have been reviled for their preference for the emotional, sensational and dramatic rather than the rational debate of the idealized public sphere (ibid., 284), but exactly this preference for popular knowledge and experience can serve to subvert elite epistemologies linked to class hierarchies. The extent of this subversion should not be overstated, since tabloid readers are themselves constructed within patterns of consumption controlled by huge conglomerates. But although tabloids are often criticized for being apolitical, the avoidance of politics-as-usual ought to be read in terms of the disconnect between mainstream politics and certain sections of the public (Bird 1992, 130). As such, tabloid news has been seen as a way to make news relevant to a section of society that would otherwise reject or ignore it (Sparks 2000, 9). At the same time, tabloid readers have been known to engage in what Hall (1970) would refer to as an "oppositional" or "negotiated" reading by knowingly choosing what tabloid stories to believe in. Stories were considered true only when they fit a reader's frame of reference (Bird 1992, 121).

If one agrees that tabloid readers actively engage with tabloid content rather than passively receive these media "messages," and if this engagement is studied from a holistic perspective (as offered by the cultural studies or media-anthropology approaches), there are two implications: First, the causal link between tabloid content and audience behavior or attitudes, suggested by some of tabloid media's critics, becomes untenable. For instance, the fact that tabloids publish pictures of semi-nude women on page three cannot automatically be taken as an indication that this will lead to increases of domestic violence, rape, or similar "social ills" (Rabe 2007, 29–30). Similarly, a fantastical story about a supernatural occurrence being published in a tabloid newspaper does not necessarily mean that this story will be taken as the literal truth by its readers in the same way as, for instance, a factual account of an accident, using conventions like the "inverted pyramid" of news reports. This means that the journalistic-ethical value of "truth" should not only be understood in terms of its correspondence with an assumed objective reality, but as part of the complex social and cultural framework through which people navigate their daily lives. In order to be in a position to better assess the value (or lack thereof) of tabloid content, an attempt should be made to understand the different interpretations of tabloid stories, influenced by a range of circumstances including the type of story, the particular tabloid in which it was published (because there are different types of tabloids and they should not be treated as a monolithic group), and the social or class position of the reader.

Second, the consumption of tabloid media will be seen as part of people's daily lives in contemporary society, not merely as texts but as points of reference within the dense texture of their lived experiences. Understanding what tabloids mean in post-apartheid South African society is therefore not identical to understanding what tabloid *texts* mean in this society. To be sure, the reading of tabloid texts forms part of audience interaction with these media, but these newspapers also play other roles in people's lives—they facilitate social interaction, serve as markers of class or ethnic identities, feature in daily social rituals and routines, and so forth. Audience preference for tabloids might not even have anything to do with their content, but with their role as objects signifying a certain social position or as markers of taste (this could explain why South African tabloids are also consumed by people who cannot read). These distinctions of taste (Bourdieu 1984; see also Glenn and Knaggs 2008) in terms of media style and genre and related expectations of the role and functions of journalism in post-apartheid South African society are linked to socio-economic, cultural, and political power. In the context of the South African media, the class positions to which these value judgements and preferences are linked also largely map onto the racial and ethnic categories inherited from apartheid that continue to shape South African society in the second decade of democracy.[3]

To understand South African tabloid media in this holistic way is to understand popular media as a "locus of contestation," where the choice of media in itself can represent an act of resistance against dominant discourses and practices (West and Fair 1993, 105). In the sense that tabloids are enjoyed by a mass population, they form part of popular culture that is "majoritarian in a way that elite culture is not" (Glynn 2000, 8). In the South African context, an examination of how readers engage with tabloids can therefore also be seen as a study of the potential and limitations of popular democracy mediated through popular texts.

It has been said at the outset of this study that in order to understand tabloids more fully as part of the social, cultural, and political life in contemporary South Africa, they should be studied as a social phenomenon which demands a multi-leveled approach (suggested by Steenveld 2006, 20). Such a study should include a textual examination of tabloid content, an investigation into the location of tabloid newspapers within the political economy of the South African media, and a study of audience responses to tabloids. What is important from the perspective of an approach to audiences informed by the tradition of cultural studies and media anthropology is that these different levels are not considered as somehow separate or self-contained dimensions of tabloid newspapers, but as inextricably linked. It is from this assumption of production and consumption as interlinked rather than dichotomous, and of this process as located in relation to a complex set of other social, political, and economic processes, that the responses of tabloid audiences should be understood.

Speaking to Tabloid Readers

South Africa's tabloids are significant phenomena for understanding the post-apartheid mediated public sphere. To gain such an understanding, it is necessary to study the connections among the political economy within which these tabloids operate, the textual representations they contain, the processes and conditions under which they are produced, and the ways they are consumed. Because this book aims to touch on all of these levels, it has opted for a broad exploration of these dimensions and their interconnections rather than an in-depth study of any one of them. In this and the following chapter, the last two dimensions (the production and consumption) of the tabloids will be discussed. By means of a series of focus groups of tabloid readers in various parts of the country, representing both urban and rural audiences and corresponding to the target markets of the various tabloids as well as different class positions within these markets, an attempt was made to map broad themes emerging from reader responses. Because it was conducted as an exploratory study rather than as an attempt at an exhaustive ethnography—and in acknowledgement of Spitulnik's (1993, 298) criticism of the label "ethnographic" being appended to audience studies where participant observation and immersion in the daily life-worlds of audiences is minimal—it remains for future research to provide a more textured picture of the use of tabloids in everyday life in South Africa.

However, although not an ethnography in the methodological sense of the word, the interviews with tabloid audiences were approached from an ethnographic perspective. That is to say, the interviews attempted not only to elicit responses related to the reception of tabloid content, but also to locate the reading of tabloids within readers' wider social and cultural lives.

The aims of the audience study were as follows:

a) to identify key themes emerging from readers' responses to the tabloids;
b) to establish how these themes relate to the discourse about tabloids in South African scholarly and journalistic criticism;
c) to locate these themes in terms of the social, political, and cultural context within which South African tabloids are read; and

d) to explore how these responses compare to patterns of tabloid reading found elsewhere as documented in the literature.

Self-reflexivity is always a necessary component in the research process. In the practice of knowledge production in a transitional society like South Africa, marked by the continuation of severe inequalities inherited from apartheid, the researcher should be especially aware of his/her position in terms of the categories of race and class. In the case of this study, the fact that the researcher belonged to the historically advantaged class and racial group, and as an academic occupies a social position which in most cases set him apart from the interview subjects,[4] should be factored into an analysis of the responses. The possibility that the researcher could be seen as an "authority" and that respondents might present their answers so as not to come across as uneducated or socially inferior because of their preference for tabloids was difficult to avoid. Where possible, an attempt was made to minimize the impact of these differentials by setting up the focus groups with the help of an intermediary who would also form part of the group. This intermediary was asked to approach potential focus group members who would feel comfortable in each other's company (after establishing the general parameters regarding the composition of the group, such as age and gender) and invite them to participate. These intermediaries also attended the focus groups as participant-observers (in Limpopo, the intermediary also translated the questions and responses into and from TshiVenda. Where interviews were conducted in Afrikaans, translations were done by the author).

Five focus groups in total were constructed using a combination of a convenience and purposive sample (Du Plooy 2001, 180). The groups consisted of seven to twelve participants of mixed gender.[5] Although a mixed-gender sample presents certain problems (ibid.), it was decided in the context of this study that a mixed group could elicit varied responses and bring to light gendered readings of tabloid content. Especially since the controversies regarding South African tabloids were in part related to gender issues, it was hoped that a mixed group would allow contesting gendered perspectives on these issues to emerge.

The groups were sampled in such a way that "they have shared some common experience, so that the interview focuses on the effects of the experience from the subjects' perspective" (ibid.) and because they "possess certain characteristics and are recruited to share a common quality or characteristic of interest to the researcher" (Wimmer and Dominick 2006, 129). Although it was recognized that tabloid readers occupy multiple identity positions, the sampling of focus groups sought to follow the market segmentation used by the media industry—that is, defining audiences in terms of their economic and demographic positions. To avoid treating the tabloid audience as a monolithic group, allowance was made for different demographics within the tabloid readership. The first demographic aspect was the geographic area where the different tabloids were distributed—the strongest concentration of readers of the *Kaapse Son/Cape Son* and *Daily Voice* was in the Western Cape province, and the *Daily Sun*'s in Gauteng. But further distinctions in terms of language, ethnicity, social class, and "race" also came into play to necessitate further distinctions among the readers of these various tabloids. For instance, two focus-group interviews were conducted in the Western Cape among readers of the *Kaapse Son/Cape Son* and the *Daily Voice,* one among working-class respondents in the peri-urban setting of Stellenbosch, a town approximately fifty kilometers from Cape Town, and one with a group consisting exclusively of Muslim readers (mostly urban professionals) in Rondebosch East, a suburb of Cape Town. The latter group was chosen because of the particular attention that tabloid editors and journalists in this province paid to avoid offending Muslim readers (through nudity and lewd content), to the extent that a special English-language version of *Son* was established in the Western Cape which excluded the notorious page-three girl for fear of offending Muslim readers (Koopman, pers. comm. 2007).[6]

In Gauteng province, two focus-group sessions were conducted with readers of the *Daily Sun,* one with farm workers in a peri-urban area of Tshwane and another with Black urban professionals working for a media-analysis company in the city of Tshwane. The aim in constructing these two different groups was to obtain responses from the two ends of the class spectrum that the tabloid attempts to address—on the one hand the poor, unemployed, or working class, and on the other young, socially mobile readers. It was assumed that, because in this case the second group consisted of professional university graduates working for a media-analysis company, they would be able to provide a contrasting perspective on tabloid content to that offered by the farm workers in the same larger geographic area whose lived experience differed quite substantially from theirs.

Lastly, a focus group was conducted in a deep rural area, Makhado in Limpopo, South Africa's northernmost province (on the border with Zimbabwe), among a group consisting of informal traders, manual laborers, and unemployed workers. The *Daily Sun* is also widely read in rural areas such as this one, and has correspondents in those areas. The assumption was that such a rural audience could contribute another important set of perspectives to those of the other focus groups, who were based in urban or peri-urban areas.

The focus-group work was designed following the type of study conducted by Bird (1998), which attempted to establish "how audiences actually view news, how they define it, and what they do with it" by asking questions such as:

> What kinds of stories do people find memorable? What do they do with them? How does an understanding of what readers and viewers actually do with news help us in understanding both the value and the dangers of the tabloidization trend? (ibid., 35–36)

In order to attach importance to the conceptual framework of the respondents themselves rather than impose pre-conceived theoretical categories on them, the approach followed could be described as an "ethnography of discourse," that is, "an analysis of talk about experience rather than an observation of experience itself" (Bird 1992, 111, citing John Fiske). Such an approach, while not a "classic" ethnography using fieldwork and observation, is still an attempt to "understand experience from the point of view of those involved" (ibid.). The aim of the interviews with tabloid readers, journalists, and editors was to give them the opportunity to express their relationship with tabloids, the way they incorporate the production and consumption of tabloids into their lives, and how their production and consumption of tabloids are informed by their view of the media's role and their own place in post-apartheid society.

The following overarching research questions underlaid the focus group study:

1. Why do readers of a particular tabloid have a preference for this paper (as opposed to other tabloids or mainstream print media), and how is this preference related to their social position and experience?
2. What type of content succeeds best in capturing the readers' attention? What meanings do readers derive from this content and to what use are these meanings put in their lives? Can tabloids function to construct a form of community (Gripsrud 2000, 299)?
3. What reading strategies are used by tabloid audiences when incorporating tabloid content into their everyday lives? Can any strategies of subversion or transgression of dominant cultural, social, or political norms be noted? How do readers use information for guidance and to help them cope with their everyday lives, marked as they are by the "uncertainties characteristic of modernity" (ibid., 297)? What entertainment or surveillance uses do the tabloids serve? Do the readings of tabloid media provided by these audiences suggest that the South African tabloid media can serve as "sites of cultural struggle, transgressive pleasures and media visibility for ordinary people and common culture" (Biressi and Nunn 2008, 10)?
4. Can the tabloids help readers make sense of the social, economic, and political conditions in post-apartheid South African society and enable them to exercise their roles as citizens and engage in political or public life not only as spectators but also as participants (see Lewis, Inthorn, and Wahl-Jorgensen 2005, 8)—a function not often associated with the consumerist and entertainment-focused tabloid media (Biressi and Nunn 2008, 10)?

Based on these research questions, the specific discussion questions were formulated, but these questions were departed from when participants' responses provided clues or suggestions for different or further lines of inquiry (Wimmer and Dominick 2006, 129). These broad questions—which were elaborated on and contextualized for various focus groups—were as follows:

- Do you read a tabloid?
- Do you also read other newspapers?
- What other newspapers do you read? What other media do you use?
- Would you prefer a tabloid to other newspapers? Why/why not?
- What recent tabloid stories can you remember that stood out particularly?
- If you see someone reading a tabloid, what would your impression be of that person?
- Would you like to be seen reading a tabloid?

- Some people say that tabloids are bad, without morals, and sensationalist—what do you think?
- How often and where do you read a tabloid? Do you sometimes share someone else's copy?
- Has a tabloid helped you in your daily life? If so, what information did you use?
- What feeling are you left with after you have finished reading a tabloid—happy, relaxed, concerned, angry, etc.? Why?
- Is there something in the tabloid that you do not like?
- Is there something in the tabloid that offends your religious or moral feelings?
- What do you think about the use of language in the tabloids?

Readers on Reading the Tabloids

Responses from tabloid readers were grouped into several main categories, linked to the research questions above. In interpreting these responses, comparisons were made with similar audience studies among tabloid audiences elsewhere (mostly the United Kingdom and the United States) to see how the South African situation displayed similarities or differences with the cases noted in international scholarly literature.

On Media Preference and Choice

Tabloids in other regions of the world have been seen to provide an additional dimension to audiences' use of media like newspapers, magazines, or television rather than to replace other media (Bird 1992, 137). This was also found to be the case among some South African tabloid readers, although there was no uniform pattern throughout. In some cases, it was the visuality of the tabloid medium that made it stand out, as in the case of a group of farm workers who indicated that while they also read the *Sowetan* and *Sunday Sun,* they prefer the *Daily Sun* because "it has more pictures than the *Sowetan*."

For some Afrikaans readers, reading the news in their own language seemed to be the deciding factor in choosing to consume tabloids, more than the style used in these papers. For readers in Stellenbosch, a town where Afrikaans is dominant, *Son* added to the range of media available in this language. Language, rather than genre, seemed to be the deciding factor for members of this group, who read *Son* alongside popular magazines like *Huisgenoot,* the elite newspaper *Die Burger* and the local newspaper *Eikestadnuus,* but not the other Cape Town–based tabloid *The Daily Voice.* Not only was it important that *Son* is published in Afrikaans, but also that it uses the linguistic variant spoken among Black speakers of the language ("Coloureds" in apartheid nomenclature). While this group constitutes the majority of the Afrikaans language community, their linguistic variant was excluded from the "standard" version of the language that was formalized in discourses of Afrikaner nationalism and apartheid. Social capital still attaches to the "White" variant of the language, which still dominates the elite media. The "bastardised language" used in the tabloids has been cause for criticism from media academics (Rabe 2007, 31):

> The fact that the tabloids use a bastardised language—please note—not creolised—can also be seen as racist. South African poor whites in the 1930s were elevated from their socio-economic situation by aspirational reading offered by Naspers (which owns Media24), a company which at that time published mainly for white Afrikaners. The question needs to be, why then give poor coloured people sleaze to read—in a language worse than they themselves are speaking?

The type of language used in the Afrikaans tabloids provided some cause for debate among the reader respondents. While respondents in the peri-urban setting of Stellenbosch enjoyed the fact that *Son* "speaks Afrikaans the way that we speak Afrikaans" (as one respondent put it) and cited this as one of the main reasons for their preference of Afrikaans tabloids rather than the Afrikaans "quality paper" *Die Burger,* the responses from the urban-based group in Cape Town differed somewhat. The respondents in the latter group were more comfortable in switching between Afrikaans and English (and also did so during the interviews), and read both the English and Afrikaans tabloids as a substitute for the English-language broadsheet the *Argus* that had been the print medium of choice before the tabloids arrived. In this case, tabloid content rather than language was the deciding factor in reader preference, as respondents noted:

> The *Son* brings us news that the *Argus* doesn't, especially as concerns the Coloured community.

> Bigger newspapers [broadsheets] are more concerned with world news [than the tabloids, which focused on local news].

> *Son* and *Voice* cover sports, especially soccer, better than broadsheets. They have more local sport than the *Argus.*

Although language was not the deciding factor in this urban group of readers, a discussion did ensue about the language politics of the tabloids. When one member of the group pointed out that the tabloids' attempt at colloquial language was not convincing, others responded by debating the merits of using colloquial language in print:

> F: The language in Afrikaans tabloids is not convincing. This is how the *skollies* [thugs] speak. I grew up there [on the Cape Flats], if I go there now, people change the way they talk to me because I am educated.
> A: *Son's* Afrikaans is more informal, what we call "Kitchen Afrikaans." This is how people talk to each other, but it is going to affect the way children learn the language, their language standards are going to drop.
> N: But what is wrong with speaking like that? Who says that's the correct Afrikaans? That's your identity, that's the way you speak. Why do you have to speak like the Whitey speaks, because he speaks the "proper" Afrikaans? That is the language that the White man created for himself. They brainwashed you

all these years. That is how the White person wants you to believe it should be spoken.

A: But then they are going to associate you with a certain stigma. There is still a stigma associated with Coloured Afrikaans.

The above conversation reflects how cultural identities in post-apartheid South Africa are shifting and are articulated through media.[7] More media-savvy readers (what Bird 1992, 116 refers to as the "self-conscious reader") of tabloids viewed the attempt to produce tabloid content in a marginalized variant of the language (albeit spoken by the majority) as a cynical commercial ploy, a "vernacular ventriloquism" (Conboy 2006, 14) aimed at creating a rapport with a target market.[8] At the same time there was also an acceptance of this strategy as a way to reclaim the linguistic variant from the elite, even while social capital is still attached to the "standard" variant.

A similar ambivalent preference for an indigenous language was also noted in audience responses to the *Daily Sun* recorded in the rural town of Makhado. Here, the use of English was seen as a missed opportunity for the *Daily Sun* to serve as a marker of local identity and to facilitate communication among members of a language community. Yet at the same time, the benefits derived from the social capital associated with English were also recognized. Readers remarked that while the *Daily Sun* covered stories directly relevant to their lives and had a strong local focus, the fact that tabloid content was produced in English put some distance between them and the paper.

One respondent stated it in terms of what was seen as the tabloid's utilitarian value in local communities: "If the *Daily Sun* could be in local languages, more people would understand it, and the newspaper would help more people." This localized view of language is in sharp contrast to that of the *Daily Sun*'s publisher, Deon du Plessis, who, in response to my question on why his tabloid uses only English and no indigenous languages, asserted (pers. comm. 2007) the language's role in facilitating social mobility within the capitalist economy:

> It's what we have in common. English is the language people want to learn. There's not a single mom and dad in this country who want their children go out speaking Northern Sotho. That's what you speak at home. They're not dumb, they know you don't have a chance in hell in the world if you don't speak English. No, this whole language thing is bullshit. English is a combining factor. There's no longer an argument, English has won.

Du Plessis' comments seem to link his paper—which also publishes regular language tips in a feature called "Speaking English"—with the emergence of new consumer-based identities in post-apartheid South Africa, stimulated by a market-led economy and the dominance of neoliberal discourses. For the working class and the unemployed poor in rural Makhado, however, this promise of social mobility remarked upon by Du Plessis might be so elusive or alien to their everyday experience that using an indigenous language in tabloids would be more useful as a communication tool in an environment that is literally miles—and in some ways a world—away from the urban capitalist economy, with its lingua franca of English, that Du Plessis might have had in mind.[9] An unspoken implication of publishing the *Daily Sun* in an indigenous language would be that the control Du Plessis and his White sub-editors wield over the final presentation of the content (Du Plessis himself frequently rewrites front-page copy and the banner headline) would be diminished. At the *Son* this is not the case, as the paper's editor, Andrew Koopman, has Afrikaans as his first language.

In the way South African readers compared tabloids with other media, they displayed the opposite reading strategy than that noted in, for instance, the case of the UK *Sun* (Pursehouse 2008, 288). Where readers in the latter context judged tabloid coverage by the standard of mainstream television news (BBC and ITV),[10] which they saw as "truer" reports that gave the news to you "straight," tabloid readers in South Africa seemed to trust tabloids more than they did mainstream news. While respondents often indicated that they also read other newspapers, they pointed out that they did not get from those papers what they wanted. There was a widespread preference for tabloids because they were seen as not hiding anything, or because they paid attention to matters relevant to readers' lived experience that had been neglected by mainstream newspapers.

A reader in Makhado summed it up thus: "The *Daily Sun* gives us the full view, everything is covered, there are no secrets. The *Sowetan* only gives a summary. The *Daily Sun* stays with a story and tells us everything." This "staying with a story," more typical of the long-term engagement with community issues associated with civic or public journalism than of the conventional, event-based journalism of commercial media, is an important aspect that sets the South African tabloids apart from their "quality press" counterparts. This indication of community involvement leads readers to reciprocate with a remarkable level of trust in the tabloids. Another respondent in the Makhado group pointed out the local focus of the tabloids as opposed to elite newspapers: "Newspapers like the *Citizen* cover things that happen in the metropolitan areas. The *Daily Sun* covers what is happening in this [part of the] country." The only group that did not seem to trust tabloids more than mainstream papers was a group of young, Black urban professionals who, working as media analysts for a media-analysis company, were exposed to a wide range of media and whose choices were informed by their social mobility.

Where participants mentioned television viewing, it was mostly in terms of entertainment or diversion (similar to the reaction of *Sun* readers in Pursehouse [2008]). Sometimes a link was made between reading the tabloid and watching a soap opera on television: "*Son* is like a soap opera. If I get home after having read it, I am ready to go watch television" (female respondent, Stellenbosch focus group). This link between the narrative style of both the tabloids and television soap operas is also borne out by the editor of *Son* (Koopman, pers. comm. 2007), who likened his paper's coverage of a murder trial to that of the soap *Days of Our Lives*.

Tabloids as Companions and Facilitators of Sociability and Social Mobility

Tabloids and other popular media have been known to provide a form of "daily companionship" (Pursehouse 2008, 290; Griffen-Foley 2008, 304) for their readers. For readers, the tabloids become like acquaintances, members of their social circle that provide points of reference for social interaction. In his study of tabloid newspapers in Britain, Conboy (2006) reflected on how tabloids in that country could "construct a community through language." This construction takes place through narratives that reinforce boundaries between insiders and outsiders, often identified in terms of race and ethnicity, with xenophobia as an extreme form of prejudice against outsiders (ibid., 94). While Conboy's study of tabloid discourse points toward a nationalistic discourse, Gripsrud (2000, 299) also sees the positive potential in tabloids creating "some minimal sort of community, an elementary sense of shared conditions and a shared agenda." Conboy sees the "idealization of community" (2006, 10) as textualized, taking place through the rhetorical patterns deployed by tabloids. Gripsrud's view of the community-building potential of tabloid newspapers is based on a ritual perspective of the role of journalism in society. This perspective

> regards media communication primarily as modern society's communication with itself about itself, in ways that reproduce and instill in all its members a sense of community and identity, of shared conditions, values, understandings, and so on. The media are storytellers, reiterating stories that, like ancient myths, serve as ways of thinking about existential and social matters individuals and groups have to deal with in their everyday lives. (Gripsrud 2000, 295)

From this perspective, the information conveyed by media is not as important as the way that media consumption of a repetitive repertoire of story categories (identified by John Langer [1998] as those about the especially remarkable, victims, communities at risk, ritual, tradition, and the past that produce "politics, pleasure, and other spin-offs") forms part of a daily routine. Bird (1992, 199) draws a link between tabloid media and folkloric communication, both processes "during which narratives are constructed from familiar themes that repeat themselves over time." Elsewhere, Bird (1998, 37) views tabloid news as part of people's daily lives, becoming a topic for conversation and speculation. Tabloid content is made relevant to people's own lives, and as people speculate on the meaning of tabloid stories, they draw upon their own experiences (ibid., 40). The important aspect of this interpretation of tabloid content from the point of view of readers' own lives is that they involve others in this process—reading tabloids and speculating about their meaning becomes a *participatory activity* (Bird 1992, 41), thus creating a sense of community among tabloid readers. An "imaginary relationship" (Johansson 2007, 96) (similar to the imagined community envisaged by Anderson, 1983) between tabloids and their readers is formed, a relationship which tabloids constantly remind their readers of.

In the case of tabloids in the United Kingdom and the United States, this companionship and sociability are often associated with celebrity news. Gossip about celebrity love affairs, scandals, and their glamorous lifestyles provides a source of amusement but also forms part of the social negotiation of moral norms, as Johansson (ibid., 142) indicates with reference to UK tabloids like the *Sun* and the *Daily Mirror*. The difference between the glamorous lives of celebrities and the daily slog of tabloid readers provides an opportunity to indulge in fantasy even as it reminds them of their own, much harsher, circumstances and "exclusion from the symbolic social centre of the media" (ibid., 144, 145). This comparison also provides readers with the opportunity to pass moral judgment on celebrities.

In African contexts, the sense of community created through media consumption often is the result of the sharing of limited resources. The communal or collective use of media in African societies occurs in varying levels and forms across media platforms. Examples of such media sharing elsewhere in Africa include passing on or even selling second-hand copies of newspapers after they've been read, "renting" a paper, photocopying articles (Frère 2007, 47), or retrieving information from the internet via intermediaries who have access to the web (see Wasserman and Kabeya-Mwepu 2005; cf. Nyamnjoh 2005).[11] Jennifer Hasty's (2005, 1) description of the "collective exercise of interpretation" of Ghanaian newspapers resonates with the social practices around South African tabloids as they emerged from the audience interviews that will be reported on in more detail in the rest of the chapter. Hasty illustrates the social discourse around news in Ghana as follows:

> At neighbourhood markets and most major intersections, crowds gather every morning and afternoon to peruse and compare the lead stories of all the newspapers currently for sale, hung in a vibrant collage across the frames of the wooden kiosks that sell them. Top stories from the major newspapers are reported on and analyzed on the morning shows of many television and radio stations. People who buy newspapers often read out the stories to those around them, punctuating the news with their own editorial comments, drawing their listeners into the collective exercise of interpretation. Once read, a paper is never thrown away but passed around for others to read, reaching as many as ten readers who may relay that news to a network of hundreds. Whether you walk, take a taxi, or ride the bus to work, someone around you is reading, listening, or discussing the news, usually adding context and commentary and inviting your own participation.

One can find similarities between Hasty's description of the social practices of news consumption in Ghana and the way news enters the public discourse in South Africa. In South Africa, news headlines are also often reported on in radio bulletins, and newspaper reports often find their way into private conversations and public debates. A key difference between the situation in Ghana as described by Hasty and the picture emerging from interviews with South African tabloid readers is how the social practice of collective newspaper interpretation in South Africa differs across newspaper types and according to social position. The type of newspapers that receive recognition in other mainstream media in South Africa (e.g., television or radio talk shows) is usually the elite broadsheets, and tabloid reports mostly only enter public debate in other media when they are being criticized. The collective interpretation of newspaper news in the mediated public sphere is therefore largely limited to broadsheets. However, from the responses by South African tabloid readers, it becomes clear that the second type of collective interpretation of newspapers is evident in the way tabloid readers interact with each other and with the medium. Through the passing on or sharing of newspapers, the discussion of tabloid stories in social circles, and the creation of rumor and gossip around tabloid news, South African tabloid readers are involved in forming interpretive communities outside the mainstream.

In the case of South African tabloids, both sociability and social mobility seem to form an important part of reader preference for and interaction with tabloids. Conversations with readers revealed similarities between their reading habits and those displayed by tabloid readers in other international settings. However, as with other aspects of the South African context, these are similarities rather than direct comparisons. The close relationship and sense of companionship between South African tabloids and their readers is predicated upon conditions in these communities. All the South African tabloids run projects involving the community. For instance, both the *Daily Voice* and the *Son* are involved with anti-"tik" (methamphetamine) campaigns in the Western Cape. The papers offer services for readers to deal with household problems like leaking roofs or broken toilets—the *Daily Sun* has "Mr Fixit," whose services can be requested by readers, and the *Daily Voice*'s "Captain Voice Power" coordinates donations from readers to members of communities struck by tragedies like fires or floods.

But the South African tabloids also provide entertainment and diversion from daily struggles, serving as a form of entertainment that can be enjoyed in interaction with others—a way to strengthen social bonds and create feelings of belonging connectedness with fellow tabloid readers (as noted by Johansson 2007, 148–149 in the UK context). Reading the paper formed part of readers' daily routines, usually as a means to share leisure time with others or to escape the drudgery of work, as a farm worker in Bronberg described: "When I finish my day job, I get the time to read the *Sun*." A Makhado respondent described how the companionship provided by the tabloids can come at a price, but is important enough to make sacrifices for: "Even though I am unemployed I sell empty bottles to buy the *Daily Sun*—I read it every day." Several respondents described reading the tabloids on their way to or from work in the car, on the train, or in a taxi. These spaces create the opportunity for tabloids to facilitate social interaction through shared or simultaneous consumption of the paper:

People often share the *Son*—we will divide the pages between ourselves. If I get home, someone will ask me if I bought the *Son*, or in a taxi on the way home, I will be sitting reading the *Son* and then someone will shout from behind "give it here quick, let me see!" (respondent, Stellenbosch)

Sometimes five of us will be sitting in one car and everyone will be reading his own copy of the *Daily Sun*, because we don't want to wait until the others are finished before we can read it. (respondent, Bronberg farm)

In Makhado, respondents also indicated that reading tabloids was a socializing process. Moreover, tabloids not only provided the opportunity to socialize with other members of a community; they also provided the social capital needed for mobility within that community. The social-mobility function of tabloids has been remarked upon by scholars researching British tabloids. Johannson (2007, 144–145), also citing the work of Nick Couldry (2003) on media rituals, again points to the importance of celebrity culture in British tabloids to create the "hope of social mobility and self-transformation." Langer (1998, 45, 151) sees the typical tabloid story on "especially remarkable" people as holding out the hope to tabloid readers that although social inequality is inevitable—and therefore the political-economic system has to be consented to—"individuals of talent and ability can, with effort and determination, rise above their circumstances" (ibid., 151). Some South Africans buy tabloids for the social capital they provide, even if they are unable to read them. This process was explained by two respondents in Makhado:

> Some people can't read but they look at the pictures and pretend they're reading, or they memorize what other people have said about the news. They think that being seen reading the *Daily Sun* will make them look decent, not like a *tsotsi* [thug]. It makes them look important, educated, like someone with status in the community.

> The elderly will take their copy to their children to read it for them and explain the pictures to them.

The social capital provided by the *Daily Sun* was also remarked upon by a respondent in the Bronberg farm group:

> [Reading the *Daily Sun*] makes us look like someone who wants to increase their knowledge.

But this social capital was closely linked to certain social contexts (or what Bourdieu would refer to as "habitus"). While reading the tabloids can signify upward mobility for some, it can stymie social mobility for others who have already accumulated a measure of social capital. Consider these responses from young urban professionals in the Tshwane group:

> I sometimes feel that it [reading the tabloids] degrades me. I buy the *Daily Sun* every day for the [media-analysis] company [I work for]. When I am traveling from where I come from, in the location [township], it is not a problem to be seen with a *Daily Sun*, but if I pass through the suburbs I don't want to be seen with it, because the quality is low.

> When I was a student, I found *Daily Sun* interesting, but as you grow you start wanting other newspapers like *City Press, Sunday Times*. I now want more opinion. I don't identify with it anymore. People who are a bit learned see it as something for people who are a bit illiterate.

The responses in the focus groups suggest that a sense of belonging to a tabloid community is created on the level of *content* and *ritual*. The tabloid *content* strikes a chord with readers' lived experience and interprets the world from a perspective familiar to them. This creates a sense of trust and identification between readers and the papers, as if the tabloids hear their complaints and speak on their behalf. Crucially, the tabloids do not speak down to their readers, but limit the distance between themselves and their readers. Because tabloid content reflects the concerns and interests of readers, it creates a sense of proximity between readers and tabloids—more so than the elite media, whose agendas might be experienced by tabloid readers as being far removed from their own.

Concerning ritual communication, the responses from the focus groups made it clear that the tabloids function as a focus point for conversation, interaction, and participation among members of the reader community. Reading the paper and sharing its stories enabled a sociability among its readers and contributed to social cohesion. Respondents sometimes alluded to a sense of feeling left out or forgotten in post-apartheid society, where they remained on the margins, and said that forming part of a community of tabloid readers countered that sense of alienation. This sociability was primarily marked in terms of ethnicity and class, because tabloids validate the experiences of those sectors of society that have been marginalized historically precisely on those grounds. However, the interactivity and cohesion created among members of the tabloid reading community also mapped onto geographic spaces. Readers remarked that tabloids created links between people living in different areas or neighborhoods. These spaces are still marked by the fragmentation and polarization caused by apartheid (e.g., the Group Areas Act, which dictated where people were allowed to live according to their "race"), as can be seen in the response from the young Black professional who contrasted his life in the township with his work in the suburb.

Many respondents remarked on the tabloids' focus on local news, and were drawn to these papers because of this focus. But tabloids also contributed to social cohesion by creating topics for discussion among readers. One respondent in Stellenbosch remarked, "I live in Eerste River, and if I see something in *Son* [that happened here in Stellenbosch], I would ask people if they know the people reported on in the story."

In this focus group, it also became evident that tabloid stories served as a way for the respondents to connect and bond across neighborhoods. Respondents shared stories, asked each other if they remembered a particular story, reminded each other of aspects of these stories and had a laugh about them among themselves. These responses seemed to support Bird's (1998, 44) observation, albeit in a society marked by different historical circumstances underlying social ties:

> The conversations that viewers and readers have about news stories serve to bind people together, and given [sic] them common topics of conversation in a world in which common ties are getting fewer and fewer. News stories of scandals . . . offer an entry point to everyday discussions of morality, boundaries and appropriate behaviour.

Talking about tabloid content can also help readers to connect tabloid stories with their everyday lives. Stories about scandals have proven to be especially popular for such post-reading gossip (Pursehouse 2008, 291): "The *Sunday Sun* is for if you want to gossip with your friends, to say 'look at what somebody did'" (respondent, Tshwane). Familiarity and sociability were also created by the character of Antie Mona (a pun on "moaning," i.e., complaining), a typical "agony aunt," to whom readers could send queries and complaints. The *Son*'s agony aunt was described by a respondent in Stellenbosch as "like someone you know well," while for a respondent on Bronberg farm, the *Daily Sun* even seemed to function (potentially, at least) as an extension of the family: "If my family saw that I was missing they would tell the *Daily Sun*. The *Daily Sun* would then publish the information in the paper, and people who know where I am working will call my family so they can find me." For another respondent, the information provided by the tabloid enabled her to fulfill her own role within the family, but clearly also served a normative moral function:

> *Son* warns us about what is going on in the world. It warns us to keep our children safe. I see things happening like rape, then I tell my daughter "look, this is what is going to happen if you are on the streets late at night." I like reading the stories about Tik [methamphetamine]—I show it to my children and warn them about the dangers. (respondent, Stellenbosch)

While the act of reading tabloids can itself take the form of collaboration or social interaction, their contribution to social cohesion probably occurs mostly because these papers covers news that is relevant to readers' lives. Recognizable news confirms their identities and validates their membership in a community. This function was summarized in an exchange between two members of the group of urban professionals in Tshwane. These respondents have both managed to "move on" from township life to the city. They reflect upon their reasons for not identifying with tabloids anymore, while at the same time recognizing why some readers still would:

> A: Stories that are important to people in the townships are like "looking for my child's head," or trainsurfing.[12] I don't find those stories interesting.
> B: But you know, if you're living in Soweto, and you've lost a brother, somebody you know, you are likely to pay more attention to it because you know more about it. In every story there's an element . . . media has to do with identity. The fact that a story like that is printed is because for somebody it means something.

The downside of creating a community of tabloid readers is that this community is often constructed in opposition to an Other. For tabloid readers, who find themselves at the bottom of the socio-economic ladder, groups like foreign nationals or gays can be preyed upon as more vulnerable groups than themselves in order to prop up their communal identity. The responses in the focus-group discussions seem to confirm the accusations (e.g., Roberts 2007) leveled against South African tabloids that they (similar to their UK and U.S. counterparts, see Conboy 2005; Hogshire 1996, 64) foster an exclusive nationalism. (Media commentators have pointed out that xenophobia has been a worrying tendency among all media in the country, however, not only tabloids.)[13]

On News, Information, and Citizenship

While the popular press internationally is often associated with "laughter and the lighter side of life" (which can also be subversive—Conboy 2008a, 113) and with entertainment and diversion (cf. Pursehouse 2008), South African tabloids are, for the most part, taken very seriously by their readers. The overwhelming response from South African tabloid readers was that they trusted the tabloids to bring them reliable information and up-to-date news that that enables them to negotiate the sometimes harsh and precarious conditions of everyday life:

We read [in the tabloids] about murders, drugs, baby rapes—things that happen every day. The other newspapers don't give enough attention to those problems. Drugs is a big problem here on the Cape Flats. The small newspapers [tabloids] spell it out for you: this is the problem, what is the government doing about it. The big newspapers don't have many stories about it. (respondent, Rondebosch East)

These are things that happen to us, man. (These are) people that live our type of lives. (respondent, Rondebosch East)

Readers trust the tabloids to provide them with detailed news that keeps them informed, but also makes them feel connected to larger society. Surveillance of society leads to empathy and identification with members of a community. A Bronberg farm worker responded that reading about crimes like rape and murder in the *Daily Sun* made him "feel sad, because I think how I would feel if something like that happened to me. But I read it because I know what goes on in the world." By providing this socially connective tissue, the South African tabloids, similar to their counterparts elsewhere, contribute to a "shared idealization of community," a sphere for the exchange of ideas and opinion that, unlike the Habermasian version of the public sphere, is constructed through ritualized, shared experiences of everyday life rather than abstract, rational debate about social issues (Conboy 2006, 10). Tabloid readers also seem to experience that they are being addressed as citizens, as members of a larger community or even of a nation. These comments resonate with Benedict Anderson's (1987) views on the role of print media in the construction of an "imagined community." The fact that the reconstruction of citizenship and nationhood—even when limited to the civic dimensions of everyday life—is facilitated by the highly commercial enterprises of tabloid newspapers supports his foregrounding of "print capitalism" as a foundation of the modern nation. As members of this imagined community, tabloid readers are compelled to reciprocate by performing their roles as citizens in the social compact:

My boyfriend was kidnapped a while ago. The detectives told him to approach the *Son* so that everyone can become aware of the danger—they had to be on the lookout for a red car that came from Mitchells Plain. He phoned *Son* and they came to his house personally, they reported on it and took his photo. So he was very happy. (respondent, Stellenbosch)

If there was something that happened in my community, something that I wanted the world to know—something like child molestation—I would phone *Son*. (respondent, Stellenbosch)

These responses indicate a level of trust in the tabloids that one might expect to be reserved for public institutions like the police, the courts, and the government. Readers' claims that they would phone the tabloids with matters concerning crime and/or social evils confirm tabloid editors' remarks that readers would call them before they would call the police—resulting in tabloid reporters often arriving at crime scenes well before the authorities would.

While the function of community surveillance and information about society might be taken for granted as a minimum requirement of democratic media, it must be remembered that in the post-apartheid context, the fulfilling of these functions by tabloid papers constitutes the *restoration* of a notion of citizenship that the majority was deprived of under apartheid. This reconstruction of citizenship is of central importance to the country's continued democratic transition, seeing as the experience of marginalization is still very real in post-apartheid South Africa. As Von Lieres (2005, 23) explains,

> In contemporary South Africa the introduction of democratic political arrangements has gone hand in hand with the unmasking of widespread marginalization. While the majority of people's legal status is assured, their experience of citizenship remains ambiguous. They continue to be excluded from economic equality and empowerment and effective, democratic participation in the public sphere. If the South African case is emblematic of anything, it is the intertwining of democracy and marginalization in contemporary life.

The fact that tabloids have contributed to the restoration of a civic presence for their readers also means that these readers can lay claim to civic privileges and hold officialdom accountable. As such, tabloids have provided what they experience as a crucial link between themselves as citizens and a government who still seems absent from their daily lives:

> One thing that the Baby Jordan story does, is it focuses a lot of attention on the police force, so that they can do their job properly.[14] Whereas in the past, none of this would have [come out]. (respondent, Rondebosch East)

> There are people that do not even know who is their ward councillor. The average Joe on the street wants to know what is happening. To whom do they complain. Say there are potholes in the street, they don't know who they should complain to, so they complain to the newspaper. (respondent, Rondebosch East)

> The *Daily Sun* addresses issues like the home affairs department, struggles to get ID books. The *Daily Sun* mediates between people and the government. (respondent, Makhado)

The last comment pertains to the widespread struggle for people to obtain an identity document, as described in chapter 5. Although it seems that tabloids presume that their readers are the "rights-bearing individual inscribed in the new Constitution (Comaroff and Comaroff 2005, 34) with a right to be acknowledged as such, it is less clear if and how they allow for a contestation of this identity from other perspectives of belonging. As Comaroff and Comaroff (ibid., 35, cf. Mamdani 1996) remind us, identity in postcolonial settings is often a site of contestation between citizenship and "policulturalism," where "various sorts of identity struggle to express themselves in the politics of everyday life."

Being addressed as citizens also entailed being in a position to make claims to government services. Readers in a focus group in the rural town of Makhado felt that while the *Daily Sun* did important work to keep government accountable, it still tended to focus on Gauteng province and neglected problems in rural areas. They listed a number of issues which they would like the *Daily Sun* to bring to the attention of government:

> The police do not do their job properly. There have been muti [traditional medicine, for which body parts are sometimes used as ingredients] killings where nobody has been arrested even if they know who it is. The *Sun* should write about that.

> A lot of the villages around here do not have electricity and water. That's why it is important that the *Daily Sun* does stories on social delivery. Some areas here go for three weeks or sometimes even three months without water. People sometimes have to hike for miles to get to an area where there is water. We get no response from the authorities when we complain. We don't know where to go to speak to the government. The *Daily Sun* should tell Mbeki that we were told we would get houses, but there's nothing.

> The *Daily Sun* should write stories about crime on trains and unemployment.

> Jobs should be created, and the *Sun* should expose that.

The group of farm workers outside Tshwane conveyed a similar wish list, connecting demands for the *Daily Sun* to pay attention to everyday living conditions with an unlikely nostalgia for the apartheid past:

> When I came here 20 years ago the old government used to fix the road. But since there is a new government and new ward councillors, the roads are no longer fixed. That kind of politics is what I want to read about. The *Daily Sun* does not do enough stories about this. The *Daily Sun* does not come here to our place to do these stories.

> I would phone the *Daily Sun* to come, they should come here and look at how we live—the condition of the roads, the crime, the working hours, the pay.

While tabloids are often seen as apolitical, the avoidance of formal politics can also be read as an indication of readers' alienation from mainstream politics because of its irrelevance to them. This theoretical point, made by critics such as John Fiske and Colin Sparks, has also been borne out in interviews with tabloid readers in the United Kingdom (Pursehouse 2008, 293) and the United States (Bird 1992, 130). While it could be argued that South African tabloids do provide conventional political coverage (the election of Jacob Zuma as ANC president being a case in point, as discussed in chapter 5), the sense of alienation from mainstream politics as it is covered in the elite press can also be seen in the responses from South African tabloid readers. This does not necessarily indicate a lack of interest in politics or the absence of a political position, but rather a disillusionment related to elite agenda setting by the mainstream press. The tabloids seem to validate their readers' view that the powerful can get away with anything and that different rules apply to them—as one respondent in Stellenbosch remarked with reference to the *Son*'s coverage of Jacob Zuma's rape trial:

> *Son* said he had to be punished. If it was somebody else, not as high up in the ANC, he would've been punished. It's true what they say—if you have a lot of money, you get things done. If you have a little money, you don't get anything done.

Surveillance of the powerful also takes on a political dimension when tabloid readers engage with stories like the government abuse of tax money, cover-ups or corruption (ibid., 128ff.). One respondent in Makhado complained, for instance, that "there is government corruption, they are filling their pockets and do not care whether other people have enough food."

The sense of powerlessness or alienation from the mainstream that tabloid readers experience, linked to their class position in society, gives them a preference for the type of story where the underdog has proven victorious, where fate and luck smiled upon someone with whom they could identify (ibid., 125), as a Makhado respondent described: "When we see stories about women becoming prosperous, selling fruit, when we see successful women it inspires us." This response is also interesting considering that tabloids are often criticized for their stereotyping of women, a point that we will return to shortly.

Readers' sense of powerlessness can also lead them to derive pleasure from seeing members of the establishment elite, such as celebrities or politicians, falter and prove fallible (ibid., 125–126.) Such stories validate the reader's resistance, outrage, or anger against the powerful and the rich (ibid., 131). Even when stories provide an entertainment function, like the case of the Baby Jordan murder trial that the tabloids covered like a soap opera, they are interpreted by readers as proof that justice was served. In the Baby Jordan case, such interpretations went further than providing vicarious revenge, but also made readers feel that they were participants in the judicial process. This sense of participation reaffirmed the civic rights of the focus-group members, as expressed by a respondent in Stellenbosch:

> I buy the *Son* every day because I want to know what happens with a story. I want to follow a story from the beginning to the end, like the Baby Jordan story. . . . If I could have made a book with all the articles on the Baby Jordan murder right from the beginning up until the end, I would have done it. I keep the copies of the *Son* in which they cover the Baby Jordan trial. Because when the trial is finished, and they get sentenced, I want to go back to the story (from the beginning) and see if it is right, if they got the punishment they deserved for all the things they did.

In summary, the South African tabloids, with their focus on social-delivery issues and the relationship of trust that they have established with their readers, have created a platform where readers can vent their feelings of marginalization. Whether this articulation of disillusionment will translate into political mobilization or instead act to defuse mounting political pressure on the government is yet to be seen. An ironic outcome of these stories might be that they serve to create consent that the current political arrangement is inevitable, yet flawed,[15] prompting readers to seek "correction" of the symptomatic flaws rather than engaging with the structural root causes.

On Negotiating Truth within the Reality of Everyday Life

In South Africa, academic and journalistic responses to tabloids have often focused on the truthfulness (or rather the perceived lack thereof) in the tabloids (e.g., Krüger 2006). Some critics (like the editor of the influential *Sunday Times,* Mondli Makhanya) have considered the possibility that readers do not believe everything they read in tabloids, but saw this disbelief as an indictment against the untrustworthy tabloids (ibid., 31). Belief in the truthfulness of stories is, however, a "more subtle and complex" (Bird 1992, 122) matter than journalistic debates often allow for.

Conventional approaches to the relationship between journalism and audiences tend to think of the interaction as a process of transmission of information and facts. A different approach would be to measure the validity of tabloid content not by how well it conveys certain facts, but by the position and status these stories occupy in people's lives, becoming, as Bird (1998, 37) describes, "the subjects of speculation and discussion."

Such stories, usually dramatic or personalized views of events, in the form of chronological narrative with a moral lesson, take on a life of their own and are remembered and retold in other contexts (ibid.):

> While journalists and media critics wring their hands because the public "needs" to be informed and is apparently perversely resisting this need, people themselves say, "why do I need to know this; what difference does it make to *my* life?" (ibid., 40)

Another perspective on readers' disbelief would be to acknowledge that readers engage in a process of discernment to assess stories' truthfulness, based on their own experiences, or that they offer negotiated and oppositional readings of stories that they find dubious. Stories that they doubt to be true could be read in an ironic or playful fashion as entertainment or diversion, bearing in mind the nature of the genre (Bird 1992, 122; Pursehouse 2008, 289). While making judgments about the credibility of tabloid content can be a source of pleasure (Pursehouse 2008, 290), it can also provide a sense of empowerment. An ironic or playful reading of tabloids is more likely among those readers that come to tabloids as occasional readers, who self-consciously engage with tabloids primarily for amusement or entertainment (Bird 1992, 124). The following comment was offered by a Rondebosch East focus group participant who works as a journalist:

> Reporters can't just write lies, a newspaper doesn't work like that. They can just report what someone told them. If they say there was a tokoloshe [mischievous, dwarf-like mythical figure] on the roof, it means someone phoned in and told them they saw a tokoloshe on the roof.

But this skepticism can also be related to an awareness of the commercial nature of the media industry, even among outsiders. A respondent working on Bronberg farm outside Tshwane said, "People lie to the *Daily Sun*. They tell them stories so they will pay you, even if it is a lie."

Devoted tabloid readers, although not gullible or passive receivers of news messages, are more like likely to trust tabloid stories as the truth. This is probably because of their closer relationship with the paper in terms of their daily routine, but also because it relates more closely to their life-worlds. The majority of the focus-group respondents did express their trust in tabloids to tell the truth. There were, however, a number of respondents who indicated that they allow for a degree of fabrication on the part of the tabloids and that, in fact, they enjoyed not having to take all stories at face value.

The power readers have to "play with definitions of reality" in order to gain a certain measure of control over news narratives (ibid., 123) was also noted among the South African tabloid readers with whom I spoke. When asked whether he believed everything he reads in the tabloids, a participant in the Rondebosch East focus group responded, "No! But that's the fun part of it. We know that the guy talking such a lot of nonsense in the paper only did it because he wanted his face or his name in the paper." The leisure function of negotiating truth (Purse-house 2008, 290) can also be seen clearly in this response from a member of the Bronberg farm group:

> There was a story in the paper about a man rising from his grave—I don't think it's true. If you're dead you are taken to a mortuary. This is made up just so we can buy the newspaper. But I will still read it—in fact I've read it twice to make sure I understand it. To me it was a bit like a movie. It was entertaining. The *Daily Sun* helps me to relax and keep my mind busy.

Respondents in Makhado distinguished between fabricated stories that were intended as entertainment and others that were to be read as factual accounts—and trusted the paper would correct mistakes in the latter type:

> Sometimes some of the stories are not real—but we take that as jokes. Sometimes the editor Themba Khumalo would apologize in the paper if they made a mistake. (respondent, Makhado)

One area in which this negotiation seemed to prove complex was in stories related to witchcraft and the supernatural. Readers from the Makhado group offered specific examples of stories where they seemed to have read between the lines to decide that witchcraft was involved.[16] When trying to understand South African tabloids as a phenomenon of post-apartheid society, the point is not so much whether all the stories contained in them are true, but whether readers believe they *could* be true (Griffen-Foley 2008, 309), and why this is the case. In other words, how does the belief that readers invest in tabloid stories relate to their experiences, and how do these experiences differ from those of the readers of the elite press? Furthermore, how do the discrepancies among various sets of experiences map onto the hierarchies and power imbalances in post-apartheid society? In the case of stories related to witchcraft, much reviled by mainstream commentators, one should ask how such stories relate to the precariousness of life in post-apartheid society and serve as an explanation for life events that seem beyond people's control. As Vincent (2007) argues, the appeal to culturally familiar frameworks such as magic to interpret everyday experience (or, in the context of reading tabloids, news events) should not be seen as a retreat into "tradition" or a remnant of a "dark and savage past," but as having to do with the conditions of the present. In post-apartheid South Africa, these conditions are marked by material inequality, desperate poverty, high crime rates, and an HIV/AIDS pandemic:

> South Africa's occult economy can thus be understood as an attempt to re-create a sense of orderliness and predictability in an unruly post-apartheid, late capitalist world of rapidly changing markers of identity, failed political expectations, massive economic deprivation amidst the sudden and conspicuous enrichment of the few, rampant criminality and the seemingly inexplicable rise in the death rate of once healthy adults. (Ibid.)

Judged from the point of view of mainstream South African journalism, with its high stake on values such as truth, accuracy, and verifiability (the first item in the South African press code reads, "The press shall be obliged to report news truthfully, accurately and fairly" [SA Press Council 2008]), news reports of supernatural events go against the grain of ethical and responsible journalism.[17]

Berger,[18] who has on several occasions accused the tabloids of eroding the credibility of South African journalism, is therefore correct in identifying the contradictory and competing professional value frameworks within which mainstream, elite media and the tabloids respectively operate. Berger remarked on the reluctant acceptance by the South African National Editors' Forum (SANEF) of tabloid editors within the ranks of the organization while reaffirming the organization's commitment to "journalistic integrity, tolerance and accountability" as a "two-handed, and potentially contradictory" move. He points to opposing views among editors on tabloid reporting of the supernatural as one area where the two genres might diverge strongly in terms of their views of truthfulness. While Berger admits that tabloid reports on the supernatural can be seen as "harmless fantasy and fun," similar to "astrology columns and news of the bizarre" in mainstream newspapers, the opposing view would be that "journalists have a responsibility to promote realism, not ignorance, and that they should balance myths with comments from professionals and scientists" (ibid.). Berger correctly recognizes that SANEF's position is at heart contradictory and untenable—it upholds in its Press Code an Enlightenment view of rational truth as based on facts and their correspondence with an external, observable reality, yet wants to acknowledge diversity and be an inclusive organization, and therefore had to extend membership to tabloid papers. This inclusionary stance does not, however, allow for the dominant journalistic paradigm to be challenged or altered under the influence of tabloid newspapers—it is, rather, a matter of tolerance and acceptance of journalistic difference (see chapter 4). In the long run, this double position might result in an impasse of either having to censure tabloids for contravening the notions of truth, accuracy, and privacy as they have come to be understood in the dominant normative discourse in the country (a discourse that largely mimics journalism ethics in Western liberal democracies; see Wasserman 2006a), or adapting the paradigm itself.

The *Daily Sun* justifies its reporting on the supernatural by restricting it to the realm of religious belief, and motivates its coverage by comparing it with the way mainstream media report on religion. The publisher of the *Daily Sun,* Deon du Plessis (pers. comm. 2007), therefore sees the supernatural and witchcraft as being to tabloid readers what Christian doctrine is to the readers of Afrikaans newspapers. Upon being asked how he would respond to critics who lambast tabloids for not verifying stories on "superstition or bestiality,"[19] Du Plessis responded as follows:

> My answer to that is the time we ran the story out of Bloemfontein of a chap that woke up in his bed on the roof. And all his neighbors said no that is to be understood, because a white horse had been seen there. And my answer would be, would you go down to Mangaung, go there, and you tell them they're talking shit. You tell them. And then I ask also, would he go to the *Hoë Kerk* [High Church] in Potchefstroom and tell them that their *Heilige Drieeenheid* [Holy Trinity] is all bullshit? (pers. comm. 2007)

Neither of three these positions—that the reporting on witchcraft and supernatural events in tabloids should be viewed as "harmless fun"; that it should be allowed in the name of inclusivity and diversity; or that it represents "a missed opportunity to contribute to communications in South African society"[20]—provides a satisfactory explanation of the role that such reporting plays in the lives of tabloid readers. Stories of the phantasmagoric and otherworldly are a well-known characteristic of popular culture in general and tabloids in particular, and are linked to the social function of popular media. As Glynn (2000, 143) points out:

> Popular culture has a long historical association with the fantastic, which is the "other" of the regime of truth established with the modernization of Western societies and the Westernization of modern societies. Their "otherness" largely constitutes the "unbelievability" of fantastic knowledges, which are often labeled "superstitious" and are primitivized and juvenilized in a variety of other ways. Fantastic knowledges can be understood as *evasive* ones, for they evade the explanatory powers of official truths that serve to extend the *social* power of dominant interests and alliances.

While stories about witchcraft and "other" knowledges can therefore be seen to conform to the genre-specific content of tabloids more generally, these stories should also be understood within the specificities of the South African context as a society undergoing transition. Reporting on witchcraft and the supernatural in South African tabloids should be understood as a form of symbolic mediation that is embedded within social, cultural, and economic conditions and that articulates particular lived experiences within this society. Viewed from this perspective, witchcraft and magic are neither seen as harmless, fun activities to be dabbled in as diversion, nor as simply religious beliefs or superstitions that fly in the face of rational thought. As Ashforth (2005, 3) has indicated, witchcraft in South African society forms part of a "complex set of relations that constitute the lived world of humanity." A dichotomy between modernity and traditional beliefs would fail to capture the ways in which Africans are "Africanizing their modernity and modernizing their Africanity" (Nyamnjoh in Wasserman 2009a, 287) through the use of media. While what Ashforth (ibid.) terms "spiritual insecurity" does have a religious dimension, it also has a *social* and a *material* dimension:

> Spiritual insecurity may be a universal feature of human life. It is related to, but not reducible to, other forms of insecurity such as poverty, violence, political oppression, and disease. It is not merely a form of benightedness that disappears with enlightenment and modernization. Nor is it simply a matter of belief that can be relegated to a distinct sphere of human concerns: religion. (Ibid.)

Viewing tabloids' reports on witchcraft from the point of view of tabloid readers—as has been the overarching aim of this chapter—means that they have to be understood as part of the multiple dimensions of lived experience in postapartheid South Africa. This experience is often one of "poverty, violence, and general hardship" and a "pervasive sense of social injustice" that makes the belief in evil forces plausible—even if such belief is sometimes combined with a measure of skepticism (ibid., 14, 17, 58). When residents of a Black township therefore tell the *Daily Sun* that their homes are haunted by the ghosts of dead White people ("mlungus") who occupied the area during the apartheid years when it was still farmland, it is not quite an adequate analysis that sees these tales as a combination of "racial fears with supernatural fears" as Goldstuck (2008) does. Nor is the reporting of these stories by the *Daily Sun* merely ruthless sensationalism that "plumbs the depths of human gullibility." Instead, one can see the relating of this tale of witchcraft in terms of the use of melodrama by tabloids (not only in the South African context) to enable readers to make sense of a modern society which to them is increasingly abstract and alien to their daily reality (Gripsrud 1992, 84, discussed in Johannson 2007, 46). What Goldstuck sees as "naked racism" (using the term "mlungu" to refer to Whites)[21] is more likely an attempt to understand the persisting marginalization and precarity experienced by many in the postapartheid democracy by drawing on the familiar explanatory framework of racially determined power relations which has been internalized by Black subjects after centuries of subordination.[22]

The result of the multi-dimensionality of witchcraft, Ashforth (2005, 11–12) shows, is that witchcraft cannot be "easily sequestered in the institutional categories—particularly those of politics, medicine, and religion—that are taken for granted in liberal democratic thought." It follows that it would be just as difficult to judge tabloid reports on witchcraft by using the evaluative apparatus of liberal democracy. This framework views the function of journalism primarily as that of a watchdog, acting as a conduit for verifiable information and facilitating rational deliberation.

Witchcraft would be seen from such a conventional journalistic perspective (grounded in assumptions about the media's role in rational deliberation in the

Habermasian public sphere) as a system of belief or superstition, and therefore the antithesis of the rational deliberative functions of journalism. Nevertheless, it would be possible to identify in witchcraft some of the same functions of social mediation that are usually associated with the mass media. In his discussion of witchcraft in another African country, Malawi, Harri Englund (2007) considered witchcraft itself as a form of mediation that competes with mass mediation like radio. This finding resonates with West and Fair's (1993, 95) observation that the communicative arena in Africa is a contested one, and that an understanding of this arena requires an expansion of our definitions of media "to encompass the matrix of social, political and economic relations that constitute contemporary African society." Media should be located within the realm of social relations of power and by historically situating media forms" (ibid.). In terms of the social boundaries of township dwellers in Malawi, Englund found that a "mass-mediated report proved to be less consequential than arguments about witchcraft" (2007, 298). For members of these communities, witchcraft "becomes an aspect of experiencing and imagining the world, comparable to other modalities of mediation" (ibid.).

Normative discourses that describe tabloids' stories on witchcraft as "falsehood," "inaccuracy," or "superstition," pitting it against the assumed rational, objective, informational function of mainstream journalism, are therefore mistaken on two levels. First, these normative critiques are based on a liberal-democratic view of journalism, rooted in Enlightenment-based, correspondence theories of truth telling, that excludes other conceptions of truth (rather than, for instance, coherence or performative theories of truth). Witchcraft discourse in tabloids may still appeal to readers' understanding of "truth"—for instance, by confirming their experience of life as beyond their control or their circumstances as inexplicable through rational means. Criticism of tabloids as engaging in "superstition" also resonates with the outdated and discredited modernization paradigm of development, where media were seen as a way to assist societies in Africa to make the transition from traditional to modern (West and Fair 1993, 91). When witchcraft discourse is referred to as proof that tabloids are reneging on their duties in a transitional democracy, the underlying assumption is that tabloids are obstacles preventing their readers from escaping their backward, traditional ways of living on the dark continent and stepping into the light of modernization, progress, and rationality (ibid.).

Second, criticism that witchcraft discourse in tabloids undermines the informative function of journalism in society and therefore confirms that "tabloids are not really journalism" underestimates how witchcraft discourse in itself can serve a mediation function. Tabloid reporting on witchcraft might therefore not be a case of misinformation as much as it is an attempt to tie into an alternative form of mediation based on a different set of experiences and ways of making sense of the world. Such mediations may indeed be in conflict with dominant understandings of the world as they are articulated in mainstream journalism, but that does not take away from the fact that they could be viewed as forms of mediation in their own right. This mediation often takes place as a subtext on different levels, as Ashforth (2005, 12) points out:

Witchcraft discourse, with all the possibilities of nefarious interactions with invisible agencies it expresses, serves primarily as subtext—that which is not said but without which one cannot comprehend what is spoken.

One could therefore assume that witchcraft discourse will not always be made explicit in media texts, and might only emerge in the interpretive act. This was suggested by the comments made by focus-group respondents in Makhado, who indicated that they had drawn their own conclusions about certain stories in the *Daily Sun* as having had to do with witchcraft without it being specifically stated as such. Such examples show how meaning is created within the act of reading, and why a study of the meaning of tabloid newspapers within post-apartheid, transitional South African society needs to include a view from the readers' perspective.

The negotiation of truth by readers of South African tabloids seemed to correspond with the reading of ostensibly far-fetched tabloid stories in other contexts, like the United Kingdom (cf. Pursehouse 2008, 300). South African readers also seem to know how much truthfulness they can expect from tabloids, and read these papers with that expectation in mind. This selective decoding of tabloid content also pertained to issues of gender, which remain a highly controversial aspect of tabloids. The perceived stereotyping of women in the tabloids forms a central point of concern for tabloid critics.[23] But as with many other aspects of the South African tabloids, the question of gender representation is fraught with contradiction and irony. While the tabloids often present stories with the ostensible aim of titillation or sexual innuendo, readers engage with these representations in more complicated ways than is often assumed. Reference was made earlier to the inspiration women readers derive from success stories about women in the *Daily Sun*. The *Daily Voice*, while publishing a topless page-three girl daily, also devotes a regular full-page feature to advice on motherhood and child-rearing. But the irony remains: this feature is titled "Ma se Voice," literally meaning "Mother's Voice," but unmistakably punning on a well-known (especially in the Western Cape) obscenity referring to a mother's genitals. The same tabloid also offers advice to women at another end of the social spectrum—like explaining over a two page-feature (headlined "Oh What a Night") how "a male strip show can be a great way to unwind with your fellow ladies," complete with photos and pointers on how to prepare "naughty invites" and "jugs of pre-mixed cocktails" (*Daily Voice*, March 6, 2008, 16–17). Although certainly titillating and risqué, if there was objectification in this depiction it was turned around. Of course, the odd feature on male strippers could act as an alibi to divert attention from the more regular objectification of women, which did not go unnoticed among female readers of the tabloids. A female respondent in the Rondebosch East focus group criticized the page-three girl and the tabloids' general lack of social responsibility, saying, "Sex crimes are spiraling, and the tabloids with their page-three girls and sex ads contribute to it. The tabloids are immoral newspapers because they make heroes out of criminals and drug addicts."

However, as was the case with some female readers of the UK tabloid *The Sun* (Pursehouse 2008, 295), some women readers of the South African tabloids reluctantly accepted the presence of the page-three girl as part of the tabloid package as well as an inevitable manifestation of the dominant cultural values of South African society. A Muslim respondent in the Rondebosch East group explained this attitude, saying, "If you are so against this nakedness and that, then you have to go live in Saudi Arabia. This is a Christian country that we're living in, we have to accept what is happening here, you can't change it." The most resistance one could offer in such circumstances was to perform a negotiated reading. A Muslim woman respondent in the same focus group voiced her disagreement with the page-three girl in the *Voice,* but said that she covers up the image on the page and then reads the copy around it.

South African tabloid readers are active participants in meaning-making and not the guileless, gullible victims that they have often been made out to be in journalistic and academic debates. In creating meaning in the act of reading, readers do, however, have to choose from among the available options. In this regard, one should remain critical of the type, scope, and range of content that the South African tabloids offer their readers, as well as the professional values underpinning tabloid journalism. The attention paid to audience agency in cultural studies approaches to tabloids (such as the one followed in this chapter) can therefore benefit from more critical attention to structural factors and the political economy of tabloid media as well as from an examination of journalists' and editors' attitudes and value systems.

The acknowledgement given in this chapter of tabloid readers' critical capabilities to offer negotiated and oppositional readings of tabloid content should not be taken as an argument for uncritical acceptance of all tabloid content. The focus on readers' interpretations of and attitudes toward tabloids should instead be seen as an attempt to counter the widespread assumption by critics of South African tabloids that these readers are helpless victims who are at the mercy of exploitative media. The information gleaned from reader interviews furthermore challenges the notion that tabloids only serve as entertainment and diversion. Tabloid readers have indicated that they invest a significant amount of trust in these papers, and take the information they provide seriously. While they do derive light relief and entertainment from tabloids, readers know where to make the distinction between serious news and entertainment. But readers have also shown that even when tabloid content does not overtly pertain to serious content like politics or hard news, it can still provide them with guidance as they negotiate their way through everyday life. Because tabloid news provides legitimacy to their everyday experiences and confirms their status as citizens, tabloids also provide readers with a framework for engaging with the political dimensions of everyday life. What has also become clear from interviews with tabloid readers is that these newspapers fulfill mediation roles that cannot be limited to a conventional notion of the rational, individualized public sphere. Tabloids also fulfill roles as ritual communication, creating communities of readers, acting as signi-fiers of social mobility, and creating cultural capital.

Perhaps the most significant insight yielded by the readers' interviews, when taken as a whole, is that the South African tabloid newspapers offer a clear and viable alternative to the mainstream "quality" papers. From the point of view of the reader, the mainstream press in post-apartheid South Africa constructs a social reality that is largely disconnected from the everyday life experiences of the majority of South Africans. The evidence from this exploration of reader re-sponses is that tabloids, for all their problems and faults, have stepped into a void of the mainstream press's own making.

Having considered the media landscape and political economy within which South African tabloids are located, the responses from the mainstream profes-sional community, the content of tabloid papers and its relation to political and public life, and the ways readers interact with tabloids in their daily lives, the only roleplayers remaining are the journalists and editors. In the next chapter, we turn to them.

7. Often They Cry with the People: The Professional Identities of Tabloid Journalists

The previous chapter explored the responses of tabloid readers to establish how they relate to the much-maligned tabloid media and to evaluate claims by critics that the tabloids serve to de-politicize their readers. It was found that tabloid readers, in most instances, take tabloids very seriously, but that they negotiate the truthfulness of tabloids' claims in relation to their own daily lives and often engage in negotiated readings in which they distinguish between different parts of the paper that variously provide entertainment and serious news. The dynamic ways readers engage with tabloids were often missed from sight in the critical views expressed by the mainstream professional journalistic fraternity, as discussed in chapter 4. Although tabloids were first rejected and later reluctantly accepted into the South African professional fold, critics mostly spoke on behalf of readers who were often assumed to be the gullible victims of "trash" journalism.

If tabloids are viewed as the epitome of trash journalism, and their readers as trash consumers (Bird 1992, 107), it would follow that the journalists working for these papers are viewed as trash journalists. But if tabloids can, upon closer inspection, have redeeming qualities that mitigate against a too-easy dismissal of them as non-political and superficial, and if tabloid readers prove to be more discerning than elite media consumers give them credit for, tabloid journalists also deserve closer attention than the cursory criticism or rebukes they often receive from their counterparts in the mainstream. Their views can provide a perspective of the role of tabloid journalism within contemporary society and popular culture and the relationship of this genre with the mainstream, as Deuze (2005, 862) explains:

> Listening carefully to those within the profession who operate in the margins and thus (sometimes) deviate from what the current consensus about what good or real journalism is offers us insight into how journalism organizes and defines itself, how this process of definition is structured, and how, in turn, this influences how journalism functions.

Tabloid editors and journalists occupy a double positioning in terms of their professional status. They are usually reviled by their colleagues in the elite media, seen as having sold out to trashy commercialism or engaging in shady journalistic practices. But while their colleagues in the mainstream view tabloid journalists as complicit in a downward spiral of the global trend toward tabloidization and infotainment (cf. Thussu 2008), and tabloid journalists are, in many regards, outcasts in the professional realm, having to "operate in the margins and along the edges of professional journalism" (Deuze 2008, 861), their work is often immensely popular among their readers. The editor of the *Daily Voice,* Karl Brophy, relates that journalists working for that tabloid were "treated like heroes coming home" when they visited a nightclub in Cape Town (cited in Glenn and Knaggs 2008): "The DJ got up into the box and announced that the *Daily Voice* was in the house. And the place went crazy. And it's madness, it's crazy; I have never seen a reaction like that to a publication before."

Tabloids' contradictory status of readers' hero versus professional outcast raises questions around professional identities and journalistic standards. Norms and standards held by mainstream media commentators and professional journalists might not be shared by publics; and if the professional identities of mainstream journalists are not shared by a significant section of the country's journalistic community, these identities might not be as universal as their proponents sometimes claim them to be. The dominant professional ideology can either include or exclude journalists from the professional field (Deuze 2005, 862). As discussed in chapter 4, the discourse of journalistic professionalism within a transitional society has enabled the mainstream press to use tabloid journalism as a scapegoat to deflect attention from its own shortcomings.

This process is not unique to South Africa. Deuze (2005) has demonstrated how tabloid journalists in the Netherlands negotiate their professional identities and their own subjectivity and self-understanding of their role and contribution. Such negotiation of identity takes place within professional structures and frameworks. In South Africa, these include the professional organization of journalists, SANEF, which sets the contours for the normative discourse on journalism standards in the country; the ethical watchdog the Press Ombudsman; and the media companies that tabloid journalists work for. The latter structural element is particularly interesting in the South African case, since the tabloids are owned by big commercial conglomerates seeking to exploit a niche market, while the journalists working for these papers often present themselves as mouthpieces of working-class communities. A central paradox in the assessment of the role and position of the tabloids in post-apartheid South Africa is that their journalists and editors consistently claim that South Africa's tabloids are "different" from tabloids in other parts of the world, and that they are focused on community interests rather than crass sensationalism and profit seeking.

This chapter will explore how tabloid editors and journalists view their professional identities and their relationship with the journalistic establishment; how they negotiate key professional values such as freedom, "objectivity," and independence, coupled with the often explicitly articulated aim of social responsibility and community involvement, within the highly circumscribed commercial environment within which they work. In terms of South African tabloid journalists' professional self-understanding, the focus will fall mostly on how they view their role within South African society, their orientation toward the profession, and how they view the ethical framework within which they operate. The responses analyzed here are derived from in-depth interviews with journalists and editors at all the main tabloids in the country (*Son, Daily Sun, Daily Voice,* and *Sunday Sun*) in 2007 and informed by a limited participant observation in the newsrooms of *Son* and the *Daily Sun.* The analysis will loosely follow the method of thematic analysis that Deuze (ibid., 863) outlines, which involves first, identifying the topics and issues addressed by journalists in the interviews; second, grouping and labeling these topics; and third, summarizing what interviewees said about these topics. The result is a set of themes that can be analyzed to bring to light the "repertoires used by participants (like theatre actors) to perform certain roles in everyday life and to give meaning to the issues at hand" (ibid). Some reference will also be made to Bird's (1992) interviews with journalists in the United States.

Categories

In his study of tabloids in the Netherlands, Deuze identified the following categories of responses from tabloid journalists and editors: gossip attitude, skills and standards, truth vs. "untruth," the public/readers/people, ethics, the magazine *Party* (a benchmark on how "not to do" popular journalism), and the low status in journalism from which many tabloid journalists in that country suffer. Within these broad categories, Deuze identified the themes of irony, morality, commercialism, and popular journalism ideology.

Many of these categories and themes also emerged in discussions with South African journalists, although they were often prioritized differently or articulated differently because of the unique contours the debates about popular journalism and the public sphere took in post-apartheid South Africa. The main categories identified in discussions were relationship with readers, journalistic skills, news values, ethics, a tabloid attitude, and low status.

A closer look at journalists' discussion of these categories revealed starker differences between Dutch and South African tabloid journalists. For instance, where for Dutch journalists "popular journalism is all about having fun" (ibid., 873) and tabloid journalists in the United States must be able to "revel in the 'fun' of tabloids without being cynical" (Bird 1992, 82), South African tabloid journalists were, for the most part, very serious about their work. They tended to express their professional identities more in terms of the ideals of public journalism or community journalism that had been forsaken by the mainstream, rather than in terms of irony or fun (although the more relaxed atmosphere in tabloid newsrooms were sometimes remarked upon). Where a commercial attitude was cited by some Dutch journalists as "the be-all-end-all of their work" (ibid., 877), South African tabloid journalists saw commercialism as a factor that had to be negotiated in order to bring their community-oriented messages across. While this analysis is not intended as a direct comparison between Dutch and South African journalists, these different thematic nuances within what may seem to be broadly corresponding categories again highlights how South African tabloids can be considered a hybrid between a global genre and a localized genre, with its own journalistic practices, identities, and attitudes.

Within the broad categories of responses provided by South African tabloid journalists, further themes emerged: community involvement and journalistic attachment, seriousness, failure of mainstream journalism, and the racial determinants of news and newswork. These categories and themes will be discussed next.[1]

Findings

Categories

RELATIONSHIP WITH READERS AND SOURCES

Tabloid journalists tended to see their interaction with the communities on which they report, the relationship with their readers, and the potential to positively influence the living conditions of their readers as their primary sources of professional motivation. The editor of the *Daily Sun,* Themba Khumalo, expressed this motivation as follows:

> A number of things drive us. You look at the readership that we serve, how they're changing, socio-economic changes, and you have to move with that, come up with new strategies, content that is exciting. We constantly have to be on the lookout for stuff that is exciting. You never know what might happen with the competition.

While Khumalo's concern for his readers' interests is evidently motivated by a desire to be commercially successful and to defeat the opposition, Andrew Koopman, editor of *Kaapse Son,* saw the role of tabloid journalists more in terms of lending an ear to the marginalized in the community and establishing a relationship with them:

> What we try to do is write for the ordinary people—their suffering and their joys. We give people unique news, news that *Die Burger* might not take seriously.... People can come and sit here and tell us something happened, and we will pay attention to them. At *Die Burger* they won't even give those people a hearing.

Khumalo in turn emphasized how tabloid stories are amplified within social networks in townships, being passed on orally. Tabloids not only reinforce circuits of communication within communities, but also benefit from the awareness created around the media product through these discussions. In the process, Khumalo claims, a dialogic relationship between reader/journalist and consumer/producer is created:

> It's about local people, a person who lives in KwaMashu—people who have a sense of attachment to a story, something that happens in their neighbourhood, the person who lives next door. The stories resonate through the township.... People get in the train in the morning, by the time they get to work in the morning they have something to talk about. So it creates a conversation. That sense of community, people can

identify with most if not all of the stories that we publish in this paper. No mumbo-jumbo, academic analyses. If you write about things they understand they begin to trust you.

This dialogic relationship seems to instill in tabloid journalists a sense of their role as one of stewardship, of acting on behalf of their readers. A former sub-editor at the *Daily Sun* described the newspaper (and by implication the journalists working for it) as "being owned by the readers—they feel the newspaper belongs to them":

> The relationship with the readers is genuine. Every month around 12,000 letters arrive. Every day Mr Fixit goes to fix someone's toilet and a photo gets published. Whenever I see someone on the street reading the *Daily Sun,* I ask them why they read it. And they are inspired. These are people that don't count anywhere. This is their life. Or if they're a little more bourgeois, it's the lives of people living next door to them, or it is their lives ten years ago. I don't think people realize how arrogant it is to tell 80 percent of this country's people that their lives are trash.

A journalist at the *Son* who had previously worked at a commercial community newspaper believed that tabloid readers had much more faith in the power of the paper to solve their problems than had been the case at the other newspapers she had worked at: "The perception is that we are the people's paper. They would phone about anything, and they believe that if *Son* does the story their problems will disappear. This wasn't the case at community newspapers." This statement was echoed by a journalist at the *Daily Voice,* who had also worked for a number of mainstream newspapers:

> While I was working in the mainstream, I always wondered: "Is this a story that my editor would want?" Here I'm wondering, "Is this a story my readers would want?" Here you don't have to sell a story to the editor. If the readers close their kitchen doors and sit in their own private space, and they speak to their children, or they scold their children, or they hear about shootings and murders, then they can tell each other "I read it today in the tabloids." You don't read the stories we write in the *Argus* or *Die Burger.*

The relationship of trust between tabloid journalists and their community of readers and sources also benefits journalists, who are given information withheld from mainstream journalists, enabling them to "scoop" their mainstream rivals, as a journalist for *Son* recounts:

> In the communities people like tabloid journalists more (than mainstream journalists), they tell us the whole business, and they tend to give us certain types of stories. We are part of the tug-of-war between the haves and have-nots—we are a hero for the have-nots because they can see we look out for them and care for them, and they like very much to embarrass the guys who are more privileged than they are. . . . We often find that people would rather come and talk to us than to the mainstream media. An example was a recent housing crisis in [the Coloured Cape Town township] Delft where the police fired on people with rubber bullets, shock grenades and tear gas. People were more likely to come and speak to *Son* to tell us what had happened. They almost ignored the mainstream media. Also where it concerns more sensitive stories,

for example one I did about boys between the ages of 9 and 12 who had been sexually abused, people trusted *Son* so much that they told us the whole story but did not even want to give their names to the mainstream papers.

The remarks by the editor of the *Daily Voice,* Karl Brophy on his readers being "massively loyal" have been noted in chapter 5. Like the editors of *Son* and the *Daily Sun,* he too testifies to high levels of interaction with readers, receiving a "massive amount" of phone calls every day. For Brophy there is no tension between his tabloid's commercial interests and those of the community:

> We do have a community role, we have to embed ourselves in the community—there is no false dichotomy between serving our interests and our readers' interests, it's a perfect match. . . . I'm not saying we are heroes, but we are a paper for the community.

Even when tabloids construct their readers as consumers by providing information on how to draw up a business plan or buying a first house or a car (see chapter 5), this role is constructed by journalists as "one hell of a service you're providing" to the community (Mike Vink, *Sunday Sun*).

JOURNALISTIC SKILLS

The dominant view of "tabloidization" is that this process causes a decline in journalistic standards. But contrary to this view of tabloid journalism as an inferior practice showing a disregard for the skills required for "proper," mainstream journalism, South African tabloid journalists seem to pride themselves on an even higher standard of journalism than their mainstream counterparts. Tabloid journalists repeatedly emphasize that tabloid journalism requires the kind of legwork that the deskbound journalists working for elite newspapers have long ago squandered in favor of telephone-and-press release-journalism. Tabloid journalists often describe their work as a kind of investigative journalism which depends on carefully nurtured community contacts and time spent "on the ground." Recognition for this work seems to be forthcoming slowly—while tabloids have been criticized by the mainstream journalism fraternity (see chapter 4), a young tabloid journalist from the *Daily Voice,* Lauren Kansley, was awarded the regional Editor's Choice award in the Vodacom Journalist of the Year competition in 2008. Kansley was one of four journalists who were recognized as the "future of journalism" in the country.[2] She attributed the award to her exclusive interview with Najwa Petersen, the widow of the popular musician Taliep Petersen, who stood accused of her husband's murder. Kansley got the interview because she met Taliep's sister at the murder location, maintained contact, and so gained the family's trust over time.[3]

More unpleasant recognition of the investigative work done by tabloid journalists has also been noted, for instance when a *Kaapse Son* journalist was arrested on a spurious claim after he had reported on allegations of police brutality.[4] Such clampdowns seem to indicate that tabloid reports are taken seriously when they report on abuses of power and are not dismissed as trivial or trash journalism.

The journalistic skills of patiently nurturing contacts on a news "beat," observing life on the streets and finding stories by talking to people, are often lamented as having disappeared from journalism in a time of fast-paced 24-hour news cycles, staff cutbacks, juniorization, and the commercialization of news values. Yet the editor of the *Kaapse Son* claimed that he was instilling these values in his staff:

> I told the news editor that if the journalists don't have stories to cover, let them get in a car and go and drive through [the poor Cape Flats neighborhoods] Hanover Park and Manenberg, talk to people on the street. That's how you get your stories. At *Die Burger* they will never do that. But the best stories don't come to you, you have to go find them in the community. You have to have an extensive contact network. We are trying to expand our correspondent network. We are now also zoning specifically for areas, to create the community feel.

The emphasis that the editor of the *Kaapse Son* places on reporting "on the ground" is in line with the paper's national policy, as the national editor of the *Son*, Ingo Capraro, explains:

> We have the policy that we do not use PR press releases. Those releases usually pertain to news that people want to keep out of the paper, so we do not do PR. Secondly, if it can be avoided at all, we do not do telephone journalism. You go out and you talk to the people themselves.

A journalist at *Son,* who had previously worked in a wide range of mainstream media, including newspapers, radio, and television, confirmed that tabloid journalism demanded from her a new set of skills and a keener sense of observation:

> The first thing I realized was that it demands a lot from you and your personality. One of the skills you need is a relatively good measure of life experience, and a good sense of humor to see the other side of the picture. You need an intelligent creativity in order to present stories different from mainstream newspapers, not from A to Z but to look at what is the odd situation in a specific story. And then to present it just that little bit different from other media, so that you do not present it like a modified community newspaper. You need a sharp eye, a good knowledge of human nature, you have to build a good network, you have to keep in good eye contact with the photographer so that he or she can show you where something is busy happening. It is then that you find those little gems in a story that otherwise would have passed unseen. You also need this ability in the mainstream media, but at a tabloid you can exploit those little gems much more and use them as the intro to your story while at other newspapers with their political baggage, you have to smuggle them in. A good example was today when I was reporting a run-of-the-mill court case. One of the biggest drug lords in Cape Town was appearing in court, and he stared down the investigating officer and pretend to spit at him. It is that offbeat, unusual element that will make your story unique. You have to have a great deal of knowledge of human nature, you have to know people's behavior and their personalities, how their personality traits are going to manifest in public in order to know where to look to find those little things.

A court reporter at *Son* who previously had worked at mainstream broadsheets and commercial community papers agreed that tabloid reporting requires new skills. She also pointed out, however, that in court reporting, these tabloid skills have to be balanced with those demanded by mainstream papers because of the legal aspects involved with reporting court proceedings:

> Facts are facts, and for a court story you have to be terribly careful. But you could use a different angle, you are a bit freer to write around the case itself. You can write more widely, not only purely about what happened in the court itself. You look for something quirky or funny. That doesn't mean you can make up things, but that you can write less formal. An interesting quote and a less formal approach. But I am still a bit careful because I grew up in the old school. A tabloid journalist definitely has to think outside the box. You have to forget saying yes and amen to everything everybody says. It's not that you don't have to have respect, but you look with a sharper eye, you don't get the wool pulled over your eyes as easily. If somebody tries to bullshit me, I now ask much sharper questions. You have to be very hard-nosed.

Importantly, the amount of time journalists spend in the communities is seen to influence the perspective from which they report. Like journalists and editors of the other tabloid newspapers, Karl Brophy (pers. comm.) saw his journalists conducting an ethnographic type of journalism in which journalists are "embedded" in the community rather than committing parachute journalism whenever there is a spike in news events. This "embeddedness" leads Brophy to claim that his journalists go into townships every day to tell their readers "this is how you live," instead of reporting on events from a comfortable vantage point remote from their readers' daily lives.

News Values

When it comes to the news values that tabloid journalists employ to select stories to cover and to decide from which angle they will do so, tabloid journalists seemed to display somewhat contradictory views of their work. While tabloid journalists stressed that their reportage conformed to the definitions of news used in the mainstream, so as to emphasize that tabloid journalism is more than entertainment and diversion, they were keen to point out that their approach to news differed from that of the mainstream. This is how Andrew Koopman described the news values employed at his paper:

> As far as news values are concerned, or the practice of journalism—it's basically the same. Our approach may differ, we may use a looser language, but news is news. We often carry the same stories [as] *Die Burger,* but we try to get another angle, to keep it unique for our reader. We know *Die Burger, Cape Times* and *Argus* will have a specific angle—and they often are similar—but we take a different angle, something they might not even consider to be news.

A journalist at the *Daily Voice* had a similar view:

> We follow the same news principles as that of a daily newspaper. We also try to tell both sides of a story. People are mistaken if they think we only blow stories out of proportion. We do however tell those stories vigorously.

For some White journalists, adopting news values for tabloids aimed at a working class and/or rural Black readership required a complicated negotiation between what they considered "the basics of journalism" (which include values such as truth, accuracy, and neutrality) and other ways of looking at the world— viewpoints to which they had not been exposed to before, such as supernatural explanations for events. One journalist testified to the difficulty she experienced in avoiding condescension toward her sources while at the same time refusing to compromise her belief in "neutrality" and facticity. Ironically, this adherence to the professional values of "objectivity" and "neutrality" was understood to mean not rejecting sources' claims of supernatural causes for events, but reporting them at face value:

> This is an unbelievable challenge for me. It is a question of how far am I going to open my mind to acquire new knowledge? It is a privilege, because I am gaining new experience and knowledge, and I see it as a challenge to go out and listen to what people say. In any case I cannot bring in my own preferences, because that would compromise the neutrality of the information I receive. I must stay objective at all times. I have to listen to what someone tells me, respect his religion, but also gather other perspectives. I would not state it [the supernatural or witchcraft] as a fact, but quote a source. . . . I learnt something I would never have learnt elsewhere, namely how to be streetwise and go through life with my eyes wide open. I acquired a certain wisdom because my world was becoming broader every day.

While tabloids are often accused of "dumbing down" or sensationalizing news for commercial gain, the reverse was claimed by a journalist at *Son:*

> Here there are no holy cows. You shoot the holy cows apart. You do not care if they (news subjects) are advertisers or not. At the community papers we always had to be very careful not to offend advertisers.

Several journalists also remarked on the different news values that tabloids employ. Tabloids were said to eschew a short-term, event-based journalism. Instead of just reporting on events as and when they happened, journalists would "stay with a story," do regular follow-ups and see it through to its conclusion. *Son*'s news editor, Edwin Scott, emphasized that "We don't do a story today and let it die tomorrow. We stick with a story, we don't let it go."

ETHICS

The editors as well as journalists working at the South African tabloids consistently emphasized that they take their ethical responsibility seriously and felt offended by the criticism to the contrary that they had received from mainstream journalists and media commentators. "Truth" and "accuracy" were the ethical values that featured most prominently in journalists' discussion of their roles, even when reporting on the private lives of celebrities, according to the publisher of *Sunday Sun*, Mike Vink:

> From the reaction of other journalists one would think that publishing a tabloid is an easy way of building circulation, which it isn't necessarily. We stand very firmly on

stories being well-researched, and because tabloid stories are so much based on personalities we also stand very firmly on the right of people we write about to have an opportunity to comment before publication.

Although tabloid editors and journalists emphasize the distinctive aspects of their work compared to the mainstream, they are also quick to point out that they confirm to mainstream ethical codes. Andrew Koopman said, "Even though we're not a conventional newspaper, we still underwrite the media ethical code. We took a press code from *Die Burger* and adapted it for our purposes. We take it seriously." *Son*'s national editor, Ingo Capraro, and the *Kaapse Son*'s news editor, Edwin Scott, also, independently, mentioned that their tabloids had an ethical code which every member of the editorial staff had to sign when starting work at the paper. Capraro invoked this code when referring to one of the tabloid's most controversial stories, an exposé of allegations against a gay Dutch Reformed minister by his former partner, which culminated in the latter's suicide (as discussed in chapter 4). Capraro said the story "still haunts" him, but believed the story passed the test of the paper's ethical code because it was "true and in the public interest."

Although imposed by management, individual journalists seem to have taken ownership of the code, as articulated by this journalist:

> Your personal ethics plays an incredibly important role. Right from the start I realized that a lot will depend on you as a person and your ethical principles. There is a fine line you should not cross, you should not overdo things and become "common." It is a whole package of rules you have to apply to yourself.

A former sub-editor at the *Daily Sun* also recalled regular discussions of ethics at the paper and that the publisher would be careful not to break the law, although it would also seem that individual journalists were trusted to be his "conscience":

> But I also do think that Deon [du Plessis, publisher], unless someone has done him in, would not harm anyone, especially not the powerless. And his reader is king.

Where tabloids lack an ethical code, or are in contravention of such a code, it can also impact journalists' professional and personal identities, forcing them to choose between their work or their personal beliefs. An editorial staff member of the *Son*, who had previously worked for the *Daily Voice*, contrasted the two tabloids in terms of their ethics, having experienced the latter as less respectful of religious sensitivities. As a committed Christian, this lack of respect for religious belief on the part of the *Daily Voice* made this journalist feel "very small" while working there and eventually left him with no choice but to seek employment elsewhere. He was happier working at *Son*, where he felt a greater sense of responsibility prevailed:

> *Son* has signed a code of ethics. This includes not to mock other people's beliefs. We have taken note of some criticism that especially our posters were "below the belt." We have to be a little more careful. The South African market is still quite different

form the UK market. One can say that other nations are turning towards heathenism, in South Africa there is still quite [a] strong religious community.

TABLOID ATTITUDE

Whereas tabloid journalists in Deuze's study displayed a playful and gossipy attitude toward their work (2005, 865), South African tabloid journalists seemed to take their roles much more seriously. Although entertainment and gossip did form part of the journalistic role they envisaged for themselves, these elements were always balanced with the roles of information provider, community advocate, or intermediary. The difference between South African tabloid attitudes and those of their counterparts in other parts of the world is in large part also due to the nature of the news covered by these papers within a context of violence, extreme poverty, and social marginalization. When asked to describe a typical *Daily Sun* story, Themba Khumalo mentioned a recent story about a cross-dressing serial killer in the town of QwaQwa in the Free State province ("the type of story that would get people talking about what went wrong"), as well as stories about "empowerment" and the "little victories that will inspire other people to move on": "So there's that mix, it's not all blood and gore." Koopman explained how a similar balance between seriousness and escapism was struck at the *Kaapse Son*:

> We try to give them news that they won't find on television or another paper. You must pick up this paper and you must enjoy it. You must be able to laugh afterwards and feel good. But often we don't get to do that, because there is so much crime in the country, so much trauma, we actually had a conversation about that, how can we make the paper a more readable experience. People don't only want to read about doom and gloom, people want to feel good after they've read a paper. That's why we have jokes every day. The girl on page three is also escapism, so [are] the funny celebrity stories. Like the Baby Jordan story—initially people were sad about the baby getting killed, but now they follow the court case and it's like *Days of Our Lives*.

The *Son*'s national editor described this balance as difficult to attain given the overall serious nature of the news covered by the tabloids. For him, the ideal tabloid attitude is that of serious news mixed with light relief:

> We have moved away from the very wacky type of story. Unfortunately we have also moved a bit too much towards the heavy ones. I am trying very hard to get the fun back, the tongue in the cheek. The idea should be to bring people some cheer. Things are rough out there, you know. To brighten their day a little, to provide them with some diversion. But of course we have a serious element.

A positive attitude toward the paper and colleagues also marked the responses by tabloid journalists. A sense of loyalty and camaraderie could be gleaned from the way tabloid reporters spoke about their workplace and coworkers. A reporter at *Son* (who had experience with both mainstream broadsheets and commercial community papers) described the sense of enjoyment that journalists at this and other tabloids often remarked on:

I am crazy about *Son*. The material we write about sometimes gets me down, but the approach to stories and the editorial meetings are wonderful. In between all the gore, people are laughing, we laugh almost every day in the meetings. There are no passengers, everybody does their share. These are all professional people, but on a whole different level to that which I am used to. I enjoy it tremendously. . . . I am crazy about my colleagues and my bosses. I enjoy it tremendously to work here.

Low Status

Capraro recalled how he had received many complaints from colleagues when he launched the paper while still assistant editor at the mainstream broadsheet *Die Burger*:

> Some people stopped greeting me in the corridors. I became the sleaze bag. Initially it was meant to be a so-called synergy project with *Die Burger*, we would use their existing infrastructure and piggy-back on them. That arrangement would include that members of *Die Burger*'s editorial staff would write for me under pseudonyms. Of course that did not happen at all. Quite the contrary—there was considerable resistance, and I struggled to get people to write for me. But these days if I advertise for a post I get fourteen, fifteen applications. I don't know if the attitude has changed, but my circulation is bigger than *Die Burger*'s. I even picked up from journalism students that their classmates look down on tabloid journalists, as if they do not really need any training.

Themba Khumalo expressed similar perceptions of a superiority complex among mainstream journalists in no uncertain terms:

> For journalistic professions its a question of your dick is small mine is big. They take themselves too fucking seriously. They sit there in judgment of what we do, but what we are doing here is to serve the reader. If the reader is happy, close to 4 million people are happy, then they can go on ranting and raving. If I were to make them happy, then I would make my readers unhappy.

Although Koopman did not deny that the tabloids' colleagues in the mainstream tend to look down on them, he seemed more optimistic that attitudes were changing:

> I think they are now starting to respect us more. In the beginning we were told we do "gutter journalism," but we have scooped them so often that they are now reluctant to look down on us. Some people will have that perception, but I think most of them now see us as their equals. Often journalists from *Die Burger* phone our journalists to get contacts of ideas for stories. I think the respect is returning. There are some individuals that look down on tabloids, but we are getting respect. We are not going to win Mondi awards [for excellence in journalism], but that's OK—because those panels are also full of anti-tabloid people. But the journalists here don't do it for the money, they really are people-persons and care about people.

One of Koopman's staff journalists confirmed this attitude:

> Initially there was a situation of people looking down on us, but because we've been going for a while we have earned respect through our writing. But as a journalist you

have to deserve that respect, because tabloids [are] a new phenomenon in South Africa at this stage.

Trust emerged as an important attitude for tabloid journalists. Sources had to be trusted, but equally journalists had to earn the trust of the people and the communities they worked with, many of whom who had lost faith in the media to understand their experiences. A former mainstream journalist now working for *Son* described tabloid journalism as a "whole different ballgame":

> A lot depends on your attitude as a journalist, whether you are going to get to know people, their habits and that sort of thing, whether you are going to make yourself acceptable to them and open up to them so that they can tell you their stories.

Although journalists experienced a high level of trust among their readers and the communities they reported on, some of their sources belonging to other communities and social classes were more reluctant to trust them, as a court reporter for *Son* indicated: "The community trusts you, but the lawyers are more skeptical about the tabloids until they get to know you."

The close relationship between tabloid journalists and their community of readers and sources helps them get exclusive stories. But regardless of their newsgathering prowess, it still sometimes seems like a struggle to be taken seriously, as one tabloid reporter remarked:

> We often break stories, but because we are a tabloid people don't take us seriously, the mainstream media won't follow up on it. For instance when we broke the story of [former ANC chief whip and convicted fraudster] Tony Yengeni living like a king in jail, *Die Burger*'s people laughed at us and said where do you get this story, it's a lot of shit. And a week later it exploded all over the media. I think it's because journalists in this country haven't been exposed to tabloids they are so conditioned in their own way of thinking and writing and cannot think outside that box.

Her colleague at *Son,* however, thought that the tabloids' demonstrated ability to break exclusive stories was changing attitudes among her mainstream peers:

> I get the idea that the mainstream papers are scared of us, because they come with their straightforward little stories and then we come with a totally different angle. I don't think the mainstream papers look down on us. The community newspapers do look down on us, but they do so with fear. We come from the outside and get the stories they don't.

This "coming from the outside" to communities seems to be a departure from comments by other journalists and editors that tabloid journalists spend more time in communities than their counterparts in other commercial media. While the close ties with communities that most tabloid journalists and editors prided themselves on are indisputable in light of the high levels of community interaction, this interaction does not exclude the possibility that the same tabloids might in some cases follow more aggressive newsgathering methods, which could be experienced as insensitive toward relationships within communities.

An editor of a community paper in a town in the Boland region of the Western Cape remarked on the damage that such reporting does to the carefully nurtured relationships between community newspapers in small town. Tabloid journalists, in this editor's view, have a ruthless approach to stories and when they "parachute" into small towns, they disturb those relationships and create suspicion toward the media in general.

Not all tabloid journalists feel equally aggrieved by mainstream attitudes. In contrast to the opinion of some tabloid journalists and editors who have experienced being looked down upon by their mainstream counterparts, the editor of the *Daily Voice* underplayed the criticism his tabloid had received:

> I think one would give the criticism too much credit to call it a backlash. It was really only a few people. They don't bother me too much. I found the notion of professional journalism hard to get my head around, because we're a trade, like carpentry. It didn't surprise me either. A lot of people in journalism in this country were opposed to the apartheid regime, and they have a specific viewpoint, all left-leaning liberal, that certainly did know what was good for the country in the eighties, but not today—people don't need to be protected from themselves. I don't think the political opinions that I hear expressed in SA journalism really reflect the political opinion of people on the ground.

Themes

When analyzing the broad categories of responses from tabloid journalists in more detail, certain themes emerged. We will now examine the common tropes in the discourse about journalistic identity and professional roles.

COMMUNITY INVOLVEMENT AND JOURNALISTIC ATTACHMENT

When discussing their relationships with the community, one of the themes emerging from the discussions with tabloid journalists was the perceived higher level of involvement in the community than would usually be the case in mainstream journalism. Several tabloid journalists pointed out that attachment to communities would sometimes extend beyond reportage to include more direct intervention and participation in community issues. This role is quite different from the conventional notion of the journalist as a detached observer. It is a role that depends on interaction (*Kaapse Son,* according to Koopman, was "inundated with letters": "People often phone in or send an email with news tips. We have a lot of interaction with our readers") and a different perspective on news, as a journalist for the *Daily Voice* explained:

> I always write from the perspective of the community, asking myself how I can present the story to our community. We also delve a bit further [into their circumstances], finding out if the people involved have money for the funeral, for the court case. We try to look at the bigger picture.

Tabloid journalists repeatedly indicated that they do not shy away from becoming emotionally involved with the stories they cover. Of the effect that covering tabloid news stories had on journalists at the *Son,* Koopman said, "For the journalists it's more than a job. It's a personal experience. Many of the journalists have said, 'Gosh, I come from Vereeniging [a town in Gauteng Province] and never knew these things happen.' Often they cry with the people at the scene of a story." Even sub-editing stories at the *Daily Sun* would elicit an emotional response, as a former sub-editor admitted: "The closest I always came to tears was when you would read a letter from a reader looking for a missing person, 'I am looking for my brother Jacob Dlamini, he left home in 1983 to go to Johburg to look for a job.' "

This attachment extends beyond empathy to a recognition that journalistic work could also involve material (and not only symbolic) support. Koopman recalls how a journalist would return from an assignment to ask: "Can't we help the family, can't we give these people money, they are really poor?" A journalist at the *Daily Voice* explained that journalists at that paper saw their role as extending further than just writing a story, to putting lawyers in contact with victims to enable readers, for instance, to sue companies creating unsafe environments for children.

A journalist at the *Son* recalls a time when the paper reached out to the subjects of a news report, following offers of assistance from readers:

> Perhaps one of the biggest responses to a story I have experienced personally, was a story about two years ago of a desperately poor family whose house burnt to the ground. Three of their children burnt to death. The way the story was presented elicited such a huge reaction—and I'm talking about all levels of society—that the people were inundated with offers of help. This ranges from an undertaker [offering his services] to someone offering a new house, clothing, the works. We collected money from our readers and I personally went out to buy clothes for the survivors with that money. There were even so many advertisers that opened their hearts— money, a house, groceries. I have never worked at a news organization where I received such an overwhelming response. Because you can leave your heart in the story, because you can be more descriptive, you are able to invite that kind of reaction from readers.

The *Son*'s news editor, Edwin Scott, mentions similar examples—a weekly grocery voucher given to a poor household or individual reported on during the course of the week, a sexually abused child whose birthday party was sponsored. It is this level of involvement that led Koopman to describe his paper as a "community paper, just on a bigger scale." Although such a definition might be contentious since the paper is edited and owned not by members of the community, but by an editorial staff located in a big commercial conglomerate, the newspaper does attempt to extend its involvement in the community beyond the interaction on the letter page. This is done primarily through its anti-drug campaign, which includes sponsorship of a Klopse group (see chapter 4). Although this campaign is sponsored by the paper and therefore creates visibility for the paper in the communities to which its readers belong, its involvement is limited to sponsorship and provision of information rather than direct activism by journalists. Journalists are, in fact, cautioned by the editor not to over-extend themselves, as Koopman pointed out:

The other day I reminded the staff, remember, we are a newspaper. We get so many requests for sponsorships, and we don't have the money. We won't organize a tik march ourselves, but if people are having a march we will provide them with newspaper posters saying for instance "stop drug abuse." You will also see at court cases, people outside the court waving *Son* posters.

One could be cynical about the community involvement by these papers by pointing out, as critics of the public journalism movement in the United States have done (see, e.g., Arant and Meyer 1998; Haas and Steiner 2006), that such involvement not only sacrifices journalistic impartiality but can also become just another marketing tool for newspapers. Yet, it remains difficult to retain such skepticism when speaking to tabloid journalists and noticing their devotion to their work and their hope that it might have a positive influence in society. If this attachment is a marketing ploy on the part of the media managers or moguls, it is not experienced as such by the individual journalists. Nor is such an attachment an easy option to follow. The emotional attachment and involvement with the people they report on can indeed take its toll. The court reporter for *Son* described how she dealt with the trauma arising from having to report on the deluge of violence that makes its way to the courts and on the scenes of crime and disaster she had witnessed:

> One feels that you can mean something. But what does get me down is the type of stories we do, the repetition of violence, violence, violence—the ugly side of life, the sensational side of life. Almost every story you do is like that—there is no chance of ever getting invited to something nice like an exhibition. If you get to a scene people are either scared for you or they have invited you to come [for a reason]. There is no chance that you will have a bit of a party or have a laugh with the people. You deal with negative stuff the whole time, and especially towards the end of the year it gets to you. You have so much ugliness in your life, and although we have little money, we would stop at a stall on the way to a murder case at the courts to buy a trinket or a nice African shirt, as a counter or escape for all the murder and mayhem and guts. If I come back from the court, from another two people who wanted to kill each other . . . that's the ugly part of being human, and in one day you would have time only for one or two stories, so this is what your day consists of. At the end of the week I look at what I have done that week and it would be only violence. I think it is trauma. They gave us addresses where to go for debriefing, but they don't really make provision for that, you have to use your own initiative. After I covered a train crash they should have told us to go and speak to someone. There were 19 bodies lying around, you would work for five to six days on that story alone, you would go to visit families and talk to them about their heartbreak, you would go to the mortuary and you would be shown away. This is not the type of thing that ordinary people . . . [have to deal with]. You cannot go home and talk about it with your teenage children. So for me there is no[where to turn] . . . My friends and family, for them it is very bad, and they are more shocked about it than being able to help me. So in the end you don't talk about it. You only dream about it.

But although reporting on the poverty and misfortune of South Africa's desperately poor and marginalized communities can be emotionally taxing, it has its own rewards:

I think for the first time in my career I really reached people. My very first story at *Son* was a real tear-jerker, a nine-year old child that was killed by another child who stuck a nail into his heart. I was in Delft and I wrote that it does not matter what color or creed you are, if your child is dead your child is dead. That part of my encounter with people, with the squatter camps, when I stop working here one day I will take that with me. I am very thankful that I gained that perspective and that I can tell my two teenagers about it. There is trauma here, but it is not overall a negative experience for me.

Khumalo put this sense of attachment described by the reporters succinctly: "We're part of the story. How do you begin to understand the story when you stand outside?"

Truth and Accuracy

When discussing the ethical standards of their reporting, tabloid editors and journalists often identified the norms of truth and accuracy as their primary concern—probably because these had been among the aspects (next to indecency, stereotyping, and objectification of women) they had been criticized for most by their mainstream counterparts. Koopman stressed balance and verification in the *Son*'s reporting:

Many people say you cannot believe what it says in the *Son,* but we won't publish a story if it wasn't true. Everything is double-checked. Both sides of the story have to be given. I always warn journalists to be careful of one-source stories. Sometimes the story is so juicy that you have to go with one source—I mean even *Die Burger* does it—but we give people a chance to reply, even if it means letting the story wait 'til the following day. Absolutely at all times we have to be fair and credible.

A *Kaapse Son* journalist linked the tabloid's meticulous attention to facts with the tabloids' low status in the profession:

Because we are so closely scrutinized by other papers, we go to extremes [to ensure accuracy]. We would rather keep a story for the next day in order to get the correct facts or hear the other side, than publishing something unchecked just to be first with the story.

Another journalist at the *Son* dismissed criticism that tabloids fabricate stories as relating to critics' insular world view, and implied that this criticism was racially informed: "People who aren't streetwise or have life experience will tell you we fabricate stories. Those are people who have never made the effort of going to a township and speaking to the people."

Her colleague also emphasized the need to remain factual when reporting on the courts. The fact that there was more freedom at the tabloids to write in a colloquial language actually meant for this reporter that she could paint a more accurate and truthful picture: "The use of language is much freer than at a broadsheet. If someone was swearing in courts, you would write it like that. For me this is actually a much closer reflection of reality. . . . I write about my experience, about how I experienced and heard a story."

The importance that journalists attached to truth and accuracy might, as suggested above, be related to repeated criticism from the mainstream that tabloids do not verify stories or report on supernatural events that cannot be verified in any case. But these values were also viewed as important to retaining a close relationship with the community, a relationship that is such an important part of tabloid journalists' professional identity. As Khumalo put it, "We do not make stories up, that way you lose credibility. We tell people's stories."

SERIOUSNESS

As described earlier, the general attitude displayed by South African tabloid journalists was surprisingly serious. Care would be taken that entertainment and fun did not dominate more serious stories. Koopman enumerated the traditional journalistic functions of information, entertainment, and edutainment:

> Yes, we try to get the balance right. We don't want people to pick up the paper and say "Oh, you cannot believe it." It must also contain serious journalism. We do have stories about police brutality, but then they can also turn to the page with music and entertainment. So we try to entertain people, we also try to educate them—this newspaper is used in classrooms. For instance the map of Africa, where we show with a diagram this is what happened in that country, and so on. A lot of people did not have the education to know where Khartoum or Cameroon is, so this is also a service we provide our readers with. We don't want to do heavy politics, but we want to tell them what goes on in other parts of the world, and we show him exactly where it happened. This is also an educational task, we know many of our readers are not highly schooled, so this is why we do this. . . . We entertain, and people should feel good after reading us, but gosh, there is so much sadness, and you cannot miss it, you cannot do something other than write about it. You cannot ignore a story about a teacher raping a pupil. It cannot be swept under the carpet. It is our duty to expose those things.

A journalist at *Son* remarked on how she could display a deeper level of seriousness and emotion in her current work than when she worked at a commercial community newspaper: "These are sad stories, but I enjoy writing about them. At the *Eikestadnuus* they used to cut things out of my story, but here I can really write the snot and tears of a sad story as it happened, a mother that had to identify her child in the morgue."

Yet fun has not completely disappeared from the practice of tabloid journalism. Several journalists noted how much they enjoyed working at the tabloids, and how they enjoyed a sense of freedom and creativity that surpassed any of their prior professional experiences. One *Son* journalist said, "It is a lot of fun working here, it is not as stiff as at the mainstream papers. That is also why we decided to write like people speak . . . The whole idea was that stories should be fun. It is starting to get a bit more serious of late."

FAILURE OF MAINSTREAM JOURNALISM

The professional identity of tabloid journalists was also partly premised on their view that mainstream journalism has lost its sense of purpose and that it is left to tabloid journalists to re-establish the media's links with poor communities, most of which are made up of Coloured (in the Western Cape) or Black readers who were still being marginalized by the mainstream. Koopman described the failure of broadsheets as follows:

I think certainly they did [fail the communities]. If you look at the Western Cape, the largest part of the population is Coloured. But if you open a newspaper, you don't read about what is happening to those people, in those communities. You read about something you don't know. It's a different world you are reading about, it's not a reality to you. They never told people the truth of what is going on in the Western Cape. What you read about are things like the battle about language [of instruction] at [the University of] Stellenbosch. Is that an issue for people who are struggling to survive? People want to know how stories are relevant to them. We really try to address issues that are important to people. People should feel that the things we cover are things that concern them.

Several tabloid journalists also remarked on how they would often get exclusive stories, or cover angles of stories that mainstream journalists fail to identify, because their mainstream colleagues are not as closely involved in the community as the tabloid journalists are. This success of the tabloids in obtaining exclusive stories or angles was also attributed to the fact that the mainstream print media had largely forsaken what were considered good journalistic habits, routines, and attitudes. Ingo Capraro described his tabloid's approach to news as a return to those old-fashioned journalistic values:

Back in the late 1970s when I worked at [the Gauteng-based mainstream broadsheet] *Beeld* we were, wow, we were enthusiastic! Nobody went home before that story was finished, you didn't kill a story easily. Through the years that attitude began to fade away. I saw this happening at [the Western Cape daily] *Die Burger*. People did not have that passion anymore, they would go home at half past five, they become clock-watchers. My people [at *Son*] are absolutely inspired, they work almost like in the old days. They are proud of what they do.

Capraro thought that the emergence and popularity of the tabloids had influenced the mainstream newspapers in the country to tabloidize their content:

I must tell you it worries me a little that we have had an influence on the mainstream. In this country we do not really have a culture of quality journalism. As far as I am concerned *Die Burger* is a "broadloid." . . . There is not even a handful of quality papers in this country—the *Sunday Independent*, the *Mail and Guardian* and *Business Day* are the only ones. The rest is a hotchpotch. And I am afraid the arrival of the tabloids has made those papers dumb down.

Racial, Ethnic, and Cultural Determinants of News and Newswork

Koopman denied that *Son* was focused specifically on Coloured readers, but admitted that their social mobility made them an attractive market for advertisers:

A lot of people will say we are a Coloured newspaper. But that's not true. We are seamless. We do not look at the color of the news. But the reality is that most of our information comes from the Cape Flats, because the numbers there are bigger. We increasingly get calls from White readers with tips. You can see *Die Burger* is now also starting to include more Coloured news, I don't know if that's because they now have a Coloured editor [Henry Jeffries], but they are realizing that their readers are getting extinct. They know their readers are becoming extinct and they have to create a new market. And where is the new market? With the Coloured middle class.

From tabloid journalists' comments, it becomes clear that race, as it correlates with class and as articulated through the geographical separation of neighborhoods in the city,[5] still plays a significant role in how news is selected for mainstream newspapers. Events occurring in the affluent areas of the city, where the (still mostly White) middle and upper classes live, are favored above those happening in poorer areas. This bias is informed by a commercial model which depends on advertising targeting lucrative readerships. Tabloid journalists saw their newspapers as a platform from which to respond to the news bias they had often experienced when working for the mainstream press. A journalist at the *Daily Voice,* who had worked at a mainstream Sunday newspaper, *Rapport,* claims that he resigned from the paper because of what he had considered a racially biased news agenda:

> We were told we should write for the White people of Johannesburg. Now a child dies in [the Black township of Cape Town] Nyanga or [the Coloured township of] Mitchells Plain, cruelly murdered or raped. But a cat gets stuck on the balcony of White people in [the affluent White suburb] Durbanville. Then you write about that [the cat]. When we lost the bid to host the World Cup soccer bid [in 1999, for the 2006 World Cup], I interviewed [bid chief executive] Danny Jordaan, and we put it on the front page. Afterwards the editor warned us: "This was the first and last time you put soccer on the front page, we are an Afrikaans rugby paper." *Rapport*'s sales dropped with something like 30,000 copies that day. Myself and several other Coloured journalists left. You would arrive at a news conference with six or seven story ideas and those stories would all be shot down there and then, you would be told that those aren't the type of stories our readers would want to read. But then it would be stories that concerns your own [Coloured] community. That is why I resigned. And the [supplement aimed at Coloured readers in the Western Cape] *Kaap-Rapport* only covers soft stories.[6]

A [White] journalist at *Son* seemed to see the criticism directed against tabloids as evidence that the stories reported in this tabloid reflect a country where race and class still determine widely divergent lived experiences. Because the lived experience reported on in the tabloids is so far removed from that of (largely White) suburbia, these reports are criticized as fabricated, untrue, or sensationalized:

> It angers me that people in their ignorance make negative comments about tabloids, without a knowledge [of broader society]. A lot of people, especially Whites, can pay lip service, and if you are relatively intelligent you can do it very beautifully, but only a select few that can put words into action.

Thus, for especially the White journalists working at the tabloids, this experience has exposed them to aspects of life in South Africa that they had never before experienced in their racially-determined, sheltered lives:

> Working here made the blinkers fall from my eyes. I had known a bit of these different lifeworlds before [I started working at the *Daily Sun*], but now it has become so much a part of me.

Race continues to be a factor not only in the selection and presentation of news, but also in the way South African tabloid journalists relate to each other professionally. Working together in tabloid newsrooms seem to require some compromises and alliances. While most of the journalists at the *Daily Sun* had some training, a former sub-editor at the paper recalled how she shared her expertise with junior journalists and helped them to revise stories. As a matter of routine, however, big stories would be rewritten by senior, White sub-editors (some of whom were described as "racist" by a former colleague) or by Deon du Plessis himself, and young Black journalists would have "very little power over their work."[7]

Yet although these power hierarchies—not unusual in editorial settings—seem to still be racially informed, there were no obvious racial tensions in the newsroom, because "the young journalists were working somewhere they wanted to work." The editor, Themba Khumalo, was described as following publisher Deon du Plessis' lead rather than providing journalistic leadership of his own: "Themba does not have a background in journalism, which makes Deon super-stronger than him. And if Deon wasn't there, one of the White sub-editors would take his place."

Du Plessis readily—and somewhat condescendingly—admitted to this rewriting that the sub-editor was referring to:

> In every *dorp* [rural town] in the country there's a stringer, often working for other community papers. Often they don't do it under their own names. Getting into the *Sun* is now a cult thing. So most of our reporters are living in the communities that they write about. But everything is rewritten—I've got two middle age White *ouks* [guys] who are writers.

Du Plessis did not think this took the reporters' voice away, saying "Their voice is incoherent, it's not a voice. If we ran it as we received it, we'd sell six."

Khumalo seems to act as the paper's public face. For instance, he writes a column (with a picture byline), and he met with and interviewed ANC president Jacob Zuma. Khumalo's editorial role seemed to be largely that of advising Du Plessis on cultural matters, like how to present stories in order not to offend readers' sensitivities or how to use idiomatic language. Du Plessis claimed to rely heavily on Khumalo's advice: "Themba's advice is a non-negotiable. It's easy to get the wrong sense of a thing and then we're buggered, because the readers will know." Du Plessis admitted to—and prided himself on—the alliances between White and Black, experienced and inexperienced members of editorial staff:

When I say truly [it] is a joint effort and none of us can do it on our own, it's true. What I like about this thing is it really is an example of how this country can work.

Interviews with South African tabloid journalists made clear that these journalists consciously reflected on their professional roles and identities and had strong views of how their work related to their readers, to wider society, and to the journalistic profession in the country. These roles and identities were often compared with those of their counterparts in the mainstream, or with their own prior experiences as journalists working in the mainstream. From these comparisons, a multi-faceted and sometimes complex tabloid journalism identity emerges. While tabloid journalists were keen to emphasize their equal status as professional journalists by citing their adherence to traditional news values, compliance with codes of ethics, and level of skill, they also set themselves apart from mainstream journalists by pointing out differences between them. Tabloid journalists emphasized their closer involvement with the community, the different perspectives they brought to stories, and their greater freedom in approach and style of reporting. Perhaps most importantly, tabloid journalists often reported having been personally transformed by their experience of working for a tabloid. Instead of invoking the conventional journalistic positions of neutrality, objectivity, and detachment, tabloid journalists readily admitted to being touched by the news they reported on. They allowed themselves an emotional reaction to stories and entered into an emotional engagement with the people who form the subjects of tabloid news. This engagement sometimes extended beyond sympathetic reporting to a direct, material intervention in the situations of the victims of crime, poverty, or disaster. The refusal by tabloid journalists to remain bystanders of the often-tragic stories they witnessed and the choice to care enough about them to adopt a position showed similarities with Martin Bell's (1998) term (in the context of war reporting), "journalism of attachment." Bell distinguishes a journalism of attachment from strident campaigning or crusading journalism, which would not be an accurate term for the style of news reporting found in South African tabloids. Instead, Bell's description (ibid., 16) of a journalism of attachment resonates with the general attitude among South African tabloid journalists:

> In place of the dispassionate practices of the past I now believe in what I call the *journalism of attachment.* By this I mean a journalism that cares as well as knows; that is aware of its responsibilities; that will not stand neutrally between good and evil, right and wrong, the victims and the oppressor. This is not to back one side or faction or people against another. It is to make the point that we in the press . . . do not stand apart from the world.

Whether this journalism of attachment is practiced consistently by South African tabloid journalists, whether their professed attachment manifests in the actual reporting, how the measure of attachment differs across different tabloids, and whether the empathy elicited by this reporting is outweighed by sensation, diversion, and entertainment are question that remain. The important finding from these interviews is that tabloid journalists saw this attachment as a core part of their professional self-identity and as a characteristic that set them apart from their mainstream counterparts. While they testified to having fun and enjoying their jobs, this serious attitude differed from the typical attitude associated with tabloid journalists in other parts of the world.

Despite these differences, tabloid journalists did not display a professional identity wholly distinct from that of their mainstream counterparts. Through their careful attention to formal codes of ethics, their emphasis on the skills required for tabloid journalism, and their disappointment at the perceived snubs received from their colleagues in the mainstream, it was clear that tabloid journalists still wanted to be acknowledged as professional journalists, even if they feel unwelcome in the country's professional coterie. The alienation between tabloid journalists' everyday lived work experience and the professional identities espoused by their mainstream counterparts should be understood in wider terms than a mere spat within the local journalistic fraternity. The professional practices and ethical codes aspired to by South Africa's mainstream journalists have largely been taken over from a liberal-democratic discourse about the role of journalism in society developed in the Global North. While constant negotiation between these globalized values and local practices also occurs within the mainstream,[8] the localization (both in geographical and in political terms) of the news in tabloid newspapers is of such intensity that these tensions between globalized norms and localized practices, and the resultant glocalization of media ethics and professional norms (cf. Rao and Wasserman 2007; Wasserman and Rao 2008) become much more evident than in the mainstream. While these tensions might therefore find expression as an internal professional quarrel, they relate to broader processes of negotiation between African contextual imperatives and a globalized discourse of journalistic professionalization that positions itself as having universal validity.

Although the self-reflective discourse by South African tabloid journalists showed broad similarities with the categories and themes identified by scholars in their interviews with tabloid journalists elsewhere in the world (e.g., Deuze 2005; Bird 1992), there are also key differences. Instead of viewing popular journalism as "all about having fun" (Deuze 2005, 873; cf. Bird 1992, 82), South African tabloid journalists displayed such a serious approach to their work that their attitudes toward the material they worked with sometimes caused psychological trauma. This difference exists partly because celebrity news, associated with glamour and entertainment, forms a smaller part of South African tabloid news than it does in other parts of the world. The emphasis South African tabloid journalists placed on the skills required for the job, especially the investigative dimension of tabloid journalism, resonates with similar claims by tabloid journalists in other parts of the world, including the Netherlands (Deuze 2005, 867) and the United States (Sloan 2001, 193; Bird 1992, 83).

It remains important to remember that the responses offered by the tabloid journalists and reported in this chapter are self-constructions of identity and professional roles, and should not be taken as "proof" that their actual practice corresponds with these identity claims. As Bird (1992, 80, citing Bruner) puts it: "There may be a correspondence between life as lived, a life as experienced, and a life as told, but the anthropologist should never assume the correspondence nor fail to make the distinction." The value of examining tabloid journalists' professional identity constructions is that they provide a window into the discourse about professionalization and the role of journalism in post-apartheid South African society. The intentions of news producers cannot always be directly linked to news content, nor is it a prediction of the way news will be interpreted by audiences. Therefore, when drawing inferences from journalists' claims, care should be taken not to read these as statements of fact regarding content or consumption. However, these statements are important indicators of the professional status of journalists and their views of their roles, responsibilities, and relation to society.

8. Conclusion: Telling Stories

This book began by posing the question: why a book on the South African tabloids? If the runaway commercial success of tabloids were the prime motivation for devoting scholarly attention to them, a one-dimensional study aimed at explaining—with an eye on replicating—their successful recipe would have been sufficient. But the tabloids are a challenging subject at least partly because their commercial success seems at first glance to be counter-intuitive. They emerged at a time when newspapers everywhere around the world are threatened with extinction. In a developing country with a high illiteracy rate, a print medium would seem an unlikely vehicle to capture the trust and aspirations of a mass audience. In a country where the discourse of post-colonial modernity underpins the development of the most sophisticated new media technology on the continent, the notion that newspapers might be part of the future of journalism might have seemed absurd. In a period following years of authoritarian control over the media, the idea that press freedom should be used for sensationalism might seem sacrilegious. The consensus was that the responsibility of the press in post-apartheid South Africa would be to vigorously scrutinize government. But instead of sharing the mainstream's preoccupation with the tumultuous post-liberation politics on the big stage, the tabloids turned their attention to sensational events concerning everyday people in small towns, informal settlements, and townships. In a journalistic context marked by an increased professionalization, the tabloids seem to follow their own instincts, impervious to the ostracization by the mainstream fraternity. Where mainstream journalism embraces globalized ethical norms within a consensual self-regulatory system, the tabloids seem to either flaunt those codes or negotiate them on their own terms. While claiming their dedication to poor and marginalized communities of readers through slogans such as The People's Paper, these papers are located in big conglomerates with a ruthless hunt for profits.

It is exactly the ostensibly unlikely success of the tabloids that invites closer scrutiny and demands that they be viewed not in isolation, or as outside influences on society, but as events occurring within a transitional society itself. While the public discourse around South African tabloids thus far has been mostly couched in normative terms, this book has sought to position tabloids within the social context of post-apartheid South Africa in an attempt to understand them as complex cultural articulations of the often contradictory and shifting processes of transition taking place on various levels in the country. Such an attempt to obtain a "thicker" understanding of popular journalism should not be understood as a normative position, but rather as a way to more fully contextualize the socio-political relations within which these media operate. It is only against the background of such a fuller contextualization that one can start to revisit normative positions, allowing such norms to amount to more than mere moral indignation or markers of taste.

This book has approached tabloids as social phenomena, approaching them from the perspective of their readers, their producers, their colleagues, and their critics in the mainstream against the background of the political, economic, social, and cultural landscape. The picture that has emerged is fraught with ironies and contradictions, both in terms of the role that tabloids play in the lived experience of both their readers and the journalists that produce them, but also in terms of their political role and influence. In all these aspects, it was found that the meaning and significance of tabloids result only from a process of negotiation and compromise— between the demands of the market and the interests of the community; between the discourse of global infotainment and the stories from rural towns; between the lure of modernity and the hold of tradition; between editorial control vested in editors and publishers and the individual freedom and creativity of journalists.

The South African tabloids are clearly linked to a very specific set of circumstances and events. But while they are specific, are they also unique? This book has attempted to understand South African tabloids not only as journalistic forms linked to a particular society, but as examples of a genre with exponents in different parts of the world. Through all the various aspects of the South African tabloids that have been examined, it is evident that although the South African tabloids bear distinctive characteristics, they also show some similarities with tabloids elsewhere. But seeing South African tabloids merely as a localized manifestation of a globalized genre would miss the fact that the relationship between the local and the global is a dynamic one, a process of ongoing negotiation. This dynamic and constantly shifting relationship between the local and the global is furthermore not limited to how much South African tabloids incorporate, appropriate, or adapt global genre characteristics or stylistic elements. The tabloids should rather be understood as articulations of a larger contestation between cultural discourses, as expressions of the push-and-pull of glocalization underway in South Africa. The tabloids show us how the media can serve as both a platform for and as a product of the complicated articulations of popular culture, mediated politics, and citizenship in a young democracy.

After conducting this multi-leveled study of South African tabloids, we can briefly and provisionally make the following conclusions:

- *South African tabloids cannot be dismissed as "trash journalism."*
  No journalistic product is perfect, and the intention of this book was not to celebrate tabloids uncritically. Their insistence on ethical standards notwithstanding, the tabloids often engage in dubious reporting. They invade people's privacy unjustifiably, get facts wrong, peddle stereotypes, and offend social mores. For these transgressions they deserve criticism, as would other newspapers that do the same. However, much of the criticism these tabloids have received seems to result from a blurred distinction

between ethical standards and markers of taste. The offense caused by tabloids often seems to function as a means of classifying the offended party as belonging to a higher social class or to an elite profession, rather than as an impetus to investigate the same ethical transgressions with the same amount of vigor not just in the tabloids, but in mainstream press as well. But even if ethical considerations are left aside, the fact that popular journalism might not conform to the professional standards determined by mainstream practitioners or taught by the institutions where journalists are trained is not reason enough to view them as unworthy of serious scholarly investigation. Such an investigation should be based on the assumption that all forms of journalism and all media products are part of societal processes and located within cultural, economic, and political power networks.

When viewed in this way, South African tabloids can be seen as closely linked to the transitions that South Africa has been undergoing since democratization. This does not mean that tabloids are necessarily the most suitable or even a completely adequate journalistic response to these changes. What it does mean, however, is that a simplistic dismissal of tabloids as "trash" and of their readers as gullible victims, uneducated and simple and in danger of being unduly influenced, would lose sight of the significant body of media-studies literature which questions a direct link between media content and its "effects" on audiences. The realization that the South African tabloids should be understood in relation to a complex, changing society means that an investigation into their significance should take place on various levels and from different perspectives. This book has attempted to accomplish these things by looking at the production, consumption, and circulation of tabloids within the country's political, economic, and social circuits.

- *South African tabloids should be viewed as part of a local-regional-global dynamic.*

Understanding South African tabloids as part of a complex pattern of social and political shifts in the country does not mean that they should be viewed in isolation of trends and developments regionally and globally. The point of this book has not been to make a direct comparison between South African tabloids and their counterparts in other parts of the world, but to arrive at a deeper understanding of the South African situation. The references throughout to tabloid journalism in the United States, the United Kingdom, the Netherlands, and other parts of Africa should, however, be taken as an indication that developments in the local press are not exceptional. While the South African tabloids are the result of local shifts in the social, political, and cultural landscape after apartheid, their emergence, as well as their influence on the mainstream press, can be viewed as part of the spread of global "infotainment" which has also made its mark on other countries in Africa and elsewhere in the Global South. This does not mean that the South African tabloids are merely mirroring their counterparts elsewhere or that they have only been on the receiving end of a global process of "dumbing down." On many levels, be they the aesthetics of style and layout, the news values determining story selection and approach, or the journalists' opinions of their professional roles and responsibilities, South African tabloids are involved in an ongoing process of negotiation between global influences, local appropriations, and regional developments. They are located within a complex network of symbolic and material power relations, having entered into a context marked by the co-existence of the discourses of late modernity and post-apartheid African nationalism; where politics have become increasingly mediated and technocratic as liberation gave way to governance (Pillay 2008, 9); and a transitory local space (see Hasty 2005, 5 for a summary of a similar confluence of forces in contemporary Ghana) where social identities are increasingly inflected through patterns of consumption.

The context within which the South African press operates is not wholly unlike the role of the press in other postcolonial African settings, yet it bears its own set of characteristic ironies and contradictions. These characteristics can only be properly understood when the South African tabloids are examined as social phenomena demanding a multi-leveled approach such as the one in this book.

- *Tabloids can be read politically.*

Contrary to the type of criticism they—like tabloids around the world—have been subjected to, the South African tabloids cannot be dismissed as merely diversion or entertainment without any political or public significance. While it would be difficult to assess their influence on political behavior, evidence from reader interviews suggests that it would be a mistake to conclude that these tabloids serve to de-politicize their readers. Tabloid readers contextualize the events and topics reported on in the tabloids, however localized or community oriented, in terms that have a bearing on public life. Whether their reading of these events as related to the current political dispensation will eventually inform voting behavior, inspire social activism, or instead only defuse the frustration and disillusionment of the poor without leading to meaningful political action remains to be established in a more focused and longitudinal study. As papers owned by big conglomerates set on maximizing profit, it is unlikely that these tabloids will ever question the logic of capitalism or encourage readers to join social movements. What did become clear in the current study is that the political relevance of the tabloids lies in what has been referred to as the "politics of the everyday." The comments by tabloid readers sourced for this book seems to indicate an active interaction with tabloid content, a process in which tabloid readers contextualize politically relevant tabloid news against the background of their own lived experience, social networks, cultural horizons, and material circumstances. Such a view of audience interaction with media content is supported by literature in the cultural studies tradition which sees media influence as an often minimal part of larger social and cultural processes. Attention to the way readers interpret the political dimension of tabloid news would provide a picture of how news events are actually being interpreted, rather than taking tabloids' claims to be the "voice of the people" at face value. Although tabloids make a big display of speaking on behalf of the community, they also interpellate their readers in highly circumscribed terms as individual consumers within a neoliberal discourse of social mobility. However problematic these tabloids might be as political vehicles, the emergence of South African tabloids is closely linked to a particular set of social conditions marking the ongoing social transition in South Africa and therefore invites a political reading.

- *Tabloid journalists take their work seriously.*

Although the professional environment has become more accommodating in recent years, South African tabloid journalists initially met with much derision from their counterparts in the professional fraternity and at one point were almost ostracized from the South African National Editors' Forum (SANEF), the country's professional body for journalists. Although the common perception might be that tabloid journalists' attitude toward news is one of fun, gossip, and irreverence—as has indeed been reported in the literature about tabloid journalists in other parts of the world—South African tabloid journalists for the most part display a very serious attitude toward their work. The professional identities they exhibit seem much closer to what one would associate with community journalists than the playful approach to news one might expect from journalists working for a medium often seen as having entertainment as its primary objective. Although South African tabloid journalists do remark on the freedom they experience at tabloids as opposed to working in the mainstream, they display a remarkably strong commitment to the communities they report on. They report high levels of interaction between the papers and their readers, and they experience a significant amount of trust being invested in them by readers and communities. The attachment these journalists have to communities, while going against the grain of conventional notions of journalistic impartiality or detachment, seems to be reciprocated by readers, who provide them with exclusive information that enables them to scoop their rivals in the mainstream. Through these exclusives, also attained through editorial policies emphasizing investigative work and time spent "in the field," tabloid journalists are reportedly slowly gaining the respect of their peers in the mainstream. This attachment and serious attitude also comes with a price, and tabloid journalists report on the emotional exhaustion they experience as a result of being constantly confronted by poverty, crime, and disasters.

South African tabloid journalists are very much aware of the low esteem they are held in by the mainstream, and are keen to emphasize the ethical standards they uphold and the skills their job requires in an attempt to improve their low status. These attempts to prove their respect-ability entail a constant negotiation between the imperatives of reporting in a colloquial, tabloid style for their local communities and adhering to the globalized professional norms of the mainstream.

Together, these factors contribute to a professional identity of tabloid journalists in South Africa that differs in significant ways from that of their counterparts in other parts of the world. How these identity con-structions translate into content—in other words, how the attitudes they report shape their reporting—would have to be established by further content analysis. What one can conclude on the basis of these interviews is that the professional identities South African tabloid journalists have constructed for themselves seem to be much closer to the ideal type of serious, investigative reporting than mainstream journalists might be willing to accept.

Finally, this book has attempted to show that a study of tabloid journalism in South Africa needs a rounded, nuanced approach that take into account the positive as well as the negative aspects of this genre. It should be accepted from the outset that South African tabloid journalism displays many contradictions and complexities that require a balanced and varied approach. After all, these papers have arisen from a country which itself harbors many contradictions and complexities. Perhaps the best way to start understanding some of these com-plexities is to do as the tabloids are doing, however incompletely and fallibly: by listening to people telling their stories.

Notes

1. Shock! Horror! Scandal!

1.   See, for example, "South Africa gets the newspapers it deserves," *The Observer,* November 14, 2004, and "Tabloid grabs South African market," *BBC Two This World,* October 17, 2006, http://news.bbc.co.uk/nolpda/ifs_news/hi/newsid_6045000/6045650.stm (accessed February 2, 2009).

2.   Audit Bureau of Circulation (ABC), January–March 2008, and All Media Products Survey (AMPS), February–November 2007.

3.   "Totally tabloid," *ABC Radio National,* February 2, 2006, http://www.abc.net.au/rn/talks/8.30/mediarpt/stories/s1560445.htm (accessed February 2, 2009). The *Daily Sun*'s manager, Fergus Sampson, sees this rumored re-selling of papers once they've been read as "one hell of a compliment" (pers. comm. 2007).

4.   Karl Brophy, editor of the Cape Town daily tabloid the *Daily Voice* (pers. comm. 2007), sees the term "mainstream media" applying to tabloids rather than broadsheets: "Given that the *Daily Sun* is, quite clearly, the biggest selling newspaper in the country and accepting that the *Daily Voice* is, by far, the biggest selling newspaper in Cape Town how do we (i.e., us and the *Daily Sun*) not qualify as the 'mainstream media'? Surely we are the mainstream media and the *Cape Times* et al are 'niche media.'" Brophy has a point, but I nevertheless prefer to use the term "mainstream media" to refer to broadsheet newspapers and commercial and public (not community) broadcasters, since these media preceded the entry of the tabloids on the market and still dominate the discourse about professional journalism, as was evident from the clash between tabloid editors and other members of the South African National Editors' Forum, notably at the 2005 SANEF Annual General Meeting in Cape Town (Barratt 2006, 57). Although the tone of debate at the latter was "exclusionary" (F. Haffajee, pers. comm., 2007), SANEF issued a statement in which the tabloids were welcomed as a "vibrant part of the changing landscape" (Barratt 2006, 57). My choice to refer to broadsheets and the like as "mainstream" is therefore informed by not circulation figures but by the balance of power in journalistic discourse in the country, which might well change over time. The use of "mainstream media" for non-tabloid media is also employed by Conboy (2005,10), who also distinguishes between "elite press" and "popular tabloids" within the British context. I will, in some instances, use "elite press" interchangeably with "mainstream press," especially when referring to the sections of society served by the established (non-tabloid) print media.

5.   The ruling party, the African National Congress (see ANC 2008), has also made this point, which is seen by its critics as a ploy by government to obtain more control over the media.

6.   Johncom's name was changed in 2007 to Avusa Ltd.

7.   This criticism followed Zuma's defamation suit in 2006 for R63 million against various media after he had been acquitted of rape charges.

8. Zelizer's three-pronged typology of journalism follows the title of the new International Communication Association journal in which her article appeared—*Communication, Culture and Critique* (ed. Karen Ross).

9. The argument alluded to in these paragraphs is worked out in more detail in Rao and Wasserman (2007), which in turn draws on the important intervention by Shome and Hegde (2002).

2. Attack of the Killer Newspapers!

1. "The 'Berliner' may not be too little, but is it too late?," *Independent on Sunday*, July 4, 2004.

2. According to Grabe, Zhou, and Barnett (2001, 638), the formal aspects of sensationalism have received much less consideration in scholarly work than its content.

3. Several explanations could be offered for the difference between my qualitative study of audience responses and the U.S. effects studies by Grabe et al. (2000, 2001). One obvious difference is that of context and the difference in class and social position between the majority of my respondents and those in the U.S. studies, where the majority of the participants were educated or belonged to the middle class (although half the respondents of one of the studies were manual laborers, and, although not statistically significant, and therefore unreported, there was a difference in terms of credibility measures between the high and low education groups—Grabe, pers. comm.). Another explanation could be that the response of the South African tabloid readers should be understood on the level of emotional recall, while retention of content was not tested. Most likely, the difference in reports on credibility between the group Grabe et al. studied and group in this book's study is due to the difference in quantitative vs. qualitative methodologies. In focus groups, which provide an in-depth analysis of discourse, these small differences in credibility are amplified and brought into clearer focus. Furthermore, a focus group environment, especially when the participants are all tabloid readers from a similar demographic background, could provide support for respondents to acknowledge that they find tabloids credible, since such a position would be more socially desirable than might be the case in different contexts (my thanks to Betsi Grabe for her elucidating comments in this regard).

4. Like Glynn (2000, 13), I also find the theoretical frameworks of postmodernity useful in explaining the pervasiveness of images and superficial information in contemporary global media, the effects of which can be felt even in African journalism cultures where access to the electronic networks underpinning this postmodern media condition is much less pervasive. I further agree with Glynn that the tension between the view of the audience as passivized by theorists like Baudrillard (although I do not explicitly draw on his work to the same extent that Glynn does) and the active role given to audiences in the work of cultural studies scholars like John Fiske is not necessarily an absolute distinction which cannot be negotiated. However, since this book focuses on a context in the developing world where the activity of the audience in making meaning out of often very scarce resources is of crucial significance for an understanding of how media operate in African societies, I tend to favor Fiske's approach—even if I find his views at times overstated. Furthermore, although I see the South African tab-

loids as belonging to a genre emerging from postmodernism's tabloid culture, I would locate these tabloids within a critical discourse rooted in social and material conditions in post-apartheid South Africa, a context which at times is at odds with more radical postmodern claims of hyper-reality, self-referentiality, and free-floating signifiers.

5.   This question formed the theme of a conference in September 2007 at Cardiff University as well as the special issue of *Journalism Studies* (9[5]) derived from that conference. A previous version of this chapter appeared in that issue.

6.   See "Hard News: Daily Papers face unprecedented Competition," *Washington Post,* February 20, 2005; "Murdoch predicts gloomy future for press," *The Guardian,* November 24, 2005; "Do Newspapers have a Future?," *Time,* September 25, 2006.

7.   See also "Latest circulation numbers show decline in consumer titles," *E-Media,* August 16, 2007.

8.   Newspapers in South Africa have adopted new technologies, including tapping into multimedia, viral networks like myvideo.co.za and using Facebook and Twitter feeds.

9.   The *Daily Sun* at the time of writing had only a masthead on its website with the message "under construction" (www.dailysun.co.za); the *Kaapse Son*'s website (www.dieson.co.za) contained mostly an archive of its page-three girls, with a random selection of recent sports stories and video clips; and an internet search for the *Daily Voice* redirects the browser to Independent Newspapers' general news site, Independent Online (www.iol.co.za). Articles that have appeared in *Son* can be found in the online archives of *Die Burger,* its sister newspaper in the Naspers stable, but only via the search engine on *Die Burger*'s website.

10. A word on nomenclature: In this book, the terms "Black," "White," "Coloured," etc. will be used to denote the racial categories inherited from apartheid and that remain relevant for a social analysis of contemporary South Africa. Although it is acknowledged that the racial nomenclature of apartheid was socially constructed and imposed rather than "natural," these designations continue to be used in official South African policies aimed at redress of the past and in the segmentation of media markets. They also still largely correlate with the enormous material inequalities in that society. For these reasons, these terms remain analytically relevant, even if problematically so.

11. Or, as one South African academic has described the tabloid market, "a raw working class" that could potentially "develop" into "a new lower middle class" with the help of tabloids (Rabe 2007, 33).

12. Although tabloid content is usually socially conservative, overt support for progressive political parties might fit their overall goal of appealing to popular sentiment. The UK *Sun*'s famous switch from the Conservative Party to Tony Blair's New Labour in 1997 might be seen as an example in this respect. This move could, however, also be seen in terms of New Labour's media strategy (see Woodward 2007) and *Sun* owner Rupert Murdoch's political opportunism.

13. The *Sowetan* has a history of being a well-established paper aimed at "urban-based, relatively affluent African readers" and under apartheid challenged the ruling order (Tomaselli 2000, 378).

14. "*Daily Sun* outshines all," *The Media,* March 3, 2003.

15. "Johncom restructures 'Sowetan', 'Sunday World,'" *The Media,* August 19, 2004.

16. The English version of *Son* was discontinued in December 2008.

17. "Johncom restructures 'Sowetan', 'Sunday World,'" *The Media,* August 19, 2004.
18. There was some disappointment when *Sondag* failed to reach its initial goal to sell 50,000 copies within its first year ("'Sondag' misses mark," *The Media,* June 2008).
19. "Uncovering two nations," *The Media,* January 7, 2004.
20. Research conducted for the project on "Political Communication in New Democracies" funded by the British Academy (Ref: LRG-45511). Principal investigators on the project are Katrin Voltmer and Barbara Pfetsch. Although interviews for this project were done on the basis of anonymity, McKinley and Mngxitama waived confidentiality.
21. Mamelodi is a township in Gauteng Province.
22. These claims will be discussed in more detail in chapter 6, where reader responses to the tabloids will be explored.
23. The re-establishment of the Forum of Black Journalists (FBJ) in February 2008 and the exclusion of White journalists was condemned strongly by the racially inclusive South African National Editors' Forum (see http://www.SANEF.org.za/press_statements/957458.htm). The decision by the FBJ to exclude White journalists from its meeting with the new ANC president Jacob Zuma was also found to be unconstitutional by the South African Human Rights Commission (http://www.sahrc.org.za/sahrc_cms/downloads/Katopodis_FBJ_finding.pdf) as it constituted unfair discrimination. In the context of the current discussion on the make-up of the South African media landscape as one of the factors leading to the emergence of tabloid newspapers, the emergence of the FBJ can be seen as indicative of the perception among some media practitioners that the industry and profession is still dominated by White interests and perspectives. Moreover, the FBJ's move to immediately align itself with political power can be seen as an indication of overarching class interests in the profession that could only serve to amplify the sense of exclusion from mainstream journalism experienced by the majority, Black readership.
24. Jordan, "Uncovering two nations," *The Media,* January 7, 2004.
25. See Wasserman 2009b for a more detailed discussion.
26. "Cabinet to probe service delivery protests," *The Mercury,* September 7, 2007.
27. The MLL is seen by some (e.g., Landman et al. 2003) as a more accurate indicator of poverty than the well-known $1-a-day benchmark.
28. White households' share of consumption expenditure in 2005/2006 was 42.9% while their share of the population was 9.2%, compared to Black households which comprised 79.4% of the population but whose share of consumption expenditure was only slightly higher than that of Whites at 44.3% (SSA 2008).
29. The Gini coefficient between other groups ranged between 0.56 and 0.59, while for Black (African) households the figure was 0.63.
30. Other notable mainstream newspapers (albeit sometimes also showing a tabloid influence) aimed at an urban Black readership are the Zulu-language papers *Isolezwe, Ilanga,* and *UmAfrika.* The latter three have grown in circulation and revenue over the last few years ("Untapped markets," *Mail and Guardian,* April 6, 2005).
31. See "Sent packing by the Sheriff," *Son,* April 13, 2007.
32. See, for example, "No Mercy! Hospital bars family—then they're hijacked!," *Daily Sun,* January 2, 2007, and "Hospital of Horrors!," *Daily Sun,* January 1, 2007.

33. See "I am not a woman!" *Daily Sun*, February 22, 2007, and "She can't retire!," *Daily Sun,* May 24, 2007.

34. On violence, see "Koeëlbloedig" (In cold blood), *Daily Voice,* April 12, 2007, and "Cop Skoot" (Head Shot), *Daily Voice,* April 11, 2007. On racism, see "Wit rassis het my sus net so laat verdrink" (White racist left my sister to drown), *Daily Voice,* March 11, 2007.

35. The *Daily Sun's* editor is Themba Khumalo, but Du Plessis fulfills most of the executive editorial functions, like convening the daily news conference and deciding on the lead stories, which he often rewrites himself.

36. Du Plessis' statement bears eerie resemblance to Margaret Thatcher's infamous quote with which the neoliberal era in Britain was heralded: "And, you know, there is no such thing as society. There are individual men and women, and there are families. And no government can do anything except through people, and people must look to themselves first."

37. "Budget and You," *Daily Sun*, February 22, 2007.

38. "Kwaai Cabbies," *Daily Voice,* April 13, 2007.

39. "South Africa gets the newspapers it deserves," *The Observer,* November 14, 2004.

40. Interviews that were conducted in Afrikaans (including this one with Koopman) were translated by the author.

41. "Tabloid irresponsibility has left us in a civic Catch-22," *The Guardian,* November 14, 2008.

3. Black and White and Read All Over

The title of this chapter derives from a BBC Two *This World* program on the *Daily Sun* in 2006. See "Tabloid grabs South African market," *BBC Two This World,* October 17, 2006, http://news.bbc.co.uk/nolpda/ifs_news/hi/newsid_6045000/6045650.stm (accessed February 2, 2009).

1. These are a random selection of actual headlines.

2. Although commercial television was introduced worldwide from the 1950s, it was not allowed in South Africa until 1976. Prior to that, television was kept out of the country because the repressive apartheid regime feared that coverage of the civil rights movement in the United States particularly would provide succor for the local resistance movement. It also believed that television would have a detrimental effect on Christian mores. Ironically, the apartheid regime cloaked its rejection of television in the discourse of "cultural imperialism"—see Krabill (2002). Several other countries in Africa also only allowed television fairly recently, some as late as the mid- to late 1980s (Bourgault 1995, 104).

3. The end of communism meant that the apartheid regime no longer had the scapegoat of the "Red Peril" (*Rooi Gevaar*) to rhetorically justify its oppression of the resistance movement. Thanks to the Cold War, South Africa had also managed to enlist the qualified support of the United States during the Reagan administration—which, with its policy of "constructive engagement," was ensured of a proxy state in Southern Africa. This relationship between South Africa and the United States also had a cultural dimension and discursive connections which Nixon (1994) examines.

4. Many of the staff of the African nationalist paper *Abantu-Batho* joined *Bantu World* after the former publication's closure in 1931 (Limb 2000, 100).

5. Limb (2000, 114) points out that the White-owned Black press later did become repoliticized (alongside the emergence of an alternative press) as sympathy grew for the struggle of African workers.

6. See Switzer 1988 for a detailed discussion of the paper's content.

7. "Son sak oor moraliteit en gehalte" (Sun sets over morality and quality), *Die Kerkbode,* September 10, 2004. Unless otherwise noted, all translations in this book are the author's.

8. "*Red Pepper* sparks controversy in Uganda," *Mail and Guardian,* October 11, 2005.

9. "Media Council warns *Red Pepper*'s Tusiime," *The New Vision,* October 18, 2007.

10. The comparison between the *Daily Sun* and African storytelling traditions has already been made in a postgraduate dissertation at the Tshwane University of Technology (Joubert 2007).

11. See Flew 2007 for an outline of different theories of globalization.

12. Even shocking stories are often given headlines using puns. An example is a report on mob violence in a Cape Town township, where two alleged robbers were attacked by a crowd hurling a "massive rock" at them. The story was headlined "Stoned" on the front page and "Rock 'n Rol" [*sic*] on an inside page where it continued (February 26, 2007).

13. See BBC Editorial Guidelines, www.bbc.co.uk/guidelines/editorialguidelines.

4. Not Really Newspapers

1. See Sparks and Tulloch 2000 for an overview of how these debates have manifested worldwide.

2. See, e.g., Berger, "Headline-grabbing tabloids: Are they journalism?," *Mail and Guardian,* December 8, 2004; Froneman 2004; 2005; "SA's press becomes a table for empowerment pinball," *Business Day,* November 28, 2003; Manson 2005; Rabe 2005; Thloloe 2005; *The Media Online* 2004; "Poniepers: waar is die grense?" (Tabloid press: Where are the limits?), *Die Burger,* December 4, 2005; "Here comes *The Sun*," *Financial Mail,* July 26, 2002; "Poniekoerant galop" (Pony press on a gallop), *Finansies en Tegniek,* March 7, 2003; and "Nuwe pret op grou Kaapse dae" (New fun on grey Cape days), *Finansies en Tegniek,* May 16, 2003.

3. An example of how mainstream media have attempted to walk the tightrope between incorporating tabloid elements to satisfy readers' curiosity while distancing themselves from tabloids is the weekly column "Tabloid Week" in the *Sunday Times*. In this regular feature, selected articles and reports from the week's tabloids are discussed and often ridiculed. The same process of indirect (and later direct) reporting of tabloid news by mainstream media—while at the same time decrying their corrupt influence—has been noted in the UK context (Conboy 2006, 208, citing Bromley).

4. This section draws on a book chapter co-authored with Marie-Louise du Bois in A. Olorunnisola, ed., *Media in South Africa after Apartheid: A Cross-Media Assessment.* Lewiston, NY: Edwin Mellen, 2006, 171–186.

5. See MacDonald 2006, 126ff. for an analysis of the continued correlation between class and race in post-apartheid South Africa. Especially pertinent is his point

6. that income inequality within racial groups, especially Africans, was increasing during and after the democratic transition. This could translate in the context of tabloids to an aspirational lifestyle, which fed into the consumerist idealism offered by the tabloids.

6. A controlling stake in New Africa Publications was obtained by another Black-empowerment company, Johncom, in 2004 ("Johncom restructures 'Sowetan', 'Sunday World,'" *The Media*, August 19, 2004).

7. "Saki's side," *The Media*, April 2004.

8. The examples given here from debates about tabloids are not presumed to be representative; rather, they are chosen using a method similar to Berkowitz's (2000, 132) in his study of paradigm repair—namely, through the method of conceptual sampling, in which texts are chosen "for theoretically relevant reasons rather than through probability samples."

9. E.g., *Son*'s Ingo Capraro, "Son's shining success," *Mail and Guardian*, June 3, 2005; *Daily Voice* news editor Raymond Joseph, "Stranger than fiction," *The Media*, July 1, 2005; *Daily Sun* publisher Deon Du Plessis' speech to the Audit Bureau of Circulation, 2005.

10. "Stranger than fiction," *The Media*, July 1, 2005.

11. At a panel discussion on tabloids hosted by the South African National Editors' Forum in Cape Town in February 2007, titled "Are we true to the public trust?," Berger engaged in a heated exchange of words with the editor of the *Daily Voice*, Karl Brophy, accusing the tabloid of disregarding the tradition of struggle journalism and cheapening it with sexual innuendo.

12. Berger, "SA's tabloids rise in the ranks of journalism," *Mail and Guardian*, July 20, 2005.

13. "Mondi: And the Winners Are. . . . ," *The Media*, October 2, 2008.

14. Berger, "Headline-grabbing tabloids: Are they journalism?," *Mail and Guardian*, December 8, 2004.

15. Ibid.

16. Ibid.

17. "Die geel gevaar" (The yellow peril), *Beeld*, April 21, 2005.

18. Singer (2006), in a different context (the challenges posed to traditional journalism by the emergence of blogging), makes a similar point, albeit more extensively—namely, that normative values will come to define professional journalism and distinguish professional journalists from other information providers in an era of information overload brought on by new-media technologies.

19. "Rich Diet at the Bottom of the Trough," *Business Day*, April 12, 2005.

20. Berger, "Headline-grabbing tabloids: Are they journalism?," *Mail and Guardian*, December 8, 2004.

21. See Pressley 2005 for a summary of the events and the religious and cultural politics with which they are tied up.

22. *Die Burger*, March 12, 2005.

23. "Headline-grabbing tabloids: Are they journalism?," *Mail and Guardian*, December 8, 2004.

24. Anton Harber, "Rich Diet at the Bottom of the Trough," *Business Day*, April 12, 2005.

25. Froneman, "Son sak oor moraliteit en gehalte" (Sun sets over morality and quality), *Die Kerkbode*, September 10, 2004; "Die geel gevaar" (The yellow peril), *Beeld*, April 21, 2005.

26. One had to look no further than the front-page articles across the range of daily broadsheets on the rape trial of former deputy president Jacob Zuma in March 2006 to see how broadsheet journalism often followed tabloid tactics in presenting titillating information.

27. It is somewhat ironic that tabloids can be considered as following a more feminine approach to news than mainstream newspapers in the light of feminist critiques—in South Africa and elsewhere—of tabloid representations of women. The way tabloids represent masculinity and femininity is more complex than just their idealization of conventional models of both masculinity and femininity, as Johansson (2007, 100–106) points out.

28. The criticisms against the professionalization of journalism outlined here pertain to the normative ethical dimension of professionalization. In recent years the notion of journalism as a profession has also come under pressure from the increase in non-professional practices that lay claim to being acknowledged as journalism, such as blogging and "citizen journalism." This debate falls outside of the scope of this book.

29. Berger, "Headline-grabbing tabloids: are they journalism?" *Mail and Guardian,* December 8, 2004.

30. Examples that Garman (2005) refers to are the recent spate of plagiarism cases in the South African media, such as the controversies surrounding the columnists Darryl Bristow-Bovey and Cynthia Vongai and the criticism leveled against the author Pamela Jooste after allegations that she plagiarized from a journalistic report in her novel.

31. E.g., Thloloe, 2005; also cited by Berger, "Headline-grabbing tabloids: Are they journalism?," *Mail and Guardian,* December 8, 2004.

32. See, for example, Berkowitz (2000) on the mainstream press's demonstration of superiority (what he calls "paradigm boosterism") to the tabloid media after Princess Diana's death. Örnebring and Jönsson (2004, 283) in their historical perspective on tabloid journalism also mention that tabloids are "obvious targets when journalists themselves engage in self-reflection and media criticism": "Tabloid journalism becomes a kind of journalistic *other,* used as a warning example and symbol for all that is wrong with modern journalism" (2004, 284). Frank (2003) has shown how self-reflexivity among media professionals also goes beyond paradigm repair to a distinction drawn between individual reporters and members of a pack.

33. In 2003, a series of media ethical scandals received considerable attention. Among them were a prominent case of plagiarism by a well-known columnist, and perhaps more seriously, an allegation of espionage for the apartheid government made against the head of public prosecutions, Bulelani Ngcuka. The latter saga—involving conflicts of interest, leaking of off-the-record information and unverified reports—resulted in a public judicial inquiry, the Hefer Commission.

34. Berger (2008) makes the valid point that the notion of "paradigm repair" needs some modification in the South African context, since the media paradigm in this transitional democracy is not yet as fixed and stable as it is in more established democracies. According to this view, debates around unethical behavior by individuals in the media (as in the case Berger mentions), or responses to new genres like tabloids, are indications of a "paradigm in progress."

35. Berger, "Headline-grabbing tabloids: Are they journalism?," *Mail and Guardian,* December 8, 2004; Harber, "State warns of bottom-line threat," *Business Day,* August 17, 2004.

36. For an elaboration of this argument, see Wasserman and De Beer (forthcoming) and Wasserman 2006.

37. See Retief (2002) for the commonality of tenets such as "objectivity," "impartiality," and "independence" in South African ethical codes, both professional and institutional. While issues of race and gender are also common denominators in media ethical codes, these are limited to issues of representation ("stereotyping") rather than their intersection with class.

38. An interesting parallel can be found in the phenomenon of blogging. Gitlin (2005) has shown that blogs may be a response to public preference among U.S. audiences for point-of-view journalism. He sees this demand as underlying the demand for blogs that are "personal, argumentative, kinetic, forceful, with some relation to fact."

39. K. Bloom, "War talk," *The Media,* July 17, 2005.

40. The chairperson of The African Editors' Forum, Mathatha Tsedu, has rejected sunshine journalism in no uncertain terms as a "negation of responsibility" (quoted in Fourie 2008, 116).

41. See Frank 2003 for an international comparison.

42. "SA's press becomes a table for empowerment pinball," *Business Day,* November 28, 2003.

43. Bloom, ibid.

44. Bloom, ibid.

45. Bloom, ibid.

46. "Son's shining success," *Mail and Guardian,* June 3, 2005.

47. In a somewhat similar venture, the *Daily Sun* (in collaboration with Business and Arts South Africa) invited writers to contribute serialized stories in an attempt to "encourage people to read stories (local stories) and develop a culture of reading, leading over time to better English literacy" (Litnet 2005).

48. Bloom, "War talk," *The Media,* July 17, 2005.

49. E.g., Joseph, "Stranger than fiction," *The Media,* July 1, 2005; Koopman, pers. comm. 2005.

50. Harber (2003) also touches on the political-economic aspect of ownership, highlighting the fact that the two most successful tabloids (the *Son* and the *Daily Sun*) may be seen as manifestations of an unhealthy conglomeration of the print media in South Africa. Both are owned by the same company, Media24 (a wholly owned subsidiary of Naspers), that is "rapidly becoming the 94-pound gorilla of our newspaper industry." The size of these conglomerates makes economies of scale possible, resulting in a lower cover price.

5. The Revolution Will Be Printed

1. Froneman, "Die geel gevaar" (The yellow peril), *Beeld,* April 21, 2005.

2. The political-economy and cultural-studies approaches to media are often characterized as opposites. The view put forward in this book, however, is that both these approaches provide critical perspectives on the relationships among media, symbolic and economic power, and the way audiences negotiate these power relations, and therefore should be considered together in order to understand the various dimensions of tabloid media and their place in post-apartheid South African society.

3. Harber, "SA's press becomes a table for empowerment pinball," *Business Day*, November 28, 2003.
4. Harber, "Rich Diet at the Bottom of the Trough," *Business Day*, April 12, 2005.
5. See "How Murdoch had a hotline to the PM in the run-up to Iraq war," *The Independent*, July 19, 2007; "Spin and scandal: how New Labour made the news," *The Guardian*, June 13, 2007.
6. "A tale of Poles and prejudice," *Media Guardian*, August 11, 2008.
7. "Tabloids serve only to dumb down readers," *Business Day*, April 4, 2005.
8. "SA's press becomes a table for empowerment pinball," *Business Day*, November 28, 2003.
9. See Sparks 2000 for a summary of these positions.
10. "Tabloid fever hits Cape Town," *The Independent*, May 30, 2005.
11. The public support for causes is not unique to the South African tabloids—see for instance Tulloch's (2007) account of staff from the UK tabloid *Daily Mirror* displaying newspaper banners in a demonstration against the Iraq war in 2003.
12. A Klopse is a minstrel carnival with its roots in eighteenth-century slave culture in Cape Town, taking place on "Tweede Nuwejaar" (the day after New Year's Day, when slaves were given the day off), culminating at Green Point Stadium on the Atlantic Seaboard of Cape Town (Martin 2001).
13. "Tik" is the street name for methamphetamine, which became endemic among youth in the Cape Flats in the mid-2000s.
14. "Wife's Lust for MXit Man," *Son*, March 23, 2007.
15. As Steinberg (2007, 260) argues, the Constitution has even been interpreted conservatively in such groundbreaking cases as when Irene Grootboom, a resident of an informal settlement near Cape Town, made a case against the State in 2000, demanding that the government meet its constitutional obligation by providing adequate housing. Although the court ruled in favor of the claimants, the ruling only had vague bearing on government policy rather than bringing about concrete, enforceable action. Grootboom died homeless eight years later. See also De Vos 2008 and Wickeri 2004.
16. For a historically and contextually unrelated but interesting comparison, see Conboy and Steel 2009 on how the *Sun* in Britain is shifting from an appeal to a homogenous collective readership in its printed version to a more "atomised, self-assembling" reader of its website.
17. "Illegal connections 'overload' station," *Daily Sun*, July 21, 2008.
18. "No Mercy! Hospital bars family—then they're hijacked!," *Daily Sun*, February 1, 2007.
19. "My Oprah angels!," *Daily Sun*, February 1, 2007.
20. An example of the terrible consequences arising from the Department of Home Affairs' inability to respond adequately to applications for ID books is recounted in Sikhakhane's (2009) account of a man who was driven to suicide when he was denied full-time employment because he was unable to show an ID.
21. This research was conducted for the project on "Political Communication in New Democracies" funded by the British Academy (Ref: LRG-45511). The principal investigators are Katrin Voltmer and Barbara Pfetsch.
22. Zuma's negotiation of the tension between tradition and modernity (see Van der Westhuizen 2009) would also be likely to resonate with the social transitions being made by the *Daily Sun*'s readers.

23.　*Daily Sun,* December 18, 2007.
24.　"ZUMA—but wait for it!" *Daily Sun,* December 19, 2007.
25.　This can be translated as "Give others a chance, ten years, give Msholozi (Zuma's clan praise name, used to indicate respect) a chance" (translation by Simphiwe Sesanti).
26.　"1,5 Tons of Meat for Hungry Politicians!," *Daily Sun,* December 19, 2007.
27.　"Make Peace Thabo!" *Daily Sun,* December 20, 2007.
28.　*Daily Sun,* December 20, 2007.
29.　Deputy Secretary-General Thandi Modise, Secretary-General Gwede Mantashe, Chairwoman Baleka Mbethe, President Jacob Zuma, Deputy President Kgalema Mothlanthe, and Treasurer Matthews Phosa.
30.　*Daily Voice,* Thursday, December 20.
31.　At the time, the Western Cape premier was Ebrahim Rasool, but he was replaced not much later (in 2008) by Lynne Brown as part of a general shake-up among ANC office-bearers nationally as a fallout of the Zuma faction in the ANC gaining power.
32.　"Bloody Justice—the brutal vigilante murder of a thief," *Daily Voice,* December 20, 2007.
33.　"Frenzied injustice," *Daily Voice,* December 20, 2007.
34.　"Out you go!" *Sunday Sun,* September 21, 2008.
35.　"Dis geen boendoehof nie!" (This is no kangaroo court!), *Sondag,* September 21, 2008.
36.　"Drink op nugter regters" ("A toast to sober judges"), *Sondag,* September 21, 2008.
37.　"MBEKI I will go without a fight!," *Daily Sun,* September 22, 2008.
38.　"And How the End Came!," *Daily Sun,* September 22, 2008.
39.　"Mbeki: What you say. . . . ," *Daily Sun,* September 22, 2008.
40.　"Thabo should have seen it coming—like a 22-wheel truck bearing down on him!," *Daily Sun,* September 22, 2008.
41.　Out of the party political coverage, the ruling party, the ANC, enjoyed the bulk (55%) of the share (980 out of 1,764 statements in total), followed by the Democratic Alliance (DA), with 325 statements (18%), the SACP (256, or 14.5%), and the Inkatha Freedom Party (3.6%).
42.　See Johansson 2007, 100ff. for a discussion of the various sides to this argument in the British context.
43.　*Daily Sun,* May 19, 2008, emphasis in original.
44.　Ibid., emphasis in original.
45.　Ibid.
46.　Ibid.
47.　Ibid.
48.　Ibid.
49.　Transcript available online at http://news.bbc.co.uk/1/shared/spl/hi/programmes/this_world/transcripts/blackandwhiteandread_171006.txt.
50.　Jon Qwelane, "Call me names, but gay is NOT okay . . . ," *Sunday Sun,* July 20, 2008.
51.　"South Africa's High Court Rules in Favor of Gay Marriage," *New York Times,* December 1, 2005.
52.　"John Qwelane in trouble for gay-bashing, *The Times,* July 24, 2008.

53. "Qwelane falls foul of press code," *Mail and Guardian,* July 29, 2008.
54. Sarah Britten, "Jon Qwelane, Facebook and market forces," http://blogs.thetimes
     .co.za/britten/2008/07/25/jon-qwelane-facebook-and-market-forces (accessed
     July 25, 2008).

6. Truth or Trash?

1. "Then, we prefer not to confront ourselves with why South Africa has the highest
    rape statistics in the world, and that domestic violence is on the increase. Of
    course, one cannot state that there is a direct correlation between tabloids and
    crimes against women and children without scientific research. But what are the
    tabloids doing about these social ills?" (Rabe 2007, 29–30). "This commodifica-
    tion and stereotyping of women is not only found in the images, but also in the
    text and style seen in tabloids and therefore one can safely say that the media is
    not unguilty of why women are treated so violently in some communities" (Rabe
    2007, 30).
2. Although, as Spitulnik (1993, 299) also points out, this "ethnographic turn" has
    been criticized for disregarding or displacing earlier work in communication
    studies (like the uses and gratifications approach) in which attention had been
    paid to what audiences do with media texts, rather than the other way around.
3. An example of how the South African media continue to be marked by racial
    polarization is the re-establishment of the Forum of Black Journalists in February
    2008, which received criticism for its alleged "racism" in excluding White jour-
    nalists (who form part of the South African National Editors' Forum, a racially
    inclusive body established as part of the efforts to transform the media in the
    1990s) from its off-the-record meeting with the new president of the ANC, Jacob
    Zuma. An unrelated incident in the same month made headlines in media
    around the country and internationally—the emergence of a racist video by stu-
    dents at the University of the Free State made in resistance to integration on
    campus. This incident reminded observers how "paper-thin" South Africa's ra-
    cial reconciliation is (William Gumede, "Racial oppression will live on if there is
    no debate about the past," *The Independent,* February 29, 2008).
4. The focus groups were not always entirely homogenous in terms of class, and in the
    focus groups in Rondebosch East and Tshwane, included some members of the
    professional class.
5. Participants were briefed beforehand about the purpose of the interviews and
    asked for their consent to participate under conditions of anonymity. Detailed
    biographical data were gathered for background purposes.
6. The editor of the *Kaapse Son* describes (pers. comm. 2007) the page-three girl as
    "escapism," but explains the reason for the omission of the topless girl in the En-
    glish version as a strategy to attract more advertisers (many of whom refused to
    advertise because of the nudity) and Muslim readers, who might be offended by
    the picture. The latter, as a relatively affluent group within the tabloid's demo-
    graphic, represent an attractive market niche (Koopman, pers. comm. 2007). The
    editor of the *Daily Voice,* which has a large Muslim readership yet publishes a
    topless girl every day, dismisses the argument that "you can't sell a paper with a
    page three girl to Muslims or Black Africans because they're more conservative"

as "an assumption made in boardrooms": "Nobody in a focus group is going to admit to it [looking at the page-three girl], it's like admitting to masturbation. The portion of our readers that are hardcore Muslim is huge, and they don't mind the page three girl. The cultural value argument is a lazy one because it is never tested. Christians aren't supposed to be looking at nudity either—there is no religion that promotes nudity."

7. For a discussion of how Afrikaans media repositioned themselves in terms of the changing cultural politics in post-apartheid South Africa, see Wasserman (2009).

8. Conboy (2006, 3) provides a detailed historical account of the way language in British newspapers became a site for political contention starting in the 1830s. His point that the creation of a "market-orientated idiom" is a key factor for the commercial success of these papers, and that in achieving this aim newspaper publishers often created an "idealized voice" to speak on behalf of the working class, is also very relevant for especially the South African tabloids based in the Western Cape, where an attempt has been made to capture the local Cape vernacular.

9. It might be worth noting that Zulu-language newspapers like *Isolezwe, Ilanga,* and *UmAfrika,* positioned at higher ends of the market spectrum than the tabloids, have recorded strong growth in recent years, leading to the launch of a new Sunday edition of *Isolezwe* in 2008 ("The all new Zulu," *Mail and Guardian,* May 27, 2007; "Zulu newspaper to be launched," *The Media Online,* http://www.themediaonline.co.za/themedia/view/themedia/en/page2164?oid=4928andsn=Detail (accessed March 8, 2008).

10. A subsequent study of British tabloids by Johansson (2007, 118) brought to light slightly different findings. Her respondents also indicated using other sources of news alongside the *Sun* or *Mirror,* but these sources were often other tabloids or television.

11. As an aside, the South African short film by Dumisani Phakathi, *Waiting for Valdez* (2001), tells the fictional story of children who want to see the Western movie *Valdez Is Coming* (1971) but do not have enough money. They decide to pool their money to enable two of them to go see the film, and then come back and relate the story to the rest of their circle of friends.

12. Trainsurfing is a daredevil activity in which participants would ride on the outside (on top of or on the sides) of a moving train.

13. See, e.g., Sean Jacobs, "South Africa: A Hard Truth," *The Guardian,* May 20, 2008; William Gumede, "Mbeki must face up to South Africa's xenophobia," *The Independent,* May 21, 2008.

14. The Baby Jordan case was about a woman who ordered a contract killing of the baby daughter her boyfriend had with an ex-girlfriend.

15. Cf. Langer 1998, 151, on social inequality as inevitable.

16. One particular story that was recounted on more than one occasion was about a woman that was found on the other side of a high fence, with no particular explanation offered for her being there. The respondents interpreted that as evidence that the woman was a witch, even though they pointed out that the *Daily Sun* did not label her explicitly as such.

17. See Harber, "Rich Diet at the Bottom of the Trough," *Business Day,* April 12, 2005.

18. Berger, "SA's tabloids rise in the ranks of journalism," *Mail and Guardian*, July 20, 2005.
19. E.g., Harber, "Rich Diet at the Bottom of the Trough."
20. Berger, "SA's tabloids rise in the ranks of journalism."
21. At the end of his piece Goldstuck does acknowledge that the fear of the spirits of White people is an "appropriate source" to draw upon to explain the occurrences related in the report, since White people "had been the perpetrators of black people's misery for so many years before."
22. For a compelling example of how this internalized inferiority complex as a result of apartheid and colonialism continues to manifest in rumor and legend as a way of explaining contemporary events, see Steinberg's (2007) retelling of a legend that circulated in the Transkei village of Lusikisiki explaining the sudden short-age of long-life (UHT) milk as a result of Black people having chased White farmers off their land and ruining milk production. Steinberg sees this tale as evidence that residents see what happens to them as being determined by forces far away from them and out of their control, and at the same time as related to the erosion of that community's self-belief.
23. Cf. the special issue of the *Gender and Media Diversity Journal* published in 2007, devoted to the "Tabloid explosion."

7. Often They Cry with the People

1. Responses by editors, news editors, and publishers are identified by name, while individual journalists were kept anonymous. While none of the respondents ex-plicitly asked for confidentiality, it was decided that in order to protect individual journalists' privacy, their responses would be dealt with anonymously. Inter-views conducted in Afrikaans have been translated by the author.
2. "Editor's Choice," *Vodacom Journalist of the year/The Media*, 2008.
3. "Going places," *The Media*, December 2008.
4. "SANEF slams arrest of journalist," *Mail and Guardian*, January 17, 2008.
5. From remarks by journalists, this geographical demarcation seems to be particu-larly evident in Cape Town. One journalist who used to work for the *Daily Sun* in Johannesburg remarked on how difficult it was for her to adapt to the more seg-regated social spaces in Cape Town when she moved there after taking another job. (This also seems to be the dominant opinion among Black professionals; see Hamlyn 2009.) The way race, class, and ethnicity are still marked by the residen-tial segregation put in place by the Group Areas Act during apartheid was also remarked upon by tabloid readers, as discussed in chapter 6.
6. To understand this remark, it is also necessary to understand that historically rugby in South Africa has been seen as a White sport (although it has always had a significant Coloured support and player base). Rugby is also often criticized for its tardiness to reflect the country's racial demographics in team selections.
   Former president Nelson Mandela's donning of a Springbok rugby jersey dur-ing the rugby World Cup tournament, hosted in (and won by) South Africa in 1995, has been seen as a reconciliatory moment, while the hosting of the Soccer World Cup in South Africa in 2010 has also created many expectations among South Africans, notably for its perceived economic benefits to the country (see for instance Grundlingh 1998; Strelitz and Steenveld 1998).

7. When visiting the *Daily Sun*'s newsroom, Du Plessis also did not want these jour-
    nalists to be interviewed, instead arranging an interview with the editor, Themba
    Khumalo.
8. See Wasserman (2006a) for a more detailed discussion; see Hasty (2005, 5) and
    Ndangam (2006) for perspectives on how these negotiations take place within
    Ghanaian and Cameroonian journalism, respectively.

References

Addison, G. 2003a. "No Race Please—We're Afrikaans." *The Media,* February 15.
———. 2003b. "The Road to Populism." *The Media,* June 19–24.
Alexander, P. 2006. "Globalisation and New Social Identities: A Jigsaw Puzzle from Johannesburg." In *Globalisation and New Identities: A View from the Middle,* ed. P. Alexander, M. C. Dawson, and M. Ichharam, 13–65. Johannesburg: Jacana.
Allen, D. 2005. "Professionalization and Globalization: Ethics and the Corporate Rationalization of Journalism." Paper presented at the annual conference of the International Communication Association, New York.
ANC. 2008. "The Voice of the ANC Must Be Heard." *ANC Today,* January 18–24. http://www.anc.org.za/anc.org.za/ancdocs/anctoday/2008/at02.htm (accessed July 28, 2008).
Anderson, B. 1987. *Imagined Communities.* London: Verso.
Appadurai, A. 1996. *Modernity at Large: Cultural Dimensions of Globalization.* Minneapolis: University of Minnesota Press.
Arant, M. D., and P. Meyer. 1998. "Public Journalism and Traditional Journalism: A Shift in Values?" *Journal of Mass Media Ethics* 13(4): 205–218.
Ashforth, A. 2005. *Witchcraft, Violence and Democracy in South Africa.* Chicago: University of Chicago Press.
Bakhtin, M. 1968. *Rabelais and His World.* Trans. Helene Iswolsky. Cambridge, Mass.: MIT Press.
Barber, K. 1987. "Popular Arts in Africa." *African Studies Review* 30(3): 1–78.
———, ed. 1997. *Readings in African Popular Culture.* Bloomington: Indiana University Press.
Bardoel, J., and M. Deuze. 2001. "'Network Journalism': Converging Competences of Old and New Media Professionals." *Australian Journalism Review* 23(2): 91–103.
Barratt, E. 2006. *Part of the Story—10 Years of the South African National Editors' Forum.* Rosebank: South African National Editors' Forum.
BBC. 2006. "Ugandan 'Gay' Name List Condemned." *BBC News.* September 8. http://news.bbc.co.uk/2/hi/africa/5326930.stm (accessed August 26, 2008).
BBC. 2007. "Anti-apartheid stalwart mourned." *BBC News.* February 10. http://news.bbc.co.uk/2/hi/6349703.stm.
Beckett, C., and L. Kyrke-Smith, eds. 2007. *Development, Governance and the Media: The Role of the Media in Building African Society.* London: Polis.
Bek, M. G. 2004. "Tabloidization of News Media: An Analysis of Television News in Turkey." *European Journal of Communication* 19(3): 371–386.
Bell, M. 1998. "The Journalism of Attachment." In M. Kieran, ed., *Media Ethics,* 15–22. London: Routledge.
Berger, G. 2005a. "Current Challenges." In A. Hadland, ed., *Changing the Fourth Estate; Essays on South African Journalism,* 19–26. Cape Town: HSRC Publishers.
———. 2005b. Remarks at Mondi Shanduka Newspaper Journalism Awards. April 20. http://journ.ru.ac.za/staff/guy/fulltext/mondi05.doc (accessed March 13, 2006).

———. 2008. "A paradigm in processs: What the scapegoating of Vusi Mona signalled about South African journalism." *Communicatio* 34(1): 1–20.

Berkowitz, D. 2000. "Doing Double Duty: Paradigm Repair and the Princess Diana What-a-Story." *Journalism* 1(2): 125–143.

Beukes, W. D., ed. 1992. *Oor grense heen: Op pad na 'n nasionale pers, 1948–1990.* Cape Town: Nasionale Boekhandel.

Bird, S. E. 1992. *For Enquiring Minds: A Cultural Study of Supermarket Tabloids.* Knoxville: University of Tennessee Press.

———. 1998. "News We Can Use: An Audience Perspective on the Tabloidisation of News in the United States." *Javnost The Public* 5(3): 34–49.

———. 2003. *The Audience in Everyday Life: Living in a Media World.* New York: Routledge.

Biressi, A., and H. Nunn, eds. 2008. *The Tabloid Culture Reader.* Maidenhead: Open University Press.

Bizcommunity. 2007. *Kaapse Son* profile. http://www.biz-community.com/PressOffice/AboutUs.aspx?i=115059 (accessed August 20, 2007).

Bond, P. 2002. *Elite Transition: From Apartheid to Neoliberalism in South Africa.* London: Pluto Press.

Bonner, F., and S. McKay. 2007. "Personalizing Current Affairs without Becoming Tabloid: The Case of 'Australian Story.'" *Journalism* 8(6): 640–656.

Bourdieu, P. 1984. *Distinction: A Social Critique of the Judgement of Taste.* Trans. Richard Nice. Cambridge, Mass.: Harvard University Press.

Bourgault, L. M. 1995. *Mass Media in Sub-Saharan Africa.* Bloomington: Indiana University Press.

Buller, J. 2007. "The 'Next Generation' 60 Years Later: Civic Journalism as the Offspring of the 1947 Hutchins Commission." *Media Ethics,* 18(2): 25–28.

Chakrabarty, D. 1996. "Postcoloniality and the Artifice of History: Who Speaks for 'Indian' Pasts?" In *Contemporary Postcolonial Theory: A Reader,* ed. P. Mongia, 224–246. London: Arnold.

Chotia, F., and S. Jacobs. 2002. "Remaking the Presidency." In S. Jacobs and R. Calland, eds., *Thabo Mbeki's World,* 145–161. Scottsville, South Africa: University of Natal Press.

Cohen, S. 1973. *Folk Devils and Moral Panics: The Creation of the Mods and Rockers.* London: Paladin.

Comaroff, J., and J. Comaroff. 2005. "Reflections on Liberalism, Policulturalism and ID-ology: Citizenship and Difference in South Africa." In S. Robins, ed., *Limits to Liberation after Apartheid: Citizenship, Governance and Culture,* 33–56. Oxford: James Currey.

Conboy, M. 2006. *Tabloid Britain: Constructing a Community through Language.* London: Routledge.

———. 2008a. "Carnival and the Popular Press." In A. Biressi and H. Nunn, eds., *The Tabloid Culture Reader,* 113–115. Maidenhead, UK: Open University Press.

———. 2008b. "The Popular Press: Surviving Postmodernity." In A. Biressi and H. Nunn, eds., *The Tabloid Culture Reader,* 45–52. Maidenhead, UK: Open University Press.

Conboy, M., and Steel, J. 2009. "From 'We' to 'Me': The Changing Construction of Popular Tabloid Journalism." Paper presented at the Future of Journalism conference, Cardiff, Wales, September.

Costera Meijer, I. 2001. "The Public Quality of Popular Journalism: Developing a Normative Framework." *Journalism Studies* 2(2): 189–205.

Couldry, N. 2003. *Media Rituals: A Critical Approach.* London: Routledge.

———. 2004. "Theorising Media as Practice." *Social Semiotics* 14(2): 115–132.

———. 2005. "Transvaluing Media Studies or, Beyond the Myth of the Mediated Centre." In J. Curran and D. Morley, eds., *Media and Cultural Theory*, 177–194. London: Routledge.

Curran, J. 2003. "The Press in the Age of Globalization." In J. Curran and J. Seaton, eds., *Power without Responsibility*, 67–105. London: Routledge.

Davis, A. 2003. "Whither Mass Media and Power? Evidence for a Critical Elite Theory Perspective." *Media, Culture and Society* 25(5): 669–690.

De Beer, A. S. 2002. "The South African Press: No Strangers to Conflict." In E. Gilboa, ed., *Media and Conflict: Framing Issues, Making Policy, Shaping Opinions*, 263–280. Ardsley, N.Y.: Transnational Publishers.

De Beer, A. S., and E. Steyn. 2002. "SANEF's 2002 South African National Journalism Skills Audit: An Introduction and the SANEF Report regarding the Media Industry." *Ecquid Novi: African Journalism Studies* 23(2): 11–86.

Derby, R. 2005. "Tabloids serve only to dumb town readers." *Business Day*, May 4.

Deuze, M. 2004. "What Is Multimedia Journalism?" *Journalism Studies* 5(2): 139–152.

———. 2005. "Popular Journalism and Professional Ideology: Tabloid Reporters and Editors Speak Out." *Media, Culture and Society* 27(6): 861–882.

De Vos, P. 2008. "Irene Grootboom died, homeless, forgotten, no C-class Mercedes in sight." www.abahlali.org/node/3884 (accessed September 2, 2009).

De Waal, M. 2008. "Black Xmas for Naspers Staff." *Moneyweb*. http://www.moneyweb.co.za/mw/view/mw/en/page215466?oid=240044andsn=Detail (accessed January 17, 2009).

Dolby, N. 2006. "Popular Culture and Public Space in Africa: The Possibilities of Cultural Citizenship." *African Studies Review* 49(3): 31–47.

Duncan, J. 2003. "Another Journalism Is Possible—Critical Challenges for the Media in South Africa." Centre for Civil Society Research Report No. 10, Centre for Civil Society, University of KwaZulu-Natal, Durban, South Africa.

Du Plessis, D. 2005. "It's the Niche, Stupid." Speech delivered at Audited Bureau of Circulation Figures meeting, Johannesburg, South Africa.

———. 2008. "Our Guy in the Blue Overalls." *Mail and Guardian Online*. http://www.mg.co.za/articlePage.aspx?articleid=341602andarea=/insight/insight__comment_and_analysis/ (accessed June 12, 2008).

Du Plooy, G. M. 2001. *Communication Research: Techniques, Methods and Applications*. Lansdowne, South Africa: Juta.

Durrheim, K., M. Quayle, K. Whitehead, and A. Kriel. 2005. "Denying Racism: Discursive Strategies Used by the South African Media." *Critical Arts* 19(1, 2): 167–186.

Ellis, S. 1989. "Tuning In to Pavement Radio." *African Affairs* 88(352): 321–330.

Englund, H. 2007. "Witchcraft and the Limits of Mass Mediation in Malawi." *Journal of the Royal Anthropological Institute* 13: 295–311.

Esser, F. 1999. "'Tabloidization' of News: A Comparative Analysis of Anglo-American and German Press Journalism. *European Journal of Communication* 14(3): 291–324.

Felix, B. 2006. "Let's Hear the Voters!" http://www.journalism.co.za (accessed February 3, 2006).

Fiske, J. 1989. *Understanding Popular Culture*. Boston: Unwyn Hyman.

———. 1992. "Popularity and the Politics of Information." In P. Dahlgren and C. Sparks, eds., *Journalism and Popular Culture*, 45–63. London: Sage.

Flew, T. 2007. *Understanding Global Media*. Basingstoke: Palgrave MacMillan.

Fourie, P. J. 2002. "Rethinking the Role of the Media in South Africa." *Communicare* 21(1): 17–40.

———. 2005. "Thinking about Journalists' Thinking (and the Criticism against Journalism and Its Education)." Paper presented at the Colloquium on Journalism Education, Rhodes University, Grahamstown, South Africa.

———. 2008. "Moral Philosophy as the Foundation of Normative Media Theory: Questioning African *Ubuntuism* as a Framework." In S. J. A. Ward and H. Wasserman, eds., *Media Ethics Beyond Borders: A Global Perspective,* 105–122. Johannesburg: Heinemann.

Frank, R. 2003. "'These Crowded Circumstances': When Pack Journalists Bash Pack Journalism." *Journalism* 4(4): 441–458.

Franklin, B. 1997. *Newszak and News Media.* London: Arnold.

Franklin, B., M. Hamer, M. Hanna, M. Kinsey, and J. E. Richardson. 2005. *Key Concepts in Journalism Studies.* London: Sage.

Frère, M.-S. 2007. "Francophone Africa: 50 Years of Media." In E. Barratt and G. Berger, eds., *50 Years of Journalism.* Johannesburg: The African Editors' Forum, Highway Africa and the Media Foundation for West Africa.

Froneman, J. 1994. "Redes vir die gebrek aan 'n ingeligte, lewendige debat oor media-etiek." [Reasons for the lack of an intelligent, lively debate about media ethics.] *Ecquid Novi: African Journalism Studies* 15(1): 123–128.

———. 2004. "Dominante motiewe in die transformasie van *Huisgenoot,* 1916–2003." [Dominant motives in the transformation of *Huisgenoot.*] *Ecquid Novi: African Journalism Studies* 25(1): 61–79.

———. 2006. "In search of the *Daily Sun*'s recipe for success." *Communitas* 11: 21–35.

Garman, A. 2005. "Teaching to Produce 'Interpretive Communities' rather than just 'Professionals.'" Paper presented at the Colloquium on Journalism Education, Rhodes University, Grahamstown, South Africa.

Geertz, C. 1973. "Thick Description: Toward an Interpretive Theory of Culture." In *The Interpretation of Cultures: Selected Essays,* 3–30. New York: Basic Books.

Gitlin, T. 2005. "Blogs and the Media Emperors' New Clothes." Paper presented at the annual conference of the International Communication Association, New York.

Glenn, I. 2008. "The watchdog that never barked (or an investigation of the sin of omission)." *Rhodes Journalism Review* (September 2008): 18–20.

Glenn, I., and A. Knaggs. 2008. "Field Theory and Tabloids." In A. Hadland, E. Louw, S. Sesanti, and H. Wasserman, eds., *Power, Politics and Identity in South African Media,* 104–123. Cape Town: HSRC Press.

Glynn, K. 2000. *Tabloid Culture: Trash Taste, Popular Power and the Transformation of American Television.* Durham, N.C.: Duke University Press.

Goldstuck, A. 2008. "Haunted by White Ghosts! The Curse of Dipokong." http://thoselegends.blogspot.com/2008/03/haunted-by-white-ghosts-curse-of.html (accessed October 10, 2008).

Grabe, M. E., S. Zhou, and B. Barnett. 1999. "Sourcing and reporting in news magazine programs: '60 Minutes' versus 'Hard Copy.'" *Journalism and Mass Communication Quarterly* 76(2): 293–311.

———. 2001. "Explicating Sensationalism in Television News: Content and the Bells and Whistles of Form." *Journal of Broadcasting and Electronic Media* 45(4): 635–655.

Grabe, M. E., S. Zhou, A. Lang, and P. D. Bolls. 2000. "Packaging Television News: The Effects of Tabloid on Information Processing and Evaluative Responses." *Journal of Broadcasting and Electronic Media* 44(4): 581–598.

Grabe, M. E., A. Lang, and X. Zhao. 2003. "News Content and Form: Implications for Memory and Audience Evaluations." *Communication Research* 30(4): 387–413.

Griffen-Foley, B. 2008. "From 'Tit-Bits' to 'Big Brother': A Century of Audience Participation in the Media." In A. Biressi and H. Nunn, eds., *The Tabloid Culture Reader,* 303–313. Maidenhead, UK: Open University Press.

Gripsrud, J. 1992. "The Aesthetics and Politics of Melodrama." In P. Dahlgren and C. Sparks, eds., *Journalism and Popular Culture,* 84–95. London: Routledge.

———. 2000. "Tabloidization, Popular Journalism and Democracy." In C. Sparks and J. Tulloch, eds., *Tabloid Tales—Global Debates over Media Standards,* 285–300. Lanham, Md.: Roman and Littlefield.

Grundlingh, A. 1998. "From Redemption to Recidivism? Rugby and Change in South Africa during the 1995 Rugby World Cup and Its Aftermath." *Sporting Traditions* 14(2): 67–84.

Gunaratne, S. 2006. "Public Sphere and Communicative Rationality: Interrogating Habermas's Eurocentrism." *Journalism and Communication Monographs* 8(2): 94–156.

Haas, T., and L. Steiner. 2006. "Public Journalism: A Reply to Critics." *Journalism* 7(2): 238–254.

Hafez, K. 2007. *The Myth of Media Globalization.* Cambridge: Polity Press.

Haffajee, F. 2004a. "An incomplete freedom: The state of the media ten years into democracy." Paper presented at the Harold Wolpe Lecture Series, University of KwaZulu-Natal, Durban, May 27.

———. 2004b. Presentation at the South African National Editors' Forum seminar series "A review of the media in the first decade of democracy." Cape Town.

Hall, S. 1970. "Encoding/Decoding." In S. Hall, D. Hobson, A. Lowe, and P. Willis, eds., *Culture, Media, Language,* 197–208. London: Hutchinson/CCCS.

Hallin, D. 2000. "'La Nota Roja': Popular Journalism and the Transition to Democracy in Mexico." In C. Sparks and J. Tulloch, eds., *Tabloid Tales—Global Debates over Media Standards,* 267–284. Lanham, Md.: Roman and Littlefield.

Hamlyn, M. 2009. "Cape Town 'too white, backward.'" *Fin24.* January 22. http://www.fin24.com/articles/default/display_article.aspx?Nav=nsandArticleID=1518–1786_2457465 (accessed January 24, 2009).

Harber, A. 2002. "Journalism in the Age of the Market." Harold Wolpe Memorial Lecture. http://www.nu.ac.za/ccs/default.asp?11,22,5,188 (accessed February 1, 2003).

———. 2003. "Tabloids, Pinball and Affirmative Action." http://www.journalism.co.za/modules.php?op=modloadandname=Newsandfile=articleandsid=939 (accessed June 7, 2005).

———. 2004. "The *Daily Sun* Shines in Gore and Glory over a Changing Land." *Ecquid Novi: African Journalism Studies* 25(1): 156–158.

Hermes, J. 2006. "Hidden Debates: Rethinking the Relationship between Popular Culture and the Public Sphere." *Javnost The Public* 13(4): 27–44.

Hinerman, S. 1997. "(Don't) Leave Me Alone: Tabloid Narrative and the Michael Jackson Child-Abuse Scandal." In J. Lull and S. Hinerman, eds., *Media Scandals,* 143–163. Cambridge: Polity Press.

Hogshire, J. 1997. *Grossed-Out Surgeon Vomits Inside Patient! An Insider's Look at Supermarket Tabloids.* Venice, Calif.: Feral House.

Horwitz, R. B. 2001. *Communication and Democratic Reform in South Africa.* Cambridge: University of Cambridge Press.

Jacobs, S. 2004. "Public Sphere, Power and Democratic Politics: Media and Policy Debates in Post-Apartheid South Africa." Ph.D. diss., University of London.

Jenkins, H. 2006. *Convergence Culture: Where Old and New Media Collide*. New York: New York University Press.

Johansson, S. 2007. *Reading Tabloids: Tabloid Newspapers and Their Readers*. Stockholm: Södertörns hogskola.

Johnson, K., and S. Jacobs. 2004. "Democratization and the Rhetoric of Rights: Contradictions and Debate in Post-Apartheid South Africa." In F. Nyamnjoh and H. Englund, eds., *Rights and the Politics of Recognition in Africa*, 84–102. London: Zed Books.

Jones, A. 2002. "From Vanguard to Vanquished? The Tabloid Press in Jordan." *Political Communication* 19: 171–187.

Josephi, B. 2008. "The Potential of Journalism Education in Transitional Economies." Paper presented to the Media, Communication and Humanity Conference, London School of Economics, London.

Joubert, M. 2007. "Rewriting traditional journalism: The case of *Daily Sun*." MTech diss., Tshwane University of Technology, South Africa.

Khumalo, T. 2007. Presentation to panel debate, "Are we true to the public trust?", hosted by the South African National Editors' Forum. Cape Town.

Kopper, G. G., A. Kolthoff, and A. Czepek. 2000. "Research Review: Online Journalism—a Report on Current and Continuing Research and Major Questions in the International Discussion." *Journalism Studies* 1(3): 499–512.

Krabill, R. 2001. "Symbiosis: Mass Media and the Truth and Reconciliation Commission of South Africa." *Media, Culture and Society* 23(5): 585–603.

———. 2002. "Starring Mandela and Cosby: Television, Identity and the End of Apartheid." Ph.D. diss., New School for Social Research.

Kraidy, M. M. 2002. "Hybridity in Cultural Globalization." *Communication Theory* 12(3): 316–339.

Kraidy, M. M., and P. D. Murphy. 2008. "Shifting Geertz: Toward a Theory of Translocalism in Global Communication Studies." *Communication Theory* 18(3): 335–355.

Krüger, F. 2006. "It's Only News If It's True." In S. Bulbulia, ed., *The Tabloid Challenge*, 30–31. Johannesburg: Institute for the Advancement of Journalism.

Landman, J. P., with H. Bhorat, S. van der Berg, and C. van Aardt. 2003. "Poverty and Inequality in South Africa 2004–2014." www.sarpn.org.za/documents/d0000649/P661-Povertyreport3b.pdf (accessed August 3, 2008).

Langer, J. 1998. *Tabloid Television: Popular Journalism and the "Other News."* London: Routledge.

Lazarsfeld, P., B. Berelson, and H. Gaudet. 1944. *The People's Choice: How the Voter Makes Up His Mind in a Presidential Campaign*. New York: Columbia University Press.

Lewis, J., S. Inthorn, and K. Wahl-Jorgensen. 2005. *Citizens or Consumers? What the Media Tell Us about Political Participation*. Maidenhead: Open University Press.

Limb, P. 2000. "'Representing the Labouring Classes': African Workers in the African Nationalist Press, 1900–1960." In L. Switzer and M. Adhikari, eds., *South Africa's Resistance Press—Alternative Voices in the Last Generation under Apartheid*, 79–127. Athens: Ohio University Press.

Litnet. 2005. "Business and Art South Africa in Collaboration with *Daily Sun*." http://www.oulitnet.co.za/indaba/basa.asp (accessed July 6, 2005).

Livingstone, S., and P. Lunt. 1994. *Talk on Television: Audience Participation and Public Debate*. London: Routledge.

Louw, P. E. 2001. *The Media and Cultural Production*. London: Sage.

Mabweazara, H. M. 2006. "An Investigation into the Popularity of the Zimbabwean Tabloid Newspaper, *uMthunywa*: A Reception Study of Bulawayo Readers." M.A. thesis, Rhodes University, South Africa.

MacDonald, M. 2006. *Why Race Matters in South Africa*. Scottsville: Harvard University Press.

Makholwa, A. 2008. "Afrikaans Editors Reshuffled." *Journalism.co.za*. http://www.journalism.co.za/index.php?option=com_contentandtask=viewandid=1911andItemid=99999999 (accessed January 17, 2009).

Mamdani, M. 1996 *Citizen and Subject: Contemporary Africa and the Legacy of Late Colonialism*. Princeton, N.J.: Princeton University Press.

Mandela, N. 1994a. Address to the International Press Institute. Cape Town, February 14. http://www.anc.org.za/ancdocs/history/mandela/1994/sp940214.html (accessed March 17, 2007).

———. 1994b. *Long Walk to Freedom*. Randburg: Macdonald Purnell.

Manson, H. 2005. "No Responsibility Please, We're Journalists." *Media toolbox* 7(13). http://www.mediatoolbox.co.za/pebble.asp?relid=3325 (accessed July 4, 2005).

Marais, H. 1997. *South Africa: Limits to change? Transforming a Divided Society*. London: Zed Books.

McQuail, D. 2000. *McQuail's Mass Communication Theory*. London: Sage.

Media Monitoring Project. 2007. "Addressing the state of the media." http://www.mediamonitoring.org.za/tabid/60/ctl/ArticleView/mid/375/articleId/88/Addressing-the-state-of-the-media.aspx (accessed July 26, 2007).

———. 2008. Media Monitoring Project Submits Complaint about the *Daily Sun* reporting on xenophobia. http://www.mediamonitoring.org.za/tabid/60/ctl/ArticleView/mid/375/articleId/251/Media-Monitoring-Project-submits-complaint-about-Daily-Sun-reporting-on-xenophobia.aspx (accessed May 30, 2008).

Media Tenor. 2004a. SA Media's blind spot on AIDS. http://www.mediatenor.co.za/download.php?download_cs=3031.pdf (accessed July 7, 2008).

Media Tenor. 2004b. Media sings Black empowerment praises. http://www.mediatenor.co.za/download.php?download_cs=4445.pdf (accessed July 7, 2008).

Meyer, P. 2004. *The Vanishing Newspaper: Saving Journalism in the Information Age*. Columbia: University of Missouri Press.

Morley, D. 1980. *The Nationwide Audience*. London: BFI.

Ndangam, L. 2006. "'Gombo': Bribery and the Corruption of Journalism Ethics in Cameroon." *Ecquid Novi: African Journalism Studies* 27(2): 179–199.

News24. 2007. Zuma, Afrikaners bond at braai. http://www.news24.com/News24/Entertainment/Local/0,9294,2-1225-1242_2089873,00.html (accessed October 22, 2008).

Nixon, R. 1994. *Homelands, Harlem and Hollywood*. London: Routledge.

Nuttall, S., and C.-A. Michael, eds. 2000. *Senses of Culture: South African Culture Studies*. Oxford: Oxford University Press.

Nyamnjoh, F. B. 2005. *Africa's Media—Democracy and the Politics of Belonging*. Pretoria: Unisa Press/ London and New York: Zed Books.

Örnebring, H. 2006. "The Maiden Tribute and the Naming of Monsters: Two Case Studies of Tabloid Journalism as Alternative Public Sphere." *Journalism Studies* 7(6): 851–868.

———. 2008. "The Consumer as Producer—of What? User-Generated Tabloid Content in *The Sun* (UK) and *Aftonbladet* (Sweden)." *Journalism Studies* 9(5): 771–785.

Örnebring, H., and A. M. Jönsson. 2004. "Tabloid Journalism and the Public Sphere: A Historical Perspective on Tabloid Journalism." *Journalism Studies* 5(3): 283–295.

Ogan, C.L. 1982. "Development Journalism/Communication: the Status of the Concept." *International Communication Gazette* 29 (1–2): 3–13.

Our First Half Century. 1960. *Our First Half Century: 1910–1960.* Johannesburg: Da Gama Publications.

Penstone, K. 2005. "Sex Sells, Says Independent Newspapers." http://www.marketingweb .co.za/media/425731.htm (accessed June 7, 2005).

Pickering, M. 2008. "Sex in the Sun: Racial Stereotypes and Tabloid News." *Social Semiotics* 18(3): 363–375.

Pillay, S. 2008. "The ANC as Government: Contesting Leadership between Democracy and Development." *Perspectives,* newsletter of the Heinrich Böll Foundation. No. 12.

Pressley, D. 2005. "Scandal involving Gay Pastor Drives Wedge in South African Church." Worldwide Faith News Archives. http://www.wfn.org/2005/09/msg00295.html (accessed October 3, 2008).

Press Ombudsman. 2004. "Press Code of Professional Practice." www.SANEF.org.za (accessed May 24, 2004).

Pursehouse, M. 2008. "Looking at 'The Sun': Into the Nineties with a Tabloid and Its Readers." In A. Biressi and H. Nunn, eds., *The Tabloid Culture Reader,* 287–302. Maidenhead, UK: Open University Press.

Quinn, S. 2005. *Convergent Journalism—The Fundamentals of Multimedia Reporting.* New York: Peter Lang.

Rabe, L. 2005. License to kill? http://www.news24.com/News24/Columnists/Lizette_ Rabe/0,,2-1630-1714_1685951,00.html (accessed July 4, 2005).

———. 2007. "An Analogy between Tabloids and the Wild, Wild West: The Good, the Bad and the Ugly?" *Gender and Media Diversity Journal* 3: 26–34.

Rantanen, T. 2005. *Media and Globalization.* London: Sage.

Rao, S., and H. Wasserman. 2007. "Global Journalism Ethics Revisited: A Postcolonial Critique." *Global Media and Communication* 3(1): 29–50.

Rauwerda, A. M. 2007. "Whitewashing *Drum* Magazine (1951–1959): Advertising Race and Gender." *Continuum: Journal of Media & Cultural Studies,* 21(3): 393–404.

Rhodes Journalism Review. 1997. Special edition: The media and the TRC. May.

Roberts, S. 2007. "Reporting Refugees: The Case of World Refugee Day 2007." *Gender and Media Diversity Journal* 3: 132–133.

Robertson, R. 1997. "Glocalization: Time-Space and Homogeneity—Heterogeneity." In M. Featherstone, S. Lash, and R. Robertson, eds., *Global Modernities,* 25–43. London: Sage.

Robins, S., ed. 2005. *Limits to Liberation after Apartheid: Citizenship, Governance and Culture.* Oxford: James Currey.

Rosen, J. 2006. "The People Formerly Known as the Audience." *Pressthink.* http://journalism .nyu.edu/pubzone/weblogs/pressthink/2006/06/27/ppl_frmr.html (accessed January 3, 2008).

SANEF (South African National Editors' Forum). 2007. "Bid for Johncom and Other Concerns." http://www.sanef.org.za/press_statements/675906.htm (accessed July 28, 2008).

———. 2008. "Concern at ANC President's Attack on Print Media." http://www.sanef.org .za/press_statements/815940.htm (accessed July 28, 2008).

Scharrer, E., L. M. Weidman, and K. L. Bissell. 2003. "Pointing the Finger of Blame: News Media Coverage of Popular-Culture Culpability." *Journalism and Communication Monographs* 5(2).

Schudson, M. 2005. "The Emergence of the Objectivity Norm in American Journalism." In S. Høyer and H. Pöttker, eds., *Diffusion of the News Paradigm 1850–2000*, 19–35. Göteborg: Nordicom.

Shepperson, A., and K. G. Tomaselli. 2002. "Ethics: A Radical Justice Approach." *Ecquid Novi: African Journalism Studies* 23(2): 278–289.

Shiva, V. 1989. *Staying Alive: Women, Ecology, and Development.* London: Zed Books.

Shome, R., and R. Hegde. 2002. "Postcolonial Approaches to Communication: Charting the Terrain, Engaging the Intersections." *Communication Theory* 12(3): 249–270.

Sikhakhane, J. 2009. "S'khumbuzo Mhlongo's death a lesson for legislators." *Business Day,* August 31. http://www.businessday.co.za/articles/Content.aspx?id=80041 (accessed August 31, 2009).

Singer, J. 1997. "Changes and Consistencies: Newspaper Journalists Contemplate Online Future." *Newspaper Research Journal* 18(1–2): 2–18.

———. 2006. "The Socially Responsible Existentialist: A Normative Emphasis for Journalists in a New Media Environment." *Journalism Studies* 7(1): 1–18.

Sloan, B. 2001. *"I Watched a Wild Hog Eat My Baby!" A Colorful History of Tabloids and their Cultural Impact.* Amherst, N.Y.: Prometheus Books.

South African Press Council. 2008. The South African Press Code. http://www.press-council.org.za/pages/south-african-press-code.php (accessed June 5, 2008).

Sparks, C. 2000. "Introduction: The Panic over Tabloid News." In C. Sparks and J. Tulloch, eds., *Tabloid Tales—Global Debates over Media Standards,* 1–40. Lanham, Md.: Roman and Littlefield.

———. 2007. *Globalization, Development and the Mass Media.* London: Sage.

Spitulnik, D. 1993. "Anthropology and Mass Media." *Annual Review of Anthropology* 22: 293–315.

Spivak, G. (1985). "Can the subaltern speak? Speculations on widow sacrifice." *Wedge* 7(8) (Winter/Spring).

SSA (Statistics South Africa). 2008. Income and expenditure of households 2005/2006: Analysis of results. http://www.statssa.gov.za/publications/statsdownload.asp?PPN=P0100andSCH=4108 (accessed August 4, 2008).

Steenveld, L. 2004. Transforming the Media: A Cultural Approach. *Critical Arts* 18(1): 92–115.

———. 2006. "Tabloids a Social Phenomenon." In S. Bulbulia, ed., *The Tabloid Challenge,* 18–21. Johannesburg: Institute for the Advancement of Journalism.

Steenveld, L., and L. Strelitz. 1998. "The 1995 Rugby World Cup and the politics of nation-building in South Africa." *Media, Culture and Society* 20(4): 609–629.

Steinberg, J. 2007. *Notes from a Fractured Country.* Johannesburg: Jonathan Ball.

Strelitz, L. 2005. Discussant presentation. Colloquium on Journalism Education, Rhodes University, Grahamstown, South Africa.

Strelitz, L., and L. Steenveld. 2005. "Thinking about South African Tabloid Newspapers." *Ecquid Novi: African Journalism Studies* 26(2): 265–268.

Strydom, T. 2009. "Big jump in Rich South Africans." *Fin24.* http://www.fin24.com/articles/default/display_article.aspx?ArticleId=2452256 (accessed January 21, 2009).

Swanepoel, T. 2005. MIV/Vigsberiggewing in die "Sunday Times," "Rapport" en "Sunday

Sun": 'n etiese beoordeling. (HIV/AIDS reporting in the "Sunday Times," "Rapport" and "Sunday Sun": an ethical evaluation.) M.A. thesis, Northwest University, South Africa.

Switzer, L. 1988. "'Bantu World' and the Origins of a Captive African Commercial Press in South Africa." *Journal of Southern African Studies* 14(3): 351–370.

———, ed. 1997. *South Africa's Alternative Press: Voices of Protest and Resistance, 1880s–1960s.* Cambridge: Cambridge University Press.

Switzer, L., and M. Adhikari, eds. 2000. *South Africa's Resistance Press—Alternative Voices in the Last Generation under Apartheid.* Athens: Ohio University Press.

Taylor, A., and C. Milne. 2006. *South Africa AMDI Research Report: Newspapers.* http://www.bbc.co.uk/worldservice/trust/researchlearning/story/2006/12/061206_amdi_southafrica.shtml (accessed January 25, 2009).

Terreblanche, S. 2003. *A History of Inequality in South Africa.* Durban: University of KwaZulu-Natal Press.

Thloloe, J. 2004. "Desperately Searching for Staff." Paper presented at the Colloquium: Taking stock of 10 years of media training and education at tertiary institutions—addressing an agenda for the next decade. Rhodes University, Grahamstown, South Africa.

———. 2005. Address at annual Press Freedom Day celebration, Department of Journalism, University of Stellenbosch, Stellenbosch, South Africa. http://academic.sun .ac.za/journalism/news/mediaday_joe.pdf (accessed August 10, 2005).

Thussu, D., ed. 2006. *Media on the Move: Global Flow and Contra-flow.* London: Routledge.

———. 2008. *News as Entertainment: The Rise of Global Infotainment.* London: Sage.

Tomaselli, K. G. 2000a. "Ambiguities in Alternative Discourse—'New Nation' and the 'Sowetan' in the 1980s." In L. Switzer and M. Adhikari, eds., *South Africa's Resistance Press—Alternative Voices in the Last Generation under Apartheid,* 378–403. Athens: Ohio University Press.

———. 2000b. "Faulting 'Faultlines': Racism in the South African Media." *Ecquid Novi: African Journalism Studies* 21(2): 157–174.

———. 2000c. "South African Media, 1994–7: Globalizing via Political Economy." In J. Curran and M. Park, eds., *De-Westernizing Media Studies,* 279–292. London: Routledge.

———. 2003. "'Our Culture' vs. 'Foreign Culture': An Essay on Ontological and Professional Issues in African Journalism." *Gazette* 65(6): 427–441.

Tomaselli, K. G., and H. Dunn, eds. 2001. *Media, Democracy, and Renewal in Southern Africa.* Colorado Springs, Colo.: International Academic Publishers.

Tomaselli, K. G., and P. E. Louw, eds. 1991. *The Alternative Press in South Africa.* Bellville: Anthropos.

Tulloch, J. 2007. "Tabloid Citizenship—The 'Daily Mirror' and the Invasions of Egypt (1956) and Iraq (2003)." *Journalism Studies* 8(1): 42–60.

Ursell, G. D. M. 2001. "Dumbing Down or Shaping Up? New Technologies, New Media, New Journalism." *Journalism and Mass Communication Quarterly* 2(2): 175–196.

Van der Westhuizen, C. 2009. "'100% Zulu Boy': Jacob Zuma and the use of gender in the run-up to South Africa's 2009 election." *Heinrich Boell Stiftung South Africa.* http://www.boell.org.za/web/144-364.html (accessed September 2, 2009).

Van Kessel, I. 2007. "Trajectories of the Transition: Tracing Former Youth Activists in

Sekhukhuneland." Paper presented at AEGIS European Conference on African Studies, Leiden, Netherlands.

Van Zoonen, L. 2000. "Popular Culture as Political Communication—An Introduction." *Javnost-The Public* 7(2): 5–18.

Vincent, L. 2007. "Killing to Order: Muti Murder in Postapartheid South Africa." Paper presented at AEGIS European Conference on African Studies, Leiden, Netherlands.

Vincent, R. C., K. Nordenstreng, and M. Traber, eds. 1999. *Towards Equity in Global Communication*. Creskill, N.J.: Hampton.

Visser, W. 2004. " 'Shifting RDP into GEAR': The ANC Government's Dilemma in Providing an Equitable System of Social Security for the 'New' South Africa." Paper presented at the 40th ITH Linzer Konferenz, Linz, Germany.

Von Lieres, B. 2005. "Culture and the Limits of Liberalism: Marginalisation and Citizenship in Post-apartheid South Africa." In S. Robins, ed., *Limits to Liberation after Apartheid: Citizenship, Governance and Culture*, 22–32. Oxford: James Currey.

Ward, S. J. A. 2004. *The Invention of Media Ethics: The Path to Objectivity and Beyond*. Montreal and Kingston: McGill-Queen's University Press.

Wasserman, H. 2005. "Talking of Change: Constructing Social Identities in South African Media Debates." *Social Identities* 11(1): 75–85.

———. 2006a. "Globalised Values and Postcolonial Responses: South African Perspectives on Normative Media Ethics." *The International Communication Gazette* 68(1): 71–91.

———. 2006b. "Tackles and Sidesteps: Normative Maintenance and Paradigm Repair in Mainstream Media Reactions to Tabloid Journalism." *Communicare* 25(1): 59–80.

———. 2007. "Is a New World Wide Web Possible? An Explorative Comparison of the Use of ICTs by Two South African Social Movements." *African Studies Review* 50(1): 109–131.

———. 2009a. "Extending the theoretical cloth to make room for African experience. An interview with Francis Nyamnjoh." *Journalism Studies* 10(2): 281–293.

———. 2009b. "Learning a New Language: Culture, Ideology and Economics in Afrikaans Media after Apartheid." *International Journal of Cultural Studies* 12(1): 59–78.

Wasserman, H., and A. S. De Beer. 2005. "A Fragile Affair: An Overview of the Relationship between the Media and State in Post-apartheid South Africa." *Journal of Mass Media Ethics* 20(2–3): 192–208.

Wasserman, H., and P. Kabeya-Mwepu. 2005. "Creating Connections: Exploring the Intermediary Use of ICTs by Congolese Refugees at Tertiary Education Institutions in Cape Town." *Southern African Journal of Information and Communication* 6: 94–103.

Wasserman, H., and S. Jacobs, eds. 2003. *Shifting Selves: Postapartheid Essays on Mass Media, Culture and Identity*. Cape Town: Kwela.

Wasserman, H., and S. Rao. 2008. "The Glocalization of Journalism Ethics." *Journalism* 9(2): 163–181.

West, H. G., and J. E. Fair. 1993. "Development Communication and Popular Resistance in Africa: An Examination of the Struggle over Tradition and Modernity through Media." *African Studies Review* 36(1): 91–114.

Wickeri, E. 2004. "*Grootboom*'s legacy: Securing the Right to Access to Adequate Housing in South Africa?" New York University Center for Human Rights and Global Justice Working Paper, Economic, Social and Cultural Rights Series. http://www.chrgj.org/publications/docs/wp/Wickeri%20Grootboom%27s%20Legacy.pdf (accessed September 1, 2009).

Wimmer, R. D., and J. R. Dominick. 2006. *Mass Media Research: An Introduction*, 3rd ed. Belmont, Calif.: Wadsworth.

Zelizer, B. 2008. "How Communication, Culture, and Critique Intersect in the Study of Journalism." *Communication, Culture and Critique* 1(1): 86–91.

Index

Page numbers in italics refer to illustrations.

Bullard, David, 115–16
Buller, Judy, 89
Die Burger: appeal to Black readers, 170; editorial practices of, 61, 65, 162–63; as mainstream paper, 88, 128–29, 154–55, 157–58, 160, 162–63; website of, 183n9
Business Day, 169

Cape Son: cover design of, *25*; focus group readers of, 125–26; founding of, 24; word play in headlines, 21
Cape Times, 158
Capraro, Ingo: on British tabloids, 56; on the importance of language, 21, 75; on political coverage in tabloids, 101, 103; as SANEF member, 61; on *Son* founding, 162; on tabloid ethics, 160, 169
Chakrabarty, Dipesh, 9
citizen journalism, 109, 188n28
City Press, 3, 23, 27, 34, 135
class: Black middle class, 33–34, 169–70, 184nn27–30, 186n5; common language in early tabloids, 19; consumption as social reordering, 98; coverage of strikes and unions, 109; distinctions of taste and, 66, 123; individual vs. structural orientation and, 95–96; Living Standards Measurement as audience assessment device, 23–24; "man in the blue overalls" image, xi, 21, 74, 96, 102–103, 114; post-apartheid mainstream press readership, 59–60, 168–69; second-generation rights gap and, 33, 93, 190n15; social mobility function of tabloids, 14–15, 73, 95–96, 135, 141, 183n11; tabloid readership and, 1, 3, 6–7, 23–24, 131, 182n3, 193n9; tabloids as class depoliticization, 84; trust in tabloids and, 16–17; undermining by tabloids of social hierarchy, 35, 57, 85, 91–92
CoE (Conference of Editors), 67–68
Cohen, Stanley, 82
Comaroff, Jean, 139–40
Comaroff, John L, 139–40
community involvement. *See* localization
comparative study of journalism, 10–11
Conboy, Martin, 19, 97–98, 132, 181n4, 193n8
Conference of Editors (CoE), 67–68
Congress of South African Trade Unions (Cosatu), 105
Consortium for Refugees and Migrants in South Africa (CoRMSA), 111
content (of tabloids): overview, 15–16, 21–23; as culturally anchored media, 118–19; distribution of story genres, 56; formulaic

quality of, 82; news values, 158–59; political orientation of, 183n12; seriousness vs. escapism in, 16–17, 161–62, 168, 173, 178; "staying with a story," 131, 159; tabloid content studies, 110–11, 191n41
convergent journalism, 20, 41–42
CoRMSA (Consortium for Refugees and Migrants in South Africa), 111
Cosatu (Congress of South African Trade Unions), 105
Costera Meijer, Irene, 85–86
Couldry, Nick, 120–22, 135
court reporting, 157–58, 166–67
cover/page design (of South African tabloids): examples, *25, 26*; history of, 50; overall visuality, 128; red-tops as influence, 44, 55; scare-heads, 14; visual features of headlines, 21, 43; word play in headlines, 21, 55–56, 148
Craven, Patrick, 105
crime stories (in tabloids): anti-gender-violence campaigns, 74; court reporting, 157–58, 166–67; drug-abuse coverage, 89–90, 138, 190n13; formulaic reporting of, 18; government accountability as focus of, 36, 88; graphic depictions of violence, 35, 56, 64; reader interactivity and, 39–40, 109; South Africa level of violence, 24, 56; stereotyping of Black social pathology and, 77; as tabloid staple, 22, 109, 110–11; unreported crimes as subject of, 140; xenophobic attacks of 2008, 111–12
cultural capital, 66
cultural hybridity, 11
cultural imperialism, 53. *See also* media imperialism
cultural studies, 35, 52, 91, 94, 120–21, 189n2
Curran, James, 35, 82

DA (Democratic Alliance), 108–109, 191n41
Dagbreek, 49
Daily Continent (United States), 18
Daily Graphic (United States), 18
Daily Mail (United Kingdom), 19
Daily Mirror (United Kingdom), 11, 82, 133
Daily Mirror (United States), 19
Daily Star (United Kingdom), 11, 19, 43
Daily Sun: overview, 1; circulation figures for, 24, 181n4; cover design of, 21, 43, 128; coverage of everyday struggles, 36, *38*, 39–40, 74; criticism of, 28–29, 48, 83–84; economic coverage in, 36; editorial practices of, 49, 160, 171–72, 185n35; English language instruction in, 130, 189n47; everyday struggles in, 35–36,

Film and Publications Amendment Bill, 5
Fiske, John, 15, 35, 85, 91–92, 94, 140, 182n4
Forum of Black Journalists (FBJ), 184n23, 192n3
Fourie, Pieter J., 70
Frank, Russell, 188n32
Franklin, Bob, 17, 27
Freedom of Expression Institute (FXI), 70, 84
Friedman, Steven, 105
Froneman, Johannes, 21–23, 49, 63, 81
FXI (Freedom of Expression Institute), 70, 84

Garman, Anthea, 66–67, 188n30
Gaudet, Hazel, 120
Gaum, Laurie, 64, 160
GCIS (Government Communication and Information System), 5
Geertz, Clifford, 9, 54
gender: anti-gender-violence campaigns, 74; femininity of tabloid techniques, 66, 188n27; gender stereotyping, 192n1; homophobia as tabloid theme, 50–51, 64, 111, 115–16; tabloid ethical standards and, 64, 160; women's social mobility as tabloid theme, 141. *See also* sex
Genderlinks, 70
Ghana, 50, 133
Gill, Andrew, 75
Ginwala, Frene, 105
Gitlin, Todd, 189n37
Glenn, Ian, 115
global media industry: crisis of newspapers in Global North, 40–41; definition and scope of, 45; effect on South African tabloids, 27, 177–78; media imperialism, 44, 52–53; superficiality as quality of, 182n4; translocal approaches to, 54–55
glocalization, 45. *See also* localization
Glynn, Kevin, 15–16, 19, 66, 92, 145, 182n4
Goldstuck, Arthur, 146, 194n21
gossip, 92, 136–37
government accountability. *See* political news; social delivery
Government Communication and Information System (GCIS), 5
Grabe, Maria Elizabeth, 16, 182n3
Gripsrud, Jostein, 82, 85, 86, 100, 132
Guardian (United Kingdom), 15
Gumede, William, 192n3
"gutter journalism," 61

Habermas, Jürgen, 30, 82, 87, 138, 146–47
Haffajee, Ferial, 31, 60, 62, 69
Hall, Stuart, 52, 120–22

Harber, Anton, 28, 32, 63, 64, 74, 83, 189n50
Hartley, John, 94
Hasty, Jennifer, 133
headlines. *See* cover/page design
Hearst, William Randolph, 14, 18
Hefer Commission, 188n33
The Herald (United States), 17–18
Hermes, Joke, 87, 117
Hertzog, Albert, 53
HIV/AIDS, 32–33, 73–74, 83, 104, 111, 144
homophobia, 50–51, 64, 111, 115–16
HRC (Human Rights Commission), 5, 6, 59, 83, 116
Huisgenoot/You, 63, 128
Human Rights Commission (HRC), 5, 6, 59, 83, 116
hybridity, 11, 54

Idasa (Institute for Democracy in Africa), 105
identity documents, 99–100, 139–40, 190n20
IDs. *See* identity documents
Ilanga, 23, 184n30, 193n9
imagined community, 17, 132, 138
impartiality. *See* objectivity
Independent Group, 27, 31, 46, 51–52, 60, 74
The Independent (United Kingdom), 15
indigenization, 45
individualism, 95–96
Institute for Democracy in Africa (Idasa), 105
interactivity (reader interactivity): audience fragmentation and, 20; citizen journalism, 109, 188n28; consumption as social reordering, 98; mainstream use of interactive technology, 20–21; media citizenship and, 86, 91–94; negotiated/oppositional reading, 16–17, 72, 122, 142, 149; political clout of tabloids, 102–104; political economy of audience agency, 94; reader responses to tabloids, 6–7, 155, 164–67; tabloids as crime intervention, 39–40, 138–39; tabloids as outlet for personal grudges, 64. *See also* localization; readers; social delivery
Internet, 20, 115–16, 183n9, 188n28, 189n38. *See also* technology
Isolezwe, 23, 184n30, 193n9

Johansson, Sofia, 17, 66, 94, 133, 135
Johncom, 5
Johnnic (later Avusa), 31
Jönsson, Anna Maria, 188n32
Joseph, Raymond, 60

mainstream journalism (*continued*)
  and scope of term, 181n4; dichotomies for
  quality journalism, 58, 65–66, 78; as
  event-based journalism, 131; format/size
  changes of newspapers, 15; interpretative
  detachment and, 66; journalistic techniques
  of, 65–66, 156–57, 188n26; post-apartheid
  alienation from media, 71–72, 140–42;
  post-apartheid business model, 28; race as
  issue in, 170–72; role in tabloid debates,
  58–59; truth as quality of, xi, 144–45;
  xenophobia in, 115
Makhanya, Mondli, 142
Malawi, 48–49, 147
Mandela, Nelson, 4–5, 99, 194n6
Manson, Herman, 44, 81
Marxist scholarship, 8
Mbalula, Fikile, 106
Mbeki, Moeletsi, 106
Mbeki, Thabo: coverage of succession battle of,
  23, 104–110; economic policies of, 46; media
  scrutiny by, 5; social protests of 2007 and,
  33; views of democratic government, 91–92
McBride Report (UNESCO), 52–53
McKinley, Dale, 28–29
MDDA (Media Development and Diversity
  Agency), 3, 32
media citizenship, 86, 91–94
Media Development and Diversity Agency
  (MDDA), 3, 32
media hybridity, 45
media imperialism, 44, 52–53
Media Monitoring Project (MMP), 70, 83–84,
  111–14
media sharing, 133–34, 193n11
Media24 (subsidiary of Naspers): *Daily Sun*
  founding and, 51–52, 60; as model of
  post-apartheid success, 46; News24.com,
  105; as part of media conglomerate, 83,
  189n50; post-apartheid restructuring
  initiatives, 32; protests against homophobia
  in publications of, 115; support for
  apartheid, 5
methodology: overview of approach of book,
  7–8; audience ethnography studies, 12, 77,
  119–28, 192n2, 192nn4–5; ethnography of
  discourse approach, 125–28; interviews with
  editors and journalists, 152–53, 194n1;
  translocal approaches to global media, 53–55
Mfeketo, Nomaindia, 88
Michael, Cheryl Ann, 54
Mirror Group, 50
MMP (Media Monitoring Project), 83–84,
  111–14

Mngxitama, Andile, 29
Le Monde (France), 15
Mondi Shanduka Newspaper Journalism
  awards, 60–61
Morley, David, 52, 120–21
Motlanthe, Kgalema, 105
Mozambique, 112
Muckrakers, 16
Mugabe, Robert, 115
Munsey, Frank A., 18
Murdoch, Rupert, 183n12
Murphy, Patrick D., 54
MXit messaging software, 90

Nail, 31, 60
Naspers. *See* Media24
Nation Group, 50
National Enquirer (United States), 22, 43
National Examiner (United States), 43
National Party, 108
neoliberalism, 71, 95–96
Netherlands, 152–54, 173
networked journalism, 20, 41–42
New Africa Publications, 60
new media technologies. *See* Internet;
  technology
New York Daily News (United States), 19, 43
New York Evening Graphic (United States), 19
New York *Journal* (United States), 18
New York Post (United States), 43
New York World (United States), 18–19
News of the World (United Kingdom), 11, 21
News World Information and Communication
  Order (NWICO), 52–53
News24.com, 105
newsbooks, 17
newszak, 17
Ngcuka, Bulelani, 188n33
NGO media organizations, 70
Ngqakula, Charles, 105
Nigeria, 21, 50
Nixon, Rob, 51, 185n3
Northcliffe, Alfred Harmsworth, Viscount,
  18–19
Nunn, Heather, 127
Nuttall, Sarah, 54
NWICO (News World Information and
  Communication Order), 52–53
Nyamnjoh, Francis B., 51, 146

objectivity, 18, 66–67, 72–73
Observer (United Kingdom), 15
oppositional reading, 16–17, 72, 122, 142, 149
oral folk culture: coverage of supernatural

events and, 145–48; dichotomies of quality and, 66; origin of tabloids and, 17; post-apartheid mistrust as source of, 194n22; post-reading gossip, 136–37; radio trottoir phenomenon, 51, 92; tabloid narrative style and, 132; tabloid stories as oral narratives, 154–55

Örnebring, Henrik, 188n32

ownership (of tabloids): effects of conglomerate ownership, 3, 29–30, 189n50; global influences in South Africa and, 27; post-apartheid restructuring and, 31–32; resistance and, 47–49, 51

Pahad, Essop, 105

paradigm boosterism, 188n32

paradigm repair, 59, 67–69, 77, 79, 187n8, 188nn30,32–33

Party magazine, 153

Paver, Bertram F. G., 48

penny press, 16–18, 79

People, 63

Petersen, Najwa, 156

Phakathi, Dumisani, 193n11

Pierce, Nigel, 103

policultural identity, 139–40

political news (in tabloids): British vs. South African approaches to, 57, 97; coverage of social protests, 32–33; election coverage, 101, 103–110, 140–41; fallen celebrities as entertainment, 141; identity documents as political news, 99–100, 139–40, 190n20; individual vs. structural orientation, 36, 39, 97–100; media citizenship and, 91; personalization of politics, 35–36, 81, 86, 100–101; political advocacy in tabloids, 23, 106–109; political orientation of tabloids, 28–30, 82–83, 109–111, 183n12; reactionary views in tabloids, 111–15; South African political parties and, 191n41. *See also* everyday struggles; resistance; social delivery

post-apartheid democracy: economic shifts, 2–4; effect on alternative journalism, 28; effect on Black solidarity, 59–60, 74; freedom of expression initiative, 4–5, 71, 72; globalization as feature of, 53–54; independence as liberal-democratic framework issue, 70; media restructuring and, 27, 30–32; political shifts, 4–6, 82–83, 86; professional self-regulation of media, 69–70; public sphere in, 30; restoration of citizenship, 99–100, 139–40; second-generation rights gap and, 33, 93,

190n15; social alienation in, 136; watchdog role of media, 64, 73. *See also* apartheid

Post/Weekendpost, 50

Press Ombudsman: complaints about tabloids to, 65, 83, 111, 115–16; establishment of position, 5, 70; as ethics watchdog, 64; tabloids as focus of, 68

professionalization, 66, 69, 188n28

prosumers, 20

public interest, 76

public journalism, 73, 165

public sphere: alternative public sphere, 86–91; entertainment as corruption of rationality, 82, 87; erosion of standards of decency, 64–65, 81; governmental politics enveloped by, 117; homogenization of, 35; integration of excluded peoples into, 76–77, 85; journalistic objectivity and, 67; mistrust of mainstream media and, 71–72; popular culture and, 47, 117; "public interest" as ethical device, 76; refeudalization by market concerns, 30; ritual vs. rationality associated with, 138; superficialization of public discourse, 63; tabloids fundamental relationship with, 78; witchcraft and, 146–47

Pulitzer, Joseph, 14, 18

Pursehouse, Mark, 136

"quality" newspapers. *See* mainstream journalism

Qwelane, Jon, 111, 115–16

Rabe, Lizette, 29, 63–64, 121–23, 192n1

race: class stratification and, 33–34, 184nn27–30, 186n5; FBJ exclusion of white journalists, 184n23, 192n3; journalistic standards and, 159; post-apartheid mainstream press readership, 59–60, 169–70, 194n5; post-apartheid newspaper staffing integration, 30–31, 59, 69; racial stereotyping of readership, 77; racist writing in tabloids, 5, 115–16, 192n3; SANEF founding and, 67–68; South African racial nomenclature, 183n10; supernatural as representation of, 146, 194nn21–22; tabloid coverage of incidents of racism, 36, 83–84; tabloid readership and, 1, 3, 6–7, 23–24, 131, 169–70, 194n5; tabloids as racial empowerment, 14–15. *See also City Press; Sowetan*

radio, 3, 133–34, 147

Radio Sonder Grense, 107

radio trottoir, 51, 92
Ramaphosa, Cyril, 104
Rapport, 27, 49, 170, 194n6
Rauwerda, Antje M., 98
readers: alienation from mainstream media, 71–72, 140–42; audience ethnography studies, 77, 124, 192n2; global vs. South African reading strategies, 131, 182n3; individual vs. structural orientation, 36, 39, 97–100; literacy of readership, 175; Living Standards Measurement as assessment device, 23–24; localization of tabloids and, 57; as meaning-producing "active audience," xi, 52, 119–23; media sharing, 133–34, 193n11; political agency of, 94–95; post-apartheid readership, 3; racial stereotyping of, 77; reading as leisure, 134–35; social functions of reading, 39, 136–37; stereotyping of, 122; "tabloid readers" as stable group, xii; tabloids engagement with excluded peoples, 40, 92–94, 140–41, 164–67. *See also* interactivity; localization
Red Pepper, 50–51
red-tops, 11, 21, 44, 55–56. *See also* United Kingdom
religion: coverage of supernatural events and, 145–48; Muslim reading strategies, 126, 149, 192–93n6; resistance to television and, 185n2; tabloid ethical standards and, 64, 160
resistance: overview of political role of tabloids, 86; alternative journalism and, 28–29; anti-apartheid history as news, 36, 37; anti-gender-violence campaigns, 74; avoidance of political discourse, 73–74, 82–84, 86; individual vs. structural orientation and, 96; Marxist scholarship, 8; media as erosive of national unity, 53; personalization of political struggle, 35–36; political orientation of tabloids, 183n12; popular culture and, 47, 123; radio trottoir and, 51, 92; skeptical humor as basis for, 92; social protests and, 32–33, 83–84; struggle fatigue and, 33, 92; summary of views on, 35; tabloid ownership and, 47–49, 51; tabloids as articulation of democracy, 39; tabloids as political resistance, 11–12, 14–15; undermining of social hierarchy (by tabloids), 35, 57, 85, 91–92. *See also* everyday struggles; interactivity; political news; social delivery
Rhodes, Cecil John, 48
Robertson, Roland, 45

Rosen, Jay, 20
rumor, 92

SABC (South African Broadcasting Corporation), 5–6, 28, 71
SAHRC (South African Human Rights Commission), 111, 184n23
Sampson, Fergus, 57, 95
San Francisco *Examiner* (United States), 18
SANEF (South African National Editors Forum). *See* South African National Editors Forum
scare-heads, 14
Schudson, Michael, 19
Scott, Edwin, 159–60, 165
self-help (as tabloid theme): overview, 23; collective vs. individual orientation in reporting, 36; community-fostering effects of, 134, 155; in early tabloids, 49–50; educational function of tabloids and, 75; guidance for political involvement, 86; as political discourse, 94–95; social mobility fostered by, 73, 95–96. *See also* lifestyle journalism
sensationalism, 16–17, 21–22, 35, 58, 63
sex (as tabloid theme): overview, 21–22; anti-gay writing, 50–51, 64, 115; British vs. South African approaches to, 57; broken marriages as focus, 90–91; crimes against women and, 192n1; Muslim readers and, 126, 149, 192n6; page-three girl, 21, 43, 74, 111, 126, 148–49, 183n9, 192n6; reading strategies for, 148–49; tabloid ethical standards and, 42, 64, 160. *See also* gender
Shaik, Schabir, 109
Shiva, Vandana, 9
Sierra Leone, 50
Sikhakhane, Jabulani, 190n20
Singer, Jane B., 187n18
social delivery: accountability of government officials and, 36, 86, 100–103; assertion of citizenship status of readers, 139–41; "Bush of Evil" campaign, 88; coverage of community protests about, 33, 101; coverage of poor and working classes, 22–23, 155–56; politics of the everyday and, 30; SunSuggestions political advice, 106–107; Wall of Shame column, 102. *See also* interactivity; political news; resistance
soft news, 16
Son: British influence on, 55–56; community focus in, 74–75, 155, 157–58, 163, 165–67; cover design of, 43, 55; drug-abuse

coverage, 89–90, 134; ethics practices of, 64–65, 160–61, 167; founding of, 24, 162; language loyalty and, 128–29; news content of, 22, 129, 159, 161–62, 168; personalization of politics, 81, 101; political coverage in, 103, 107–109, 110, 141; readership of, 23, 131, 134, 136, 169–70; self-help advice in, 36, 40, 75; tabloids as crime intervention, 40, 138–39; visual features of, 21

Sondag, 27, 109–110, 184n18

South Africa. *See* apartheid; post-apartheid democracy

South African Broadcasting Corporation (SABC), 5–6, 28, 71

South African Human Rights Commission (SAHRC), 111, 184n23

South African National Editors Forum (SANEF): condemnation of FBJ, 184n23; criticism of Zuma, 6; founding of, 67–68; normative journalism and, 152; paradigm repair function of, 59; post-apartheid back-to-basics campaign, 69, 72; racial integration of newspapers and, 31; as site for tabloid debates, 65; tabloid participation in, 3, 60–62, 144, 179

Sowetan: appeal to affluent readers, 62; Black-interest stories, 36, *37;* circulation figures for, 24; community involvement initiatives, 75; *Daily Sun* founding and, 60, 98–99; news content of, 131; readership of, 3, 23, 27, 34, 183n13, 184n30; self-help advice in, 40; tabloidization and, 32, 98–99

Sparks, Colin, 45, 81–82, 86, 93, 140

spiritual insecurity, 146

Spitulnik, Debra, 121, 124, 192n2

sports news, 22, 57

The Star (South Africa), 1

The Star (United States), 43

Steenveld, Lynette, 7, 29, 92, 93, 122–23

Steinberg, Jonny, 190n15, 194n22

Strelitz, Larry, 72–73, 92, 93

struggle fatigue, 33, 92

The Sun (United Kingdom): celebrity news in, 133; as exemplar of British-style tabloids, 19; influence on *Son,* 55; page-three girl, 149; political influence of, 23, 83, 183n12; reading strategies for, 131; as "red-top" tabloid, 11; visual features of, 21, 43

The Sun (United States), 17–18

Sunday Independent, 65, 169

Sunday Sun, 23–24, 27, 95–96, 109, 111, 115–16, 137

Sunday Times, 1, 65, 103, 115–16, 135, 186n3

Sunday World, 24, 60, 75

SunLife, 30

sunshine journalism, 73, 189n40

superficialization of public discourse, 63

supernatural occurrences (as tabloid theme), 22, 63, 122–23, 142–48, 159, 193n16

Swanepoel, Thalyta, 73–74

Swaziland, 48–49

Switzer, Les, 48–49

Tabloid Column website, 15

tabloid culture, 19

tabloid debates: critical political-economic perspective, 78–79; mainstream press as site of, 58–59, 63; paradigm repair, 59, 67–69, 77, 79, 187n8, 188nn30,32–33; SANEF participation issue, 60–61; "social ills" causal thesis, 121–23, 192n1; sources of Ombudsman complaints, 65; superficialization of public discourse, 63; tabloidization as threat to journalistic standards, 62–63; United States influence on, 82. *See also* ethics; journalism

tabloid media events, 19–20

tabloidization: defined, 15–16; as African popular culture trend, 47; as crisis in global journalism, 46, 151–52; decline of ethics and, 63; post-apartheid restructuring and, 32, 47; as threat to democracy, 82; as threat to journalistic standards, 62–63, 156

Tambo, Adelaide, 36, *37,* 99

Tambo, Oliver, 99

Tanzania, 50, 92

technology: blogging, 116, 188n28, 189n38; producer/consumer interaction and, 20; reader interactivity and, 20, 115–16; tabloid websites, 15, 183n9; as threat to newspapers in Global North, 40–41. *See also* Internet

television: recognition of print journalism in, 133–34; resistance to introduction in South Africa, 53, 185n2; tabloid readership and, 131; tabloid-style television programming, 15

Thailand, 57

Thatcher, Margaret, 185n36

third-world journalism, 11

Thloloe, Joe, 48, 51, 65, 68, 71, 77, 111, 115–16

Thompson Group, 50

The Times (United Kingdom), 15

Tomaselli, Keyan G., 77

translocal approaches to global media, 53–55

TRC (Truth and Reconciliation Commission), 5, 6, 59

Treatment Action Campaign, 3, 103, 106

truth: credibility of sources and, 158, 163, 167; everyday reality and, 142; fabricated stories and, 142–43, 167; journalist views of, 153; objectivity of journalists and, 18, 66–67, 72–73; public trust in tabloids, 40, 138–41, 149, 163; as quality journalism feature, xi; social and cultural framework for, 123; supernatural occurrences and, 22, 63, 122–23, 142–48; "true story" concept, xi–xii. *See also* ethics

Truth and Reconciliation Commission (TRC), 5, 6, 59

Tsedu, Mathatha, 189n40

Tshabalala-Msimang, Manto, 6, 105

Turner, Graeme, 94

Tusiime, Richard, 51

Uganda, 21, 50–51

UmAfrika, 184n30, 193n9

Union of Black Journalists, 68

United Kingdom: British tabloids as global model, 43–44, 56; British vs. South African reading strategies, 131; celebrity news in, 133, 135; differences in South African tabloids, 57; language orientation in early tabloids, 193n8; political influence of tabloids, 83; political orientation of tabloids, 29–30, 97, 183n12. *See also* red-tops

United States: celebrity news as negotiation of moral norms, 133; civil rights movement effect on South Africa, 185n2; media imperialism and, 52–53; objectivity as concern in, 72–73; overview of tabloid features, 43; penny press development in, 17–18; political substance in tabloids, 29–30; tabloid debates in, 82; tabloid journalism as profession in, 153, 173

Unlindi we Nyanga, 49

Van Kessel, W. M. J., 97

Vincent, Louise, 144

Vink, Mike, 95–96, 159–60

violence. *See* crime stories

Von Lieres, Bettina, 139

Vongai, Cynthia, 188n30

Ward, Stephen J. A., 72–73

Weekly Mail, 27

Wessels, Douw, 64, 160

West, Harry G., 47–48, 92, 147

Wimmer, Roger D., 125

Winfrey, Oprah, 99

witchcraft. *See* supernatural occurrences

women. *See* gender; sex

xenophobia, 64, 83–84, 111–15, 137

xenophobic attacks of 2008, 111–12

yellow journalism, 14, 16, 18

Yengeni, Tony, 163

Zambia, 48–49

Zelizer, Barbie, xii, 8–9, 118, 182n8

Zhou, Shuhua, 16

Zille, Helen, 103, 108–109

Zimbabwe, 21, 48–49, 50, 110, 113–14

Zulu-language newspapers, 193n9

Zuma, Jacob: ANC democracy vs. development fissure and, 91–92; ANC election coverage and, 6, 23, 103–110; coverage of rape case of, 103–104, 141, 181n7; FBJ meeting with, 184n23, 192n3; riots of 2008 and, 112–13; social delivery protests of 2007 and, 33

Herman Wasserman is Senior Lecturer in Journalism Studies at the University of Sheffield, UK, and Visiting Associate Professor Extraordinary at the University of Stellenbosch, South Africa. He is editor of the journal *Ecquid Novi: African Journalism Studies*. His previous publications include the co-edited books *Media Ethics Beyond Borders: A Global Perspective; Shifting Selves: Post-apartheid Essays on Mass Media, Culture and Identity;* and *Power, Politics and Identity in South African Media.*